Cryptocurrencies and Blockchains

Digital Media and Society Series

Cryptocurrencies and Blockchains

Quinn DuPont

polity

The right of Quinn DuPont to be identified as Author of this Work has been asserted in accordance with the UK Copyright, Designs and Patents Act 1988.

First published in 2019 by Polity Press

Polity Press
65 Bridge Street
Cambridge CB2 1UR, UK

Polity Press
101 Station Landing
Suite 300
Medford, MA 02155, USA

ISBN-13: 978-1-5095-2023-7
ISBN-13: 978-1-5095-2024-4 (pb)

A catalogue record for this book is available from the British Library.

Library of Congress Cataloging-in-Publication Data
Names: DuPont, Quinn, author.
Title: Cryptocurrencies and blockchains / Quinn DuPont.
Description: Medford, MA : Polity, 2019. | Series: Digital media and society | Includes bibliographical references and index.
Identifiers: LCCN 2018022732 (print) | LCCN 2018037863 (ebook) | ISBN 9781509520275 (Epub) | ISBN 9781509520237 (hardback) | ISBN 9781509520244 (paperback)
Subjects: LCSH: Bitcoin. | Electronic funds transfers. | Blockchains (Databases) | Digital media. | BISAC: SOCIAL SCIENCE / Media Studies.
Classification: LCC HG1710 (ebook) | LCC HG1710 .D87 2019 (print) | DDC 332.1/78--dc23
LC record available at https://lccn.loc.gov/2018022732

Typeset in 10.25 on 13 pt Scala by
Servis Filmsetting Ltd, Stockport, Cheshire
Printed and bound in Great Britain by CPI Group (UK) Ltd, Croydon

The publisher has used its best endeavours to ensure that the URLs for external websites referred to in this book are correct and active at the time of going to press. However, the publisher has no responsibility for the websites and can make no guarantee that a site will remain live or that the content is or will remain appropriate.

Every effort has been made to trace all copyright holders, but if any have been inadvertently overlooked the publisher will be pleased to include any necessary credits in any subsequent reprint or edition.

For further information on Polity, visit our website: politybooks.com

Contents

Acknowledgments

This book is truly a collaborative, global effort. While writing it I travelled nearly constantly and met dozens of people who informed my thinking. My greatest intellectual debt goes to Bill Maurer at the University of California, Irvine, who has long supported and encouraged me. Parts of this book were written during a Fellowship at the lovely Leuphana University of Lüneburg, which was both enjoyable and productive thanks to Armin Beverungen, Paula Bialski, Lisa Conrad, and Jorge Oceja. I am also indebted to my European and American colleagues, whom I have had had many valuable conversations with—Mark Coeckelbergh, Wessel Reijers, Gianluca Miscione, Rachel O'Dwyer, Taylor Nelms, Lana Swartz, David Golumbia, and Finn Brunton. My editors at Polity Press, Mary Savigar and Ellen MacDonald-Kramer, moved mountains to bring this book to press so quickly. Similarly, the anonymous reviewers provided expedient, thorough, and insightful feedback. Special thanks to Megan Finn and Katie Shilton for providing me with the institutional support and opportunity to complete this book.

Writing would have been impossible without my friends and family and their unwavering support. Rory, woof. This book is dedicated to Alana Cattapan, my "producer" and wife who made untold sacrifices—putting up with academic wanderlust, often finding me far from home. On more than one occasion I was warned, "If you mention Bitcoin one more time, I'm hanging up on you"—a refrain undoubtedly heard by many others involved in this field, and yet the phone was never put down and encouragement and care were always forthcoming. Thank you.

I do not invest in cryptocurrencies. I do, however, buy small amounts of cryptocurrencies for experimentation. I am also an occasional advisor, participant, and employee of cryptocurrency and blockchain companies and projects. My up-to-date financial investment and conflict of interest disclosure is available at iqdupont.com/disclosure.

CHAPTER ONE

Experiments in Digital Society

I bought Bitcoin at $20. I bought Ethereum at $4. I've bought coins, tokens, and "crypto" of every kind. As I write this, Bitcoin trades near $20,000, Ethereum above $1,000. Blockchain startups launch in the millions or hundreds of millions. By the time you read this, these prices may very well seem quaint.

But I'm no investor, and this is no investment book. I lost money when the Mt. Gox exchange bankrupted, and then again when The DAO crowdsourcing experiment was hacked. I bought penny coins that stayed penny coins. Those Bitcoins and Ethers? I sold them long ago, making profit enough for a couple of nice dinners. This book is no guide to riches.

This book is a guide to understanding the wide, and yes sometimes wild, world of cryptocurrencies and blockchains.

It is remarkable how quickly the topic has grown in interest and importance. Just a few years ago cryptocurrencies and blockchains were considered fringe topics largely of interest to only a niche community of software developers. Today, banks and institutional investors are actively trading cryptocurrencies, international engineering and standards associations are helping shape the future of blockchain technologies, blue chip enterprises are leading research and development, and government agencies both big and small are deploying the technology for their constituents. By 2016, billions had already been poured into research and development. Through 2017, cryptocurrency and blockchain venture capital funding (US $3.7 billion) surpassed *the entirety* of all other technology seed funding (F. Wilson 2017), and there are no signs of investment slowing down through 2018 and forward. Hype and general interest, combined with confusion, has also grown rapidly. Issues facing cryptocurrencies and blockchains—from hacks to the hunt for Bitcoin's inventor—are regularly featured on the front pages of leading newspapers, in magazines, and in the daily television and radio news cycle. The inexact science of online search volume is also indicative of the hype and confusion—searches for cryptocurrency and blockchain keywords are now several factors greater than the big technology stories of the last decade, besting Web 2.0, Cloud Computing, and VoIP (Figure 1.1). Perhaps the truest measure of widespread interest is the number of times I have heard conversations about cryptocurrencies and blockchains at my local café or bar, and even the deli.

The key insight I develop in this book is that cryptocurrencies and blockchains are more social than technological. In fact, few technologies require as much from people as cryptocurrencies and blockchains, yet developers, advocates, critics, and users often ignore this fact and fail to see the broader applications and implications.

It all started with the digital money Bitcoin. An unknown software developer by the name of Satoshi Nakamoto started developing Bitcoin around 2007–2008 and continued to do so until 2011. Without much fanfare, Nakamoto then disappeared to let the open-source software community collectively develop the code, much like other successful open-source software products. In the early years, the bitcoins produced by the Bitcoin system were practically worthless and the whole enterprise was a fun diversion for geeks and an online community known as "cypherpunks." Within a few years, however, Bitcoin became valuable and people started treating it like the money it was meant to be (albeit money without state backing). Some retailers began accepting Bitcoin, a few Bitcoin automated teller machines (ATMs) were installed, and digital "money" started to flow across the globe. Bitcoin also

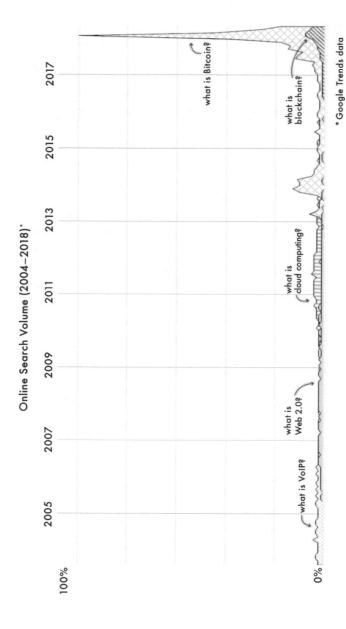

Figure 1.1 Online search volume for questions about technologies

3

facilitated illegal purchases on the "dark web" and startups claimed to offer lower transaction fees and better service than incumbents while dreaming of banking the unbanked across the globe.

Other digital "coins" soon entered the market, sometimes clones of Bitcoin, and sometimes with different philosophies, designs, or technologies. For example, Dogecoin (2013–) satirized the hype and mania of the time by issuing coins based on the Internet meme "doge." Soon, despite being a satire, the hype and mania drove the price of Dogecoins up, which eventually became valuable enough for its community to help send the Jamaican bobsled team to the 2014 Winter Olympics. Namecoin (2011–) sought to use the underlying technology of Bitcoin to create a new kind of decentralized Domain Name System (DNS) to make a more resilient Internet; Litecoin (2011–) was designed to improve on perceived issues with Bitcoin; and so on. These alternative or "alt" coins now number in the hundreds. Collectively, these are known as "cryptocurrencies" because they are currencies based on technologies derived from cryptography.

The next big shift occurred when a nineteen-year-old Russian-Canadian Bitcoin enthusiast named Vitalik Buterin decided to break away from the prevailing belief that cryptocurrencies were only useful as money. Buterin invented a generic and fully programmable system called Ethereum (2015–). Unlike Bitcoin and the alt coins previously, Ethereum was designed to be a general-purpose distributed computing environment that would sit on top of the peer-to-peer ledger technology used in Bitcoin. Because this technology used "blocks" of bundled transactions that are "chained" together, it became known as "blockchain" technology. Almost immediately large corporations recognized possibilities for Ethereum and began investing heavily.

No longer shackled to the concept of money, Ethereum and other blockchain technologies were adopted by industries to solve existing technical challenges, and by those companies that simply wanted to look "cool." The financial sector, itself going through a "fintech" moment, was especially eager to adopt blockchain technologies to facilitate transfers between banks and financial institutions (see Chapter 5). A quasi standard Ethereum-compatible token design called ERC-20 emerged and was widely deployed by startups. Blockchain technology also made possible "smart contracts," an idea first theorized in the 1990s but brought to life within the programmable and secure environment of blockchains. With blockchain-based smart contracts, lawyers could create digital notary services, or try out entirely new ideas in law (see Chapter 6). Because blockchains are so good at tracking digital things, sectors like logistics and supply chain management developed blockchains specific to their challenges (see Chapter 7). Most ambitiously, entirely new kinds of autonomous and decentralized businesses were dreamt up (see Chapter 8). Blockchain companies soon proliferated, and investment in research and development from startups and established corporations grew quickly.

Throughout this book you will find evidence of this shift from Bitcoin to blockchain. As I discuss in Chapter 2, Bitcoin was invented and popularized by a fringe community with unusual ideas about politics and economics. The turn to blockchains that I discuss in Chapter 4 was more than just a technology upgrade. Banks and blue-chip corporations liked the technology and saw many possible applications but needed to steer well clear of the illegal and unregulated use cases and the fringe politics associated with Bitcoin. To do so, these industries created a new narrative, completely eliminating any talk of Bitcoin and cryptocurrencies, and instead developed blockchain technologies that evolved out of this milieu. In fact, even the term "blockchain" was seen by some as tainted, so the banks created the hollow bowdlerization "distributed ledger technology" (DLT) as a politically safe way to describe the same thing.

To some extent, the introduction of a new, "serious"

blockchain pushed out the early community, who saw their invention morph from a technology to remake the world in their image to plumbing for dominant capital. Everything got professionalized and standardized (even major organizations like the IEEE and ISO got involved), and the idea of using Bitcoin as money faded almost completely. Today, it is nearly impossible to actually "buy" anything with Bitcoin (except for drugs), and early Bitcoin evangelists now suffer this pathos. Blockchain has no charm or revolutionary spirit, and the gears of progress and industry "disruption" are now largely owned by incumbents like IBM, Microsoft, and Intel (and the startups who want to become them). The consolation prize is that early Bitcoin users are now rich beyond their dreams.

Yet, for all of the investment and focus placed on the serious business of developing blockchain technologies to solve real-world computing problems, money and economics still matter. Even blockchains work best when their abstract "tokens" have some value. The fledgling study of this is known as "cryptoeconomics." Companies soon realized that cryptocurrencies—valuable tokens—can stand in as a kind of budget version of stocks (free from the hassle, regulation, and *safety* of existing stock markets). Launching a new "crypto" company with sellable assets became known as an "Initial Coin Offering" (ICO)—the cryptocurrency version of an Initial Public Offering (IPO), when a private company goes public. The investment returns from ICOs now regularly outperform existing stock market picks, and these companies rake in hundreds of millions in investment—sometimes for untested business models, zero sales, or no products. While the enthusiasm and potential are exciting, many of these companies go bankrupt, fail to launch, or simply steal investors' funds.

Cryptocurrency investors have also gotten more serious. Investors feverishly buy up ICOs and cryptocurrencies, even politically unsavory cryptocurrencies like Bitcoin (see Chapter 5). Hedge funds and traditional financial institutions invest alongside hobbyists and a few geeks holding out from the early days. Index funds and derivatives are now common, with more sophisticated financial instruments on the horizon. Investment activity has driven up the price of cryptocurrencies to truly unbelievable levels, shooting through bubbles on an upward and very volatile climb. But these are not investments for the faint-hearted, since cryptocurrencies regularly lose 20 percent or even 50 percent of their value in *a single day*. Of course, financial regulators, tax agencies, and concerned politicians have also noticed this, and occasionally reassert control. The danger of writing about cryptocurrency markets and prices, I fully appreciate, is that today's marvel is tomorrow's curiosity or calamity.

I have learned from studying cryptocurrencies and blockchain technologies since 2012 that there is never a dull day in this field. The fact that I am one of a few academic experts, with a mere half-decade of experience, is surprising by itself and suggests that many radical changes and interesting opportunities remain on the horizon. The academic research field is nascent and struggles to keep up with changes but is itself developing rapidly. Technical topics are actively researched and a number of previously dormant areas of computer science have since become hot topics (such as consensus systems for distributed computing). Social and behavioral topics are broadly represented too, but there are few truly unique areas of study (an exception is governance and governance systems, which are widely seen both as necessary for the success of blockchain companies, and an interesting proving ground for new ideas about coordinated action, social decision-making, and peer production).

To help visualize the history of cryptocurrencies and blockchains I have created two timelines. In the first (Figure 1.2), I show some of the notable events that have transpired since Bitcoin's inception. In the second (Figure 1.3), I offer my characterization of the relative levels of interest in use over time. Neither figure is necessarily rigorous or scientific, but these

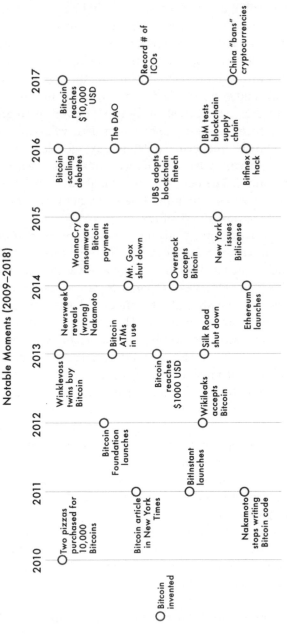

Figure 1.2   Notable events

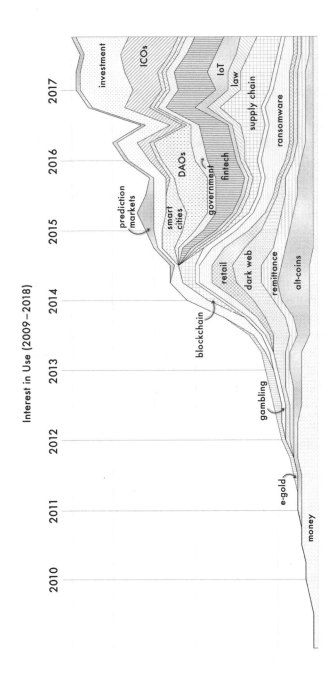

Figure 1.3   Author's interpretation of interest in use

figures do represent a long learned and *lived* take on changes in cryptocurrencies and blockchains over their early years.

But let's step back. With a market for cryptocurrencies in the hundreds of billions, and billions of research and development dollars being spent on blockchain technologies, where is all the real-world impact? A great joke told to me by Stephan Tual in 2016 supplies an answer: "What's your favorite blockchain app?" The joke worked in 2016 because there were none, and in 2018 the situation isn't much different. Today, no single "killer app" has emerged from cryptocurrencies and blockchains (among the hundreds of services and apps that have been developed) and no industries have been "disrupted." Yet, despite there being little more than hype, speculation, and possibility today, there are reasons to be cautiously optimistic about the future of cryptocurrencies and blockchains. The technology itself holds promise (even though it is constantly attacked by critics who lament that it is nothing new or unique). More consequential, to my mind, are the social changes underway that are driving innovation. With all of this *money, labor*, and *interest* there is almost no way cryptocurrencies and blockchains won't have significant impact in the future, which makes the field worthy of attention and study today.

Users

One of the most significant issues facing the study of cryptocurrencies and blockchains today is the lack of research on who users are and what they do with the technology. There are, however, dozens if not hundreds of market and technology surveys, primarily of interest to business journalists and the industry itself. There are also a number of technical analyses that focus on privacy and security, but not on users' thoughts or feelings about these issues. Measurement of cryptocurrency and blockchain peer-to-peer networks is another area of research for computer scientists and engineers (Gencer, Basu, Eyal, van Renesse, & Sirer 2018), but while these studies do provide some insights into relationships and trends, actual usage numbers are mere approximations (e.g., Yelowitz & Wilson 2015). The main challenge facing these kinds of studies is that because accounts are pseudonymous there is no way to discover basic demographics (but some research has been able to successfully de-anonymize certain aspects; see Biryukov, et al. 2014; Dupont & Squicciarini 2015; Fanti & Viswanath 2017). A small number of researchers have connected human interests—technological affordances or human-centered design—to the study and development of cryptocurrencies and blockchains (Kazerani, Rosati, & Lesser 2017; Velasco 2016). Others have studied cryptocurrency and blockchain users' discourses (Hernandez, Bashir, Jeon, & Bohr 2014). But despite a generally robust research field (see the research bibliography at http://blockchainresearchnet-work.org with its rapidly growing sets of published research articles and books covering all disciplines), there are only a few published articles focused on actual people, and none that richly engage with the activities, discourses, and beliefs of cryptocurrency and blockchain users.

The measure most regularly used as a proxy for the number of participants or to gauge general interest is the market capitalization (or "market cap") of cryptocurrencies. Market capitalization is the aggregate value of a market, calculated by multiplying the price of a single item (stock, barrel of oil, cryptocurrency token) by the number available. In traditional contexts, say stocks or bonds, the market capitalization measure is a helpful if somewhat flawed way to compare sizes. For cryptocurrencies, it is a *useless* measure. The price of a given cryptocurrency does not reflect a simple one-for-one exchange of state-issued currency (i.e., it is not the case that for every $100 of a cryptocurrency's price, $100 of state-issued currency has been invested). Nor does this figure truly reflect current market demand or any practical ability to sell at this level of market capitalization. While it may be possible to sell $100 worth of cryptocurrency for $100 of state-issued currency, it is certainly not true that $100 million of a cryptocurrency can be sold for $100 million of a state-issued currency. Even for Bitcoin, the largest market for cryptocurrencies by far, selling significant volume is difficult and liable to cause unintended market changes before transactions can be completed. This is because most cryptocurrency markets are surprisingly illiquid and "thin," with few real buyers but plenty of fabricated market demand (Stubbings 2014). Market capitalization is therefore a measure of a fictional reality, more misleading than informative.

The richest analyses of cryptocurrency and blockchain users so far have come from historical and documentary sources, either found in explicit discussions online, in whitepapers and manifestos, or from the implied commitments of users and developers (see Brunton 2018). In the early days, when there was only Bitcoin, users and developers were largely the same people (up to 2013, one half of Bitcoin users were also Bitcoin miners or had mined previously; Bohr & Bashir 2014). These early users included key and now mythic figures like Charlie Shrem (co-founder of BitInstant, later jailed for operating an unlicensed money-transmitting business), Mark Karpeles (CEO of Mt. Gox, later arrested for embezzlement charges), and Tyler and Cameron Winklevoss (former US rowing Olympians, erstwhile Facebook antagonists, early Bitcoin investors, and now multi-billionaires) (see Popper 2015). Many of these early figures and users held strong anti-authoritarian views, usually with a political and economic libertarian and right-wing bent (Golumbia 2016).

As the user base grew and the possible applications diversified (in the transition to blockchain technologies that I describe in Chapter 4), more mainstream users became involved. Today, there still remains a healthy countercultural element, and the revolutionary spirit of early "dreamers" still drives some innovation and interest (Swartz 2017), but judging from anecdotal evidence many of the newer participants no longer share or care about the political and economic aspirations of early users. In one of the few empirical studies of actual users, Caitlin Lustig and Bonnie Nardi found that from late 2013 until mid-2014, most Bitcoin users reported a distrust of human institutions (such as governments) and held that technology was more equitable and trustworthy, a political view largely in line with cyberlibertarianism and Silicon Valley–style thinking (see Fuchs 2007; Golumbia 2016; Pasquale 2015; Winner 1997; see also Doguet 2012 and Chapter 8 for the issue of trust and trustworthiness). Lustig and Nardi also found that Bitcoin users were overwhelmingly male, heterosexual, non-religious, relatively wealthy, well-educated, young, and politically Libertarian. In another study covering approximately the same time period, Jeremiah Bohr and Masooda Bashir (2014) found similar demographic results. Bohr and Bashir also found that those who used Bitcoin for illegal activities or self-identified as investors were more likely to have a larger investment (suggesting that purchasing illegal goods and investment were dominant uses). Aaron Yelowitz and Matthew Wilson used Google search data to study Bitcoin users (from January 2011 until July 2013), finding similar political and ideological interests.

Since these early (prior to 2014) studies, however, my own research and anecdotal observations suggest that the users of cryptocurrencies and blockchains have changed considerably in the intervening years. Unfortunately, there have been no follow-up empirical studies to date, but some conjectures about the changing user base can be made. For example, when I interviewed hobby and professional cryptocurrency traders in 2017 (for the research discussed in Chapter 5), I found a minority of women, but still far more than the 2 percent reported by Lustig and Nardi and the 5 percent reported by Bohr and Bashir. Women working in the industry have also become more prominent, at least self-consciously so, but it still remains depressingly common to see blockchain companies comprised entirely of men or industry conference panels with not a single woman on stage. Such gender imbalances are not unique to cryptocurrencies and blockchains, of course, but it seems that the nexus of radical politics, money, and emerging technology (all traditionally male domains) has produced a culture that has both ignored women and systematically excluded them. Nonetheless, there are some reasons to be optimistic that this proclivity is declining—during my studies I found an increasingly healthy range of worldviews beyond the libertarian/privacy/technology nexus reported in earlier studies. I even found some diversity in race and geographical location.

The discourses of users on social media portray a narrow band of interests. Cryptocurrency users tend to discuss investments and price fluctuations, often dogmatically and vocally. This focus on wealth generation still has a revolutionary twinge, but more in the spirit of a gauche *nouveau riche* than a community working towards a radical new technology to change the world (which characterized the community spirit up until about 2016). On social media there are visible examples of this shift in the community. For example, one formerly influential cryptographer and software developer (responsible for a technology that directly informed the invention of Bitcoin) as of 2018 appears to have given up on developing technologies and now focuses on maximizing cryptocurrency profits. While not all cryptocurrency users have become millionaires, the number of punks and misfits in the community has significantly declined from its early days.

Beyond Bitcoin, users are a more diverse group, ranging from software developers working at Microsoft and IBM to privacy-maximalists at Zcash (in the spirit of early cypherpunks) to international development and charity workers trying to stem corruption in developing nations. In recent years, interest in cryptocurrencies and blockchain technologies has broken out of its niche, attracting the attention of the general population (although largely for purposes of speculative investment). In late 2017, the Coinbase iOS app rose to the top of the Apple App Store sales chart, signaling broad adaption, while—somewhat inexplicably—celebrities like the rappers 50 Cent and Snoop Dogg, the pop star Katy Perry, and the boxer Floyd "Money" Mayweather all publically promoted and purchased cryptocurrencies. As with those in the Bitcoin community, this more diverse group of users still tends to believe strongly in free market capitalism. Small projects originating from innovators on the political left have been developed as well, although these have not always been met with great success or universal approval (one creative project that sought to use idle computer resources to generate funds for Americans unable to afford bail proved controversial for its side effect of wasting electricity). In general, many in the blockchain community lament the focus on investment and wish to build new technologies instead—although they recognize that soaring prices finance development work.

A study by Garrick Hileman and Michel Rauchs (2017) offers a more recent snapshot of the changing face of cryptocurrencies and blockchains. Although focused more on industry than on actual users, the study highlights a few relevant facts: 1) cryptocurrency exchanges are essential infrastructure in the industry, 2) global transfers do happen with some regularity (i.e., not *all* activity is speculative investing), and 3) cryptocurrency miners control technical development of the networks. One conclusion from the study is that the labor force developing core features of the industry is still small, employing less than 2,000 people globally across exchanges, wallets, payments, and mining companies (Hileman & Rauchs 2017). Nonetheless, the study argues that the industry is growing rapidly, and I would expect that if the study had included workers across the complete range of commercial activities, the labor force would be much larger, perhaps ten or a hundred times larger.

Hileman and Rauchs's study also highlights an important change in the user and developer community. As I described above, in the early days most participants were simultaneously advocates, developers, entrepreneurs, and users. Hilemand

and Rauchs's study suggests that cryptocurrency and block-chain miners have since emerged as a community distinct from users. Miners have always been an important part of the ecosystem because they are responsible for validating and processing transactions (see Chapter 4). This special role is part of the design first set out in the Nakamoto (2008) whitepaper describing Bitcoin. And because miners control the network, they are able to dictate protocol changes. Significant changes to protocol require miners to upgrade their software, but refusal to upgrade is tantamount to veto power, which has been effectively leveraged by Bitcoin miners in recent years. This is known as the Bitcoin "scaling debate," which has resulted in the community of miners effectively blocking a much-needed increase in network capacity, thereby resulting in slow processing times and enormously high fees. Until miners agree to upgrade the software that processes transactions, the Bitcoin network will remain hamstrung (barring clever work-arounds or alternatives like "Bitcoin Cash," a forked version of Bitcoin). Given that the community of miners has grown distinct from users, decisions made by miners impact the *user* ecosystem but hardly impact miners themselves.

The core issue facing the Bitcoin network is that miners' interests are not aligned with those of the broader community of users. Even in the early days, Bitcoin miners did not share the ideological interests of the broader community (Bohr & Bashir 2014). Rather than being motivated by an ideology of privacy and libertarian politics (and being focused on the technology to produce this vision), miners were and are mostly economically incentivized. Because processing fees are set by a market mechanism (transactions that include higher fees are processed first), network congestion is actually good for miners, who collect higher fees even though this means that users fare worse. When miners were more likely to be users themselves (only in the *very* early days), they had some interest in maintaining a healthy network. But as Bohr and Bashir found, by 2013 miners had already started to separate themselves from the rest of the community. Then, as mining difficulty went up (it is correlate to price; see Chapter 4), mining soon required specialized hardware, which caused further bifurcation between the user and miner communities. Today, the majority of cryptocurrency and blockchain mining (especially Bitcoin) is done in China (Velasco 2016), a country that has effectively banned cryptocurrencies (Wolfson 2015). Outlaw Chinese miners now control the global Bitcoin network, are economically incentivized to keep it congested (so long as the Bitcoin price stays high), and do not share the ideology or community interests of most users.

Globally, communities of cryptocurrency and blockchain users have unique and sometimes competing interests, inhabit distinct monetary and technological cultures, and live in radically different and often changing regulatory climates. The range is massive. For example, Venezuela developed a state-backed "petro" cryptocurrency (in a remarkable reversal of the libertarian ethos of Bitcoin), while Bolivia has declared Bitcoin illegal and punishes any users (most countries simply turn a blind eye or occasionally reassert control).

Even in countries where cryptocurrencies have attracted broad use, the kinds of uses are often novel and the regulations inconsistent. For example, China has long been at the forefront of digital payments, but not cryptocurrencies, which have come under scrutiny by regulators many times, despite growing use (Y. N. Lee 2017). In China, Bitcoin mining is legal (for now) but cryptocurrency exchanges are not, so Chinese miners have had to turn to nearby exchanges in Japan, South Korea, and Vietnam in order to exchange mining rewards for local state-issued currency. The governments of Japan, South Korea, Vietnam, and India have all been cautious about cryptocurrencies, despite considerable use by their citizens (largely for investment). Japan has also led several blockchain development efforts, especially in the financial technology space. Although North Korea is a political outsider, it is rumored that the country is extensively involved in cryptocurrencies—both through legitimate and hacking or cyberwar means, ostensibly to launder funds to bypass international sanctions (Zoey 2018). Russia also has a significant indigenous interest in cryptocurrencies and block-chains, although use currently occurs without clear laws (Liao 2017). The former Soviet state of Estonia—a small country that is always at the forefront of new digital technologies—has embraced cryptocurrencies and especially blockchain tech-nologies. In particular, Estonia has experimented with using blockchain technologies for offering a range of government services (Mettler 2016; Sullivan & Burger 2017). Whereas, fol-lowing the Greek economic crisis and the capital control rules imposed in 2015, it was conjectured that Greeks would flood to Bitcoin as an alternative currency, yet this has not come to fruition (Zamani & Babatsikos 2017). Europe, North America, and Australia have long been involved in the use and develop-ment of cryptocurrency and blockchain technologies. Indeed, although China now dominates cryptocurrency use (up to 40 percent globally, according to Hileman & Rauchs 2017), most cryptocurrency and blockchain software development—and its funding—occurs in the United States.

Developing nations, and in particular those in Africa, have a unique relationship to cryptocurrencies and blockchains. Hileman and Rauchs (2017) describe a fledgling industry for cryptocurrencies and blockchains in developing African nations and yet these fringe use cases have garnered an out-sized amount of (largely speculative) academic and industry attention. Providing banking services for the unbanked is seen as a key use case for cryptocurrencies (and is a particu-lar interest of technology-oriented, or ICT4D, scholars; see, e.g., Ammous 2015). In many countries in Africa, however, alternative banking structures have already arisen, such as M-Pesa, the largest and most famous of the digital "leap-frog" banking services in Africa. BitPesa, a direct competitor to M-Pesa (and incumbents such as Western Union), is cur-rently the largest cryptocurrency startup company focused on

Africa, although to date the number of transactions and users is miniscule.

Global remittances are a large and lucrative market, with over US $500 billion transferred every year. Like banking for developing nations, remittances were seen as one of the first use cases for cryptocurrencies. Today, startups compete on the belief that cryptocurrencies can provide fast, low-fee global transfers. In recent years, however, Bitcoin has failed to live up to this promise (exacerbated by high fees and difficult use; see RogomonZ 2016). Other cryptocurrencies (such as Litecoin) have done somewhat better in this regard, but it is not clear that any cryptocurrency solution will create the necessary socio-technical infrastructures to actually aid developing nations. According to researchers at the Consultative Group to Assist the Poor (CGAP), BitPesa in particular has not been able to provide a service rivaling either M-Pesa or Western Union. Instead, BitPesa is being used to facilitate global payments for African entrepreneurs, and is not used for remittance and banking services. In general, many of these efforts to bring cryptocurrencies to developing nations have been critiqued as typical of the technology-focused external "solutionism" that often characterizes aid and development (Mazer 2014; Scott 2016).

Even in the developed West, cryptocurrencies and block-chains have yet to be adopted to any significant extent outside of speculative investment. In the last couple of years, a number of early blockchain products have launched in a variety of industries (see Chapters 5, 6, and 7). While these have immense promise, few are fully operational and none can be considered critical to any industry. The adoption of cryptocurrencies as currency is even worse. No cryptocurrency has had widespread adoption for the kinds of practices usually associated with money (investment activity is, on the other hand, vigorous). Bitcoin is the most successful cryptocurrency in terms of user adoption, but the dream of retail sales, payments, or any typical use has faded to almost zero (Chaparro

2017). In Chapter 2 I discuss many of the reasons why Bitcoin has failed to be adopted as a currency; these reasons include high price volatility, economic incentives to hoard, high fees, slow transaction processing, poor user experience, and security risks. Beyond these critical socio-technical issues and limitations, there are also more subtle psychological reasons why Bitcoin has failed to be adopted as a currency. Most people simply *don't care* about alternative currencies—seeing few limitations with state-issued currency—and therefore *any* impediment or issue with an alternative is likely sufficient to prevent adoption.

If there was ever a chance for Bitcoin to flourish in the West, it would have been with the young and technologically savvy undergraduates at the Massachusetts Institute of Technology (MIT) who were given *free* Bitcoins in 2014. But, as this experiment played out, adoption has been limited. As of 2017, only 13 percent of the MIT undergraduates had actually used their Bitcoins; the remainder had exchanged them for US dollars (39 percent) or simply forgotten about them (48 percent) (Athey, Catalini, & Tucker 2017; Catalini & Tucker 2016). (Technically, these Bitcoins are simply "unused," but given the difficulty of securing Bitcoins it is reasonable to think that most are now inaccessible and effectively lost.) If MIT students cannot or will not use Bitcoin as an alternative currency, I see no reason to think that the general population will, at least not yet.

Social technologies

The single greatest innovation of Bitcoin was not the development of new software. Rather, Bitcoin solved a social coordination problem. The consensus protocol (see Chapter 4) introduced a practical way of coordinating computational activity without explicit and sustained participation, and with unknown and untrustworthy actors. In doing so, Bitcoin revitalized a dormant research field in computer science, spurring further technical development (see Lamport, Shostak, & Pease 1982). And with machine coordination came new experiments on human coordination, including the availability of social and political tools to control populations and "optimize" the delivery of services. Bitcoin, and, later, cryptocurrencies, also presented a practical solution to the challenge of creating and maintaining value online—as a form of money, as abstract tokens, and as economically incentivized behavior. Together, these innovations—consensus and value—make cryptocurrencies and blockchains powerful because they are *social technologies.*

In thinking about cryptocurrencies and blockchains as social technologies we can draw on the rich literature about money. Even though Bitcoin has largely failed to be *used* as money, it still looks and behaves a lot like money. In a classic work, Georg Simmel (2004) described money as "the purest form of the tools" with "no purpose of its own," which therefore has "unlimited possibilities" and "unpredictable uses" (210 ff.). With no purpose of its own, money is just a "means" that gains value in exchange (in Chapter 4, I develop this insight into a theory of blockchain *media*). Simmel's description of money is particularly apt for understanding cryptocurrencies and blockchains. In the shift from Bitcoin— imagined as a kind of money—to blockchain, there has been an abstraction (and elimination) of ideology and meaning. In being less about money, blockchain technologies have become purer tools, and therefore gained more possibilities. Software developers in the blockchain industry perfectly reflect this sentiment; when faced with any problem, only half-jokingly they exclaim, "Put it on a blockchain!"

Cryptocurrencies and blockchains are different than the kinds of money Simmel was imagining back in the late 1800s in an important respect—they are *computing technologies.* Mark Coeckelbergh (2015) explores what the recent rise of "money machines" means for society and finds that there is a significant moral dimension that ought to inform discussions about their development and use. Using Simmel's argument that money is a means, Coeckelbergh notes that money both bridges and creates distance (2015, p. 36). Coeckelbergh argues that technologies are often *tele*-technologies that also affect distances, sometimes helping to connect geographically distant people, but also creating further social and moral distance. Consider the ways that Facebook helps friends stay close but erodes engagement in local democracies, such as the town hall meetings of an imagined pastoral past. With this change in democratic engagement, it is possible that "clicktivism" fails to create the same kind of emotional proximity in society, thereby diminishing empathy and fueling hatred and vitriol. Yet, every new technology brings social change—both positive and negative—and moral outrage. Attending to the ways that technology changes society is complex and context specific. When it comes to questions of money and finance, Coeckelbergh draws on Simmel's claim that money objectifies, depersonalizes, detaches, automates, and alienates (2015, p. 12), and even more so when money is a creation of high technology. In so doing, money machines change our values and goals, sometimes causing us to mistake a means for an end.

In his specific reflections on Bitcoin, Coeckelbergh highlights the ways in which money has become dematerialized. This dematerialization has resulted in some puzzling issues, prompting questions about the ontology of money (what *is* money when it is just a transaction record on a digital ledger?). To resolve these quandaries, Coeckelbergh considers the social ontology developed by John Searle, who espouses a theory of "collective intentionality" to explain how we accept that a piece of paper or a transaction on a digital ledger comes to count for something valuable (the question of value is an especially thorny one for all money, but especially for those currencies that are virtual). Coeckelbergh finds Searle's theory compelling but ontologically messy, in that it adds a human and social dimension "on top" of natural reality

(Coeckelbergh 2015, p. 100). Instead, Coeckelbergh develops a relational theory of money. Using the example of Bitcoin as characteristic of the fact that *money is technology* (this holds true for all money media, including paper bills and metallic coins), Coeckelbergh introduces Martin Heidegger's (1993) critique of technology. According to Heidegger, technology reorients human relationships, subjugating our values and "ways of being." Rather than liberating humans, modern technology conceals. Bitcoin, according to Coeckelbergh, is "part of a larger transformative process . . . about how we are changing." These changes are social and political, brought about by Bitcoin's technology (Coeckelbergh 2015, p. 163).

In the next chapter, I describe the social dimensions of cryptocurrencies, but for now let's consider what is at stake with social technologies. There is a simple story that cryptocurrencies and blockchain technologies are just *used* by social actors—that is, they are *in* society. As technologies in society, cryptocurrencies and blockchains merely conform to a society's preexisting norms and values (in the extreme view, such technologies are thought to be morally inert; for a criticism of this view, see Winner 1980). The more powerful (and I think correct) characterization is that cryptocurrencies and blockchain technologies *produce* society, and, therefore, to the extent that we are able to control what we create, allow us to produce *the society we want*. This ability to *experiment* on and with society—with real social and political levers—gives us nearly unprecedented powers.

As cryptocurrency and blockchain software developers are starting to realize, these technologies must be handled with care. When, for instance, the blockchain project known as "The DAO" was hacked (see Chapter 8), the implications were not simply a loss of money. The DAO revealed the extreme importance of managing change and configuring failsafe switches; it showed why we need to align interests across communities. Or, to use another example, when we design a privacy-maximizing cryptocurrency like Zcash, we ought to recognize that we are reconfiguring powerful, perhaps *essential*, parts of human nature. This is because the structure of money dictates how human beings relate to one another and to communities and even the past (Konings 2017). Similarly, even seemingly trivial business optimizations, such as blockchain technology for logistics (Chapter 7), determine how we overcome or accept geographical limitations. For every new industry vertical that a cryptocurrency or blockchain technology is developed for, from actuaries to voting, we gain a new tool of change and inherit the moral obligations that come with this.

Managing the development and adoption of cryptocurrency and blockchain technologies in real social, political, and business settings remains a significant challenge. From a systems perspective, the methods for dealing with development and adoption are known as "change management." Change management is the organization of processes and resources to efficiently and effectively produce and sustain positive change. This change is usually focused on solving business goals, but change management processes can be directed towards any goal—social, environmental, or otherwise. The setting of these goals, and the alignment of strategies to accomplish them, is known as governance. Unlike change management, which is often a discrete task accomplished by personnel who are solely responsible for bringing about change, governance is more strategic and visionary. Governance involves the assessment of multiple options, limitations, and opportunities.

In the case of cryptocurrencies and blockchains, governance is perhaps the most important and yet critically misunderstood part of the industry. Cryptocurrency and blockchain governance is so complex and difficult because these systems are typically designed to be decentralized and community (or stakeholder) driven. For systems that have an "open" architecture (see Chapter 4), such as Bitcoin and Ethereum, aligning miner interests with those of the broader community is critically important because miners control how (and if) change is implemented. For organizations developing cryptocurrency products and services, it is important to recognize that authority—which is responsible for setting and effecting strategic vision—is not hierarchical nor equally dispersed among stakeholders. In many cases, governance of cryptocurrency and blockchain products and services is at least partially algorithmic, which sets in motion unique challenges concerning how and when change can occur, and who can effect it. In particular, cryptocurrency and blockchain governance must contend with an intermediate layer of valuable and granular tokens. Having direct access to finely individuated parts of an organization, and the ability to leverage economic prohibitions and incentives, is an awesome opportunity for designing new kinds of organizations and society. But this awesome opportunity also requires expertise and know-how that, for the most part, most organizations lack. Increasingly, cryptocurrency and blockchain companies are realizing these deficiencies, and governance and change management are areas of growth in the industry.

To deal with questions of governance and (more broadly) the social and political impact of these technologies, how should we study cryptocurrencies and blockchain technologies? There are many possible methods, some of which I have used in my own research. For quantitative research, a typical measurement study might count the volume of transactions on the cryptocurrency and blockchain networks. More sophisticated studies might create graphs of transactions or show trends over time. As mentioned above, however, due to the pseudonymous nature of cryptocurrencies and blockchains, these measurements are somewhat unreliable (even the simple measurement of transaction volume is fraught with difficulty, since it is considered best practice to create new wallet destinations after every transfer, which effectively hides the user). Survey studies of users, companies, or other stakeholders are another approach. What a survey might lack in coverage it makes up for in richness of data collection. A well-designed survey can even collect subtle data points about the thoughts and feelings of users, in addition to raw facts about how, how often, and when people are using cryptocurrencies and block-chain technologies. There is, I should point out, currently a critical lack of these kinds of studies.

Qualitative research on cryptocurrency and blockchain users is richer and rarer still. Perhaps the easiest way to gather rich qualitative data is to actually use the technology, a form of research known as autoethnography. I have myself used autoethnographic methods and learned a lot in the pro-cess. Early on, I bought a few Bitcoins and briefly tried my hand at investing. I learned that having some "skin in the game" changes one's relationship to the technology and other users (it also introduces ethical issues, something that academic researchers in this field have yet to properly attend to). I have also tried cryptocurrency mining, which I found to be oddly soothing (the hum of a machine, the satisfaction of mindless number crunching), but not particularly lucrative. In Chapter 8, I describe my effort to launch a decentralized, autonomous charity using a blockchain platform. Even just puzzling through the potential issues, without ever getting dirty in the code, can help reveal subtleties and create empathy for software developers (or conversely, it can horrify). Because many cryptocurrency and blockchain platforms are open source, and use open networks, the opportunities for action or design research are also plentiful. Working alongside devel-opers and reporting about those experiences can provide an insider's view, and much like how I learned about the psychol-ogy of cryptocurrency investors when I briefly became one, action research motivates interest and attunes the researcher to things that might otherwise go overlooked.

Interviews and ethnographic studies provide the rich-est data sets, but this kind of research is rare in this field. Interviews with important developers, either retrospective (oral histories) or contemporary, require a combination of technical know-how and expertise in qualitative research methodology, and therefore are challenging to conduct but useful. A volume comparable to Peter Seibel's (2009) classic *Coders at Work* would go a long way to explain how cryptocurrencies and blockchain technologies impact software and society. Curiously, it seems that we know even less about actual users. In Chapter 5, I describe my small sample of interviews with cryptocurrency investors, both hobby and professional. Doing interviews of this nature requires sensitivity to the concerns of users, which includes delicacy when talking about money, a preference (usually) for anonymity, and system security risks (revealing information about how much cryptocurrency a user holds and how that cryptocurrency is held creates a target for hackers and thieves).

If my characterization of cryptocurrencies and blockchains as social technologies is correct—that through such technologies developers and users have unprecedented access to experiment with social and political levers—I would argue that we can treat these environments like scientific laboratories, where tokens, ledgers, smart contracts, and distributed networks take the place of beakers, burners, and particle accelerators, and study them as such (see also Böhme, Christin, Edelman, & Moore 2015, who characterize "Bitcoin as a Social Science Laboratory"). Science studies provide a model for this kind of research—think Bruno Latour and Steve Woolgar's (1986) *Laboratory Life*, but for cryptocurrencies and blockchains. In *Laboratory Life*, Latour embedded in a biology laboratory to report the rich details about how facts come to be, how politics and everyday issues change scientific results, and how objects and inscriptions circulate with theories, facts, and experiments. Reporting on the seeming minutiae of discovering amino acids in a molecule, Latour relays one of his participant's comments:

> But at the Tucson meeting, when I heard the report of Guillemin, my God, I thought that we were on the right track all along in 1966. It came as a complete surprise to me. (Latour & Woolgar 1986, p. 141)

From this and many other discourses, and an ethnographer's sensitivity to how people are critical ingredients to the laboratory, Latour and Woolgar were able to reconstruct the very basis of how biological science works. Consider the parallel, an online discussion about how Ethereum's experimental Proof of Stake consensus mechanism might work:

> If the minimum stake deposit requirement is 1500 ETH, becoming a validator is out of reach for majority holders. While not part of Casper design, delegate services would likely arise as validator interest grows and a high barrier to entry exists. This is more of an economic topic rather than technical. Have there been any conversations on the economic design of Casper/PoS? (Loon 2018)

In both cases, the domain of discourse includes technical details and facts (the report by Guillemin; the stake deposit in ETH), but also a range of social and psychological interests and behaviors. Where Latour's scientists were discussing the impact of running experiments, calibrating instruments, and assaying peptides, the participants in the Ethereum developer community were discussing economic thresholds, validation techniques, and community interests.

The critical ingredients are again the people in the room—here, virtual, but the same could be done, to an even greater effect, by sitting in the meeting rooms of blockchain start-ups. But unlike Latour's biology laboratory, the tools and techniques of cryptocurrencies and blockchains are largely social, economic, and political. It matters if the "Casper design" sets the validator threshold at 1,500 instead of 2,500, in the same way that the three amino acids "accounted for 30 percent of the dry weight of TRF" and not 40 percent (Latour & Woolgar 1986, p. 134). The results—security of health data, transaction volumes of shipping manifests, or privacy of retail sales—depends on getting the validator threshold "right," to say nothing of the million other finer points that require action and revision, testing and troubleshooting, by the developers, miners, venture capitalists, regulators, and users.

Cryptocurrencies and blockchains, therefore, are social experiments in mediation, power, order, and time. These forces flow among people and devices, and what gets to count as fact depends on what is considered authentic and "real" for cryptocurrencies, and what is adopted and used by stakeholders for blockchains. The technological artifacts that result are emblematic of the place, time, and communities in which they are taken up.

Terminology and definitions

While it is no substitute for the full descriptions available in the respective chapters, in lieu of a glossary (see also InterPARES Trust Terminology Project 2017; Walch 2017), the following definitions cover the basic terminology of cryptocurrencies and blockchains:

- *Cryptocurrencies*: Money-like technologies that record transactions on distributed, append-only digital ledgers. Transactions are validated and chained to form secure blocks and blocks are sequentially chained to form a "blockchain." Blocks are replicated and distributed through a peer-to-peer network of computers that are responsible for independently verifying incoming blocks while creating a local copy. Local copies are kept in sync across the network by a consensus protocol. Also known as "crypto." See Chapters 2 and 3.
- *Blockchains*: Distributed computing technologies that securely record data on append-only digital ledgers and execute code. Blockchains are functionally similar to cryptocurrencies but are not tied to a system of money and therefore have enhanced code execution environments. Also known as "decentralized ledger technologies" (DLTs). See Chapter 4.

- *Mining*: Computational process of validating, storing, transmitting, and securing transactions in a Proof of Work consensus protocol. See Chapter 4.
- *Consensus*: A protocol mechanism that is required to sync digital ledgers across distributed, heterogeneous networks that lack trustworthy actors. The Proof of Work consensus protocol is used in Bitcoin, but there are others, such as Proof of Stake. See Chapter 4.
- *Coins and tokens*: Abstractions of value exchanged by cryptocurrency and blockchain systems. These terms are misnomers, as digital ledgers contain only transactions, not discrete coins or tokens.
- *Smart contracts*: Self-executing code on distributed cryptocurrency and blockchain networks. Smart contracts are notionally similar to legal contracts but may operate outside of an explicit legal context or attempt to represent or embed legal discourse. See Chapter 6.
- *Decentralized and distributed*: Descriptions of network architectures where nodes are interconnected without a single point of control. Network architectures may be either private, permissioned/consortium, or public (see Chapter 4). Terms are typically used interchangeably.
- *Cryptography*: Transposition and substitution of discrete notation (bits) to exploit combinatorial expansiveness, typically for information confidentiality, integrity, and authentication (see DuPont 2017). Includes encryption, decryption, and hashing algorithms. Cryptocurrencies and blockchains do not (typically) use encryption; rather, data are authenticated and secured by cryptographic digital signature and hashing algorithms. See Chapter 4.

Overview of chapters

Chapter 2 describes the origins and possible future of Bitcoin. This chapter sets up the discussion about how cryptocurrencies do and do not count as money, which marks a transition from the first and primary use of cryptocurrencies as money and the second and broader use of blockchain technologies for everything else.

Chapter 3 describes the common narratives of money as found in the cryptocurrency literature. After comparing the orthodox theories of money, I describe a range of alternative theories of money. This chapter provides a groundwork for thinking about cryptocurrencies beyond the typical narratives found in most literature.

Chapter 4 describes the technical components of blockchains. I describe what cryptographic hashes are, how they are used to create blocks of transactions, and how blocks are chained together to create secure records. I highlight the role of consensus protocols, focusing on the most common protocol, the "proof of work." I conclude the chapter by discussing why the proof of work consensus protocol uses so much electricity and introduce three network architectures that offer alternative designs.

Chapter 5 describes two aspects of finance: the development of financial clearance and settlement infrastructure and cryptocurrency financial investment. In this chapter, I detail some of the reasons why "disrupting" the financial clearance and settlement industry is challenging. I also detail the results of a small qualitative study of cryptocurrency and blockchain investors, highlighting how the investment market presents numerous unique challenges.

Chapter 6 describes some of the issues facing law and legal professions. I discuss possible ways to understand the jurisprudence of cryptocurrencies and blockchains and how this impacts the regulatory landscape. In this chapter I also detail the concept of "smart property" and how smart contracts potentially change enforcement from reactive to proactive, which might cause issues.

Chapter 7 describes the history and future of information technologies for logistics. This chapter details how emerging Internet of Things (IoT) and sensor networks and other "smart" devices work on blockchain platforms, and how this anticipates the shift to blockchain technology solutions for "Industry 4.0" applications. I conclude with a critique of blockchain technologies as "logistical media."

Chapter 8 describes the ambitious efforts to create new, blockchain-based organizations, focusing on the development of Decentralized Autonomous Organizations (DAOs). I frame the operation of DAOs in the context of trust and relationships and then detail a case study for evaluation. I discuss how contracts are key technologies for developing trust, which the advent of smart contracts running autonomously on blockchain platforms seeks to displace. I conclude on an optimistic note, about how the governance of blockchain technologies is a significant challenge but also an exciting one.

CHAPTER TWO

Origins and Futures of Cryptocurrencies

Bitcoin is the first cryptocurrency: a cryptographically secured, privately issued digital money. Or at least it *wants* to be money. Designed around 2008 and released in early 2009 by a shadowy and unknown inventor, "Satoshi Nakamoto," Bitcoin was a response to the 2008 global economic crisis, the worst economic crisis in decades, perhaps centuries. A whole generation of people—derided as millennials—were economically devastated (see Hobbes 2017) and unsurprisingly many are now thoroughly enticed by Bitcoin. But Bitcoin was also designed to be more than just another digital money. Nakamoto wanted to remake the entire economic system anew, from the roots of cyberlibertarian politics and extreme Austrian economics (Golumbia 2016). While Bitcoin has dramatically changed since its early days—it is now largely used for investment (see Chapter 5)—these radical economic and political origins are still visible. Literally encoded in the original (or "genesis") block, Nakamoto set his political aim: "The Times 03/Jan/2009 Chancellor on brink of second bailout for banks."

The design and architecture of Bitcoin reflects these political and economic goals. Bitcoin is issued on a predetermined schedule that reaches a maximum and then stops. This monetary cap ostensibly prevents inflation, which is the worst sin of central banks that print money with abandon, according to Bitcoin's economic logic. In reality, however, Bitcoin does not avoid inflation because inflation is not a simple monetary issue (instead, Bitcoin suffers deflation, even hyperdeflation). Bitcoin is also a peer-to-peer system that ostensibly does away with central banks and government backing, another key dimension of the ideology inscribed in its design. Since Bitcoin is passed peer-to-peer without a central clearinghouse, it is supposed to be unstoppable and impervious to censorship. This, too, in reality, is not so simple. Because Bitcoin is a complex socio-technical ecosystem and not just a technical protocol, it is shaped by many externalities, including users bent on manipulating or attacking the market, systemic risks caused by cryptocurrency exchanges, and evolving legal status dictated by government regulators (see Gerard 2017).

This chapter details the origins of Bitcoin and offers a description of its future uses and present issues. Bitcoin emerged from the panic of the 2008 global economic crisis but traces its roots through the long history of alternative and private currencies, and in particular the ways these were taken up by a subculture of "cypherpunks." The predecessors of Bitcoin that emerged out of the cypherpunk community combined recent advances in cryptography with quixotic political and economic goals. This chapter sets up the discussion that is completed in the next chapter, about how cryptocurrencies do and do not count as money, which marks a transition between the first and primary use of cryptocurrencies as money and the second and broader use of blockchain technologies for everything else. The broader arch over these three chapters is the transition from money to media.

Origins

Bitcoin was not the first private money, nor the first digital money, and not even the first to use cryptography. Money has a long history beyond the familiar stuff found in wallets (Maurer 2006). Money comes in many different forms and is used in many different ways (Maurer 2015). Some scholars distinguish between money, currency, and cash (see Agha 2017). These are, however, multidimensional categories: money is the broadest (and abstract) category of value, currency is whatever kind of money is accepted and counts for "passing current" (Brunton 2018), and cash is the physical form of currency (or "pecuniary media" that are usually state-issued banknotes and coins). While these distinctions may at first seem clearcut, they are quickly blurred, especially in the digital realm.

The variety and accessibility of money today is vast. Money has been issued by people, companies, banks, states, collectives, and groups. Sometimes, money is not "issued" at all, appearing by spontaneous social consensus (but some scholars claim that in order to count as "money," it must be *issued* by someone; see Ingham 2004, p. 12). Money has taken many shapes, sizes, and material forms, ranging from shells, stones, metal coins, paper notes, and digital data—to say nothing of the ways that abstract notions such as labor, credit, or purchasing power count as kinds of money. Nor is this variety of issuers and materials just a historical curiosity. Money is still widely issued outside of the familiar forms of state-issued currencies. Money, or perhaps "money-like" things, includes private scrips (IOUs, company money, and loyalty programs), video game currencies, monthly transit passes, and arguably the largest category of all, government bonds (Ferguson 2009).

There are also many "alternative" forms of money still passing hand to hand, as currencies in their own right. In fact, privately issued currencies are surprisingly common, usually filling some unmet need specific to their context. For example, Salt Spring Dollars can only be spent on the small island off the coast of western Canada, Euskos can only be spent in Northern Basque country, and North London LETSs (a "Local Exchange Trading Scheme") allow community members to directly trade skills and services instead of exchanging the abstract and alienating value of state-issued currency. Sometimes ready-made things or abstractions take the place of money, such as the exchange of mobile phone airtime minutes in Egypt, Ghana, Uganda, and Kenya. In Kenya, this grassroots practice grew until a major telecommunications company, Safaricom, adopted it and formally developed it into M-Pesa, now a successful alternative banking and monetary system across Africa (Dodd 2016; Harris, Goodman, & Traynor 2012).

Despite many well-established alternatives, the online world presents new challenges for money. Before Bitcoin, it was no secret that a better solution to online commerce and digital money was needed. Many companies tried to fill this gap (see Clark 2016), but credit card companies were the most successful. Credit card companies, however, left much to be desired. In addition to being rentier, for-profit companies selling parasitic credit-based solutions, actually using credit cards online was (and is) fraught with issues. Supporters of Bitcoin, the open-source, peer-to-peer, pseudonymous network controlled by no one with unblockable and immutable transactions, feel that it is just the thing the world needs.

The existing payments and digital money infrastructure has issues. First, payments companies block certain kinds of transactions. For example, in 2012, credit card companies blocked transfers to WikiLeaks, which then turned to Bitcoin as an alternative. These credit card companies were ostensibly acting on legal requirements: legitimate financial services are prohibited from working with criminals, terrorists, fraudsters, and money launderers, which includes WikiLeaks. But many saw the blockade against WikiLeaks as simply politically motivated financial censorship. Second, credit cards permit "chargebacks." That is, credit card transactions are never really "final" and can be reversed by the credit card company for any reason. Third, online credit card purchases are weakly authenticated—usually requiring only a credit card number and expiry date—so fraud online is rampant. Usually fraud is dealt with by credit card companies as a service to customers, but this cost is passed on in the form of fees. Fourth, while credit card companies filled the online payments gap, they failed to facilitate peer-to-peer transfers. Bank wires, Western

Union transfers, and other private money solutions like PayPal and later Alipay do permit peer-to-peer transfers, with some of the qualities of cash, but they also operate within the confines of laws and regulations and, like credit card companies, they are private businesses interested in profit maximization.

Early proto-cryptocurrencies solved some of these issues, but for a variety of reasons these failed to achieve widespread adoption. The most famous and successful was DigiCash, designed and launched by the cryptographer David Chaum in 1989. DigiCash was a private corporation, and it worked within the legitimate financial sector, but unlike the services offered by existing credit card and payments companies, DigiCash's "e-Cash" was designed to be much more like cash in that it permitted *untraceable* online transactions. Anonymous transactions were made possible by Chaum's own cryptographic innovation, a technique known as Blind Signatures (Chaum 1982). This anonymity was a key feature of DigiCash, which later inspired Bitcoin. However, because DigiCash was a private centrally organized company, when the company DigiCash went bankrupt in 1998, the e-Cash money system it sustained also shut down (Blanchette 2012).

In the years following DigiCash's bankruptcy, systems using similar kinds of cryptographic technology were proposed and some were even developed. Leading up to the 1990s Internet bubble, dozens of companies followed DigiCash's lead as they launched their products but found no users or interested business partners and were subsequently shuttered (Pitta 1999). The salad days of digital money have lessons for the current cryptocurrency market.

Direct antecedents to Bitcoin through the 1990s and 2000s included Adam Back's Hashcash, Hal Finney's Reusable Proofs, Nick Szabo's Bitgold, and Wei Dai's b-money, as well as numerous other commercially oriented "digital gold" systems like Liberty Dollar, Gold Money, and e-gold (Brunton 2018). Gold-like systems with "material" constraints and the perceived economic stability they entailed were popular (Dodd

2017; Maurer, Nelms, & Swartz 2013). Back's Hashcash system, for example, developed from an idea to use computational processing time (solving tough equations) as a kind of material constraint to limit sending email spam (Brunton 2013). By making it computationally expensive to send email spam, Hashcash implicitly made the virtual nothingness of solving tough equations a valuable commodity. (Back appears to have developed his system independently from an earlier one proposed by cryptographers Cynthia Dwork and Moni Naor; see Clark 2016.) In effect, the Hashcash system issued an unlimited but materially constrained supply of money. This system directly influenced the design of Bitcoin.

The materiality of traditional banknotes and coins is what makes cash work (see also Chapter 3), but this is not easily replicated by digital money. Cash solves two key issues: ownership and authenticity. With cash, the question of who owns it is usually pretty apparent; the owner is the person in physical possession of the cash (the same is true for bearer instruments). In cases where you "own" some cash not in your possession—perhaps the bank is holding on to it for you—your ownership claim is attenuated. As Bitcoin evangelists will tell you, cash in a bank isn't really yours, and it takes just one bank run to discover this brutal fact. In the same way, cash is also an efficient medium of exchange. Once you spend your cash, physically handing it to the recipient, the cash transfers ownership. There are no chargebacks or payment reversals with cash. Once spent, cash is gone.

Authenticity is more difficult. Modern banknotes and coins guarantee authenticity by using sophisticated printing techniques and special materials, but this is an imperfect science. Users of cash can check authenticity by inspecting the material item, looking for telltale anti-counterfeiting markers. However, counterfeited money is not uncommon (especially for the notoriously low-tech US notes). Even with anti-counterfeiting measures, so-called "supernotes" can be printed on machines identical to the originals using indistinguishable materials, but these notes are considered counterfeit. Supernotes are, in all but sovereign authority, identical forms of currency (see Chapter 3). This is a problem. Because the authenticity of cash is represented by its materiality, but ultimately lies in the authority of the issuing sovereign, it can never be *proven* to be authentic. One must *trust* in the general efficacy of anti-counterfeiting measures, the likelihood that cash will be accepted for payment, and that the sovereign will continue to authorize the currency.

In the digital world, ownership and authenticity are more complicated. Since digital files can be perfectly and endlessly copied and shared, special techniques are needed to make digital money behave like cash. Using cryptographic techniques developed in the late 1970s, it is easy to prove (and verify) the authenticity of digital money. Because these cryptographic techniques are considered robust, issues of authenticity are largely solved: users do not need to rely on trust for the authenticity of digital money, since, having been cryptographically generated, digital money is practically impossible to counterfeit. DigiCash and other proto-cryptocurrencies used these techniques for precisely this reason. In fact, in this regard, digital money is superior to cash since authenticity can be proven and independently verified. Bitcoin adopted these cryptographic techniques, but more significantly, Bitcoin also solved the issue of ownership that had plagued earlier versions of digital money.

Rather than trying to replicate the materiality of cash in a digital world, Bitcoin solved the ownership problem by adapting double-entry bookkeeping (in Chapter 4, I describe the specifics of the underlying transaction technology used in Bitcoin, which is called a "blockchain"). Far from a new invention, double-entry bookkeeping has been in use since the Renaissance (Poovey 1998). Traditionally, accountants kept track of incoming and outgoing finances by recording transactions on a ledger. With double-entry bookkeeping, the ledger has two columns, and every transaction has an entry in each, which must add up correctly. For each transaction, assets are "cancelled" as they are moved from the asset column to the liability column. Having two entries ensures that any errors or fraud will be caught and can traced back to the origin. Digital versions of double-entry bookkeeping were of course in use before Bitcoin, being used for tracking company finances and, in effect, issuing digital money. A digital bank, for example, can manage its digital cash by tracking and cancelling funds as they are spent. If you send me a digital dollar, the dollar is deducted from your side of the ledger and added to mine. Once the transfer is completed, you cannot "spend" that same digital dollar again (even if you make a perfect copy) because it has been cancelled from your account. The ownership of digital cash, thus, must be carefully tracked and managed by the issuing bank, to prevent "double spending," but the system works.

While double-entry bookkeeping is an elegant solution for keeping track of digital money, it also introduces a source of risk. First, to prevent users from double-spending money, transactions must be carefully tracked and cancelled. Second, those who control the ledger control the source of money. An unscrupulous digital bank could omit or censor certain kinds of transactions, or the ledger itself could be lost. Worst of all, if the bank that controls the ledger goes bankrupt, the entire system simply stops working and the digital money is rendered worthless. Accepting this risk requires a lot of trust from users, which is why traditional digital money companies have built their businesses on reputations of trustworthiness ("The Trust Machine," 2015).

The fundamental issue facing traditional digital money companies, like PayPal or Alipay, is that they are organizationally and technically centralized. Removing this source of risk (and trust) would be an obvious innovation, but without a company keeping track of transactions on a ledger, how do you prevent someone from making perfect copies and spending the same digital dollar over and over? Bitcoin's solution (described in detail below and in Chapter 4) is to decentralize the ledger. By removing the central authority, participants in the money network are responsible for validating transactions and updating their own copy of the ledger. Then, using a clever "consensus protocol," the multitude of distributed ledgers are kept in sync to produce one version of the truth about who owns what (while ensuring that no fraudulent copies of the ledger are permitted). An additional benefit to decentralizing the ledger is that by removing the central controlling authority, all of the issues about censorship, fraud, and bankruptcy are removed. This distributed and decentralized ledger, when combined with a network of recording and validating nodes, became known as a blockchain.

These are the two key components to how Bitcoin works: cryptographic authentication of digital money and decentralized record keeping. While the latter was the real innovation, and as we will see in Chapter 4 it was the idea that really caught, it was the former that provided the social and cultural roots of Bitcoin. It is through its genealogy in cryptography that Bitcoin acquired the label of "cryptocurrency." Unlike, however, the underlying cryptographic algorithms, the idea for Bitcoin did not emerge from universities or government research labs. Cryptocurrencies and specifically Bitcoin came from an anarcho-capitalist movement known as "cypherpunk."

The cypherpunk movement was not a single group or ideology. It emerged from embryonic political strands in the early 1990s, with members who were interested in finding applications of cryptography to wrest control and power from governments and states (they were punks, after all). They also had wide-ranging and eclectic interests: cryogenics, transhumanism, technological singularity, Libertarian politics, and money (Brunton 2018). Part acid-trip culture, part California ideology, and part *Wired* magazine, cypherpunks soon became a political force that would change the course of technology regulation and spur innovation. The cypherpunks were, for example, influential in releasing and proselytizing Phil Zimmerman's "Pretty Good Privacy" (PGP) email encryption software, protesting a "secure" telephone system that contained the government-mandated "Clipper Chip," and forcing the US government to transfer control and regulation of cryptographic software from the military to the Commerce Department. They also helped develop tactical organizations such as the Electronic Frontier Foundation (EFF), which emerged as a powerful ally to early Internet companies. With the help of the EFF and the cypherpunks, Internet companies such as Facebook and Google later became the dominant actors in the new media and communications industry.

For all of their eclectic interests, the cypherpunks considered money to be an essential ingredient in the realization of their punk goals and political aspirations. This meant in the first instance that cypherpunks were hostile to state-issued money. Cypherpunk theories of money were often bundled with Austrian economics, especially as these stem from the economist Friedrich Hayek. Famously, Hayek wanted money to be issued outside of national controls. But where Hayek thought private banks should be responsible for issuing money, the punk ethos ran deeper. Cypherpunks sought radical disintermediation, with no states or banks. This led them to experiment with money systems that ran like machines, or better yet, to think about *money as a machine*.

Bitcoin is a vision for digital cash, and like cash, it is supposed to be anonymous. But recall that in Bitcoin all transactions must be tracked and managed on distributed ledgers and that these ledgers must be open to inspection. Transactions are seen by all. Thankfully, in Bitcoin you are not represented by your real identity. Instead, your wallet address, where transactions go in and out, is a jumbled string of data that stand in for you. So long as you keep your real identity unlinked from your wallet address (as it turns out, this isn't so simple), you have an element of privacy. Therefore, the system is *pseudonymous* (not, as it is often mislabeled, anonymous).

But, like cash passing anonymously in the offline world, Bitcoin has also been taken up in earnest by criminals: from drug dealers to cyberwar actors and from tax dodgers to money launderers. More accurately, Bitcoin resembles Swiss or offshore numbered banking, and like these institutions, is often used illegally. These illegal use cases, however, are not the accidental outgrowth of an open system. Illegal use is an intentional and expected consequence. According to Bitcoin's early developers and advocates, illegality is a symptom of a liberated money system. Money without borders or boundaries was a conscious design decision and key to the political agenda—to create a world without state or corporate oversight and sanction.

For reasons beyond the control of cypherpunks, the influence and power of state-issued money had already been eroding over the last several decades. This was not unusual, since, in the anthropological record, state-issued money is actually something of a recent invention. State-issued money played an important role in the development of modernity and the emergence of sovereign nations (see Chapter 3), which has led some scholars to argue that we are now living in a "golden era" of state-issued money. However, inspired in part by the advent of Bitcoin and cryptocurrencies, the sociologist of money Nigel Dodd questions this claim. Dodd asks if there has *ever* been a golden era of state-issued money (Dodd 2016, p. 212). He points out that state-issued money, along with sovereign power, has never been absolute. Today, state-issued money makes up a small percentage of the total money supply (less than 11 percent. according to Ferguson 2009). In recent years, most money, or at least the stuff that has replaced money, has been bound up in financial instruments like stocks and bonds or has been invented out of thin air through the financial wizardry that produced the Collateralized Debt Obligations responsible for causing the 2008 global economic crisis, to which Bitcoin was a response. In this way, the emergence of Bitcoin, seemingly out of thin air, is quite typical.

In sum, Bitcoin capitalized on a set of geopolitical trends, political alliances, and technological affordances to create a system of privately issued digital money, without state or bank backing, which operated pseudonymously and was impervious to censorship. It accomplished this with cryptographic algorithms and decentralized ledgers.

Developing cryptocurrencies and blockchains

While it is unknown who really invented Bitcoin, how the Bitcoin software was developed is less mysterious. A person going by the name "Satoshi Nakamoto" first publicly discussed Bitcoin on October 31, 2008 and released a whitepaper (early source code was available by request). A month earlier, Nakamoto had registered the bitcoin.org domain and claimed that the software had been in development for "over the last year and a half" (according to an early forum post by Nakamoto). A discussion on the Cryptography Mailing List where Nakamoto made the announcement quickly ensued. Influential members of the cryptography community, such as Hal Finney (who later became an important contributor to Bitcoin), responded with questions about the system's design and assumptions. Nakamoto actively responded to these questions and before long the source code was available on the open-source software repository SourceForge. Like other open-source software projects, a loose-knit community of developers began making contributions to the code. Some of the early and influential figures included Martii Malmi ("sirius_m"), Laszlo Hanyecz ("laszlo," who later became famous for buying a pizza for 10,000 Bitcoins), Gavin Andresen ("gavinandresen"), Chris Moore ("dooglus"), Pieter Wuille ("sipa"), Jeff Garzik ("jgarzik"), Gregory Maxwell ("gmaxwell"), and many others. By late 2010, Nakamoto stopped personally contributing to the Bitcoin software and soon disappeared entirely, leaving the rest of the community to continue the project.

As to be expected, the software that is Bitcoin today looks very different from the first version that Nakamoto released and discussed in his famous whitepaper. In the early years of development, Nakamoto and others added features and cut superfluous ones (including a proposed decentralized marketplace, akin to eBay or Silk Road) and generally made the software more robust. Today, anyone can contribute to the Bitcoin "core" software, which is now stored on the open-source software repository GitHub. In addition to improving the software, contributions include submitting bug reports, writing documentation, and creating translations. No person or entity owns or controls Bitcoin software development, but a small group of developers have official "commit" access to the source code repository and therefore are ultimately responsible for the development of Bitcoin.

As part of the ethos of open-source software development, any person is free to "fork" the software. Software forking is a routine activity in open-source software development, but controversial forks emerge when developers with commit access refuse to integrate features or changes that some part of the community believe are important (think of software forking like a vote of non-confidence in politics). Since the source code is freely and openly available, anyone can create a duplicate version and set off development in a different direction, thereby splitting (or "forking") from the original. The results of a forked software project are two (possibly incompatible) versions that over time have grown increasingly distinct (in theory, the forks can at some point recombine, but this is very rare).

The Bitcoin software has been forked several times, mostly in response to the refusal by the developers of the original version to implement suitable solutions for scaling network capacity (an issue that has plagued Bitcoin since 2015). The result is that there are now several versions of Bitcoin software (the original Bitcoin software was renamed "Bitcoin Core"). In cases where the various Bitcoin software forks are compatible they co-exist on the same Bitcoin peer-to-peer network and therefore are part of the same monetary system. When the resulting forked software is no longer compatible with the original network protocol, as was the case with the emergence of Bitcoin Cash in 2017, the result is a fork in the distributed ledger as well. Since any transaction data stored on the forked distributed ledger are separate from the original, the new software, network, and transaction data comprise a distinct monetary system. In this way, there can be—and currently are—several competing and completely independent versions of "Bitcoin."

Of the many cryptocurrency and blockchain software projects that have emerged since the invention of Bitcoin, most take their design cues from the original Nakamoto whitepaper, but they often follow different trajectories. And while most cryptocurrency and blockchain software remains opensource (for reasons of security more than anything else—it is important that source code can be inspected and evaluated by outsiders), only a few exceptional cases can be considered truly open-source software *community* projects like Bitcoin. Ethereum is the most notable example for comparison. It, like Bitcoin, was invented by a singular individual (Vitalik Buterin) but soon became a true community project with no formal leader. Unlike Bitcoin, however, the development of Ethereum is guided and funded by a nonprofit association, the Ethereum Foundation (the comparable Bitcoin Foundation was set up *post facto* and is mostly responsible for education, outreach, and lobbying efforts). Most other cryptocurrency and blockchain software projects are developed exclusively by the companies that launch them, and therefore more closely resemble traditional software products.

For any cryptocurrency and blockchain project, the kind of software development that is required is new and difficult and there are few existing best practices or successful models to follow. In particular, the programmers creating the core blockchain infrastructures for these projects are largely without the ecosystem of tools and testing methodologies that are typical in other software environments, and the security requirements are stringent and uncompromising. Even leading computer security developers frequently make mistakes today. In Chapter 8, for example, I discuss the development of a blockchain platform (The DAO) that was hacked and lost the equivalent of US $78 million. What is unique about this case is that, unlike the slapdash programming of cryptocurrency exchanges (which are constantly hacked and tend not to even use blockchain technologies), the system was developed by a seasoned veteran with a background in high performance computing and security. The system was also vetted by numerous experts in the field, and despite all of this, a tiny unforeseen error in logic was exploited within days of its launch. What this story tells us is that the economic incentive to hack cryptocurrencies and blockchain technologies is a strong motivator, and robust, secure systems require vigilant software development practices.

An especially thorny issue facing blockchain systems that use an open network architecture (like Bitcoin and Ethereum) are the ways in which software is patched, upgraded, and deployed. In the distributed environment of open blockchain systems that use computing resources outside of an organization's or individual's control, the previously simple task of updating software becomes a balancing act of persuasion and technical development. As cases like The DAO platform or the Bitcoin scaling debates have made clear, software changes on open platforms must be guided by *social* consensus. Ultimately, the independent miners that validate transactions are wholly responsible for implementing changes and therefore are truly in charge of the network. Miners may be economically incentivized to update software but sometimes they will be reluctant to do so, and no amount of social pressure may change their decisions.

Future uses and issues

Bitcoin can be used as money, but also in many more ways. Bitcoin can be used for payments, salaries, financial services, remittances, charity, and so on. You can even "burn" Bitcoin to gin up scarcity (more boring than burning real cash—just ask the electro-avant-garde band The KLF who burned £1 million in 1994). Bitcoin can also be used in ways that state-issued money cannot. Because of the recordkeeping system powering Bitcoin—a blockchain—it can be used as a generic "token" system for side-currencies, for tracking material goods, and even for limited scripted programming. In Chapter 4 I discuss blockchain technologies that can be used for an even wider range of applications.

The "colored coins" proposal is a way to use Bitcoin for non-money applications. Early on, colored coins opened up exciting new vistas for Bitcoin, but since the widespread adoption of alternative cryptocurrencies and blockchain technologies, colored coin schemes have now become largely historical relics. Coins are "colored" by adding metadata to transactions that identify coins for an alternative use. The attached metadata (the coin's "color") distinguishes it from regular Bitcoins. Colored coins still remain Bitcoins, but users pretend that they stand in for something else, such as company stocks, voting slips, or coupons. Because Bitcoin can be denominated to 0.00000001 (known as a "Satoshi"), a portion of a Bitcoin, down to a single Satoshi, could represent a bond certificate worth thousands of dollars or just a cup of coffee. In practical terms, however, there are limits to the minimum cost of using a colored coin. Most Bitcoin software will not process "dust" transactions, variously defined as 546 Satoshi (about US $0.10 at the time of writing), and processing fees are often upward of US $20 (until the scaling debate gets settled). Therefore, colored coins only make economic sense for relatively valuable goods (the same is true, of course, for all Bitcoin transactions).

Although colored coin proposals are no longer being widely pursued, they were an important step towards more advanced cryptocurrencies and blockchains. Early software forks of the Bitcoin codebase grew the initial idea, suggesting that a powerful distributed ledger could be used to track, manage, and manipulate nearly anything. The Namecoin system (a distributed Internet Domain Name System) was the first fork of the Bitcoin software, adapting the Bitcoin system for naming websites. Others developed special purpose token systems that used "side chains" of the main Bitcoin network, and eventually alternative cryptocurrencies emerged using entirely new blockchains. With the launch of Ethereum in 2015—a generic blockchain system without a monetary design—the possible use cases expanded almost infinitely.

The difference between cryptocurrency and blockchain technology is not always clear, since most blockchain technologies retain at least some elements from cryptocurrencies, in particular the exchange of value. For example, the Ethereum blockchain system (described in Chapter 4) is the prototypical blockchain technology that is responsible for popularizing the concept and developing the terms we use today. Yet the Ethereum system makes extensive use of valuable tokens (known in the Ethereum system as "Ether"). These tokens— effectively a cryptocurrency—serve many purposes: they help secure the system from game theory attacks, they incentivize general use, they serve as a conduit of value between otherwise disparate systems, they help fund further development of the software, and so on. Other blockchain technologies make extensive use of valuable tokens for funding the organization that is developing the software, a practice known as an "Initial Coin Offering" (ICO) (see Chapter 6). Some of these blockchain technologies use their valuable tokens to economically incentivize or prohibit behaviors. In short, most blockchains utilize a cryptocurrency, and most cryptocurrencies are built on top of a blockchain.

Despite much promise, Bitcoin and cryptocurrencies have

many issues. The most significant issue is that Bitcoin is not being used as money. Instead, Bitcoin and cryptocurrencies have been taken up with vigor as a speculative investment class (see Chapter 5), but wild gambles on price fluctuations hardly live up to the world-changing rhetoric. Most cryptocurrencies also have volatile prices, illiquid markets, and appear to be largely controlled by illegal market manipulations. It is not clear what it would take for Bitcoin and many other cryptocurrencies to change tack at this point.

Replacing industry incumbents and getting real people to adopt digital money is not easy. In the 1990s, a digital money fever gripped the world, much like the "crypto" fever today, but nearly every company went bankrupt (with the notable exception of PayPal, but arguably PayPal succeeded *because* it did not change anything). Although Bitcoin has grown massively in size and value in recent years, it is arguably going in the opposite direction of its own goals. Today, the concentration of wealth in the Bitcoin market is at levels almost unprecedented for modern comparisons. A mere 1,000 people own 40 percent of the Bitcoin market (Kharif 2017). This concentration of wealth allows these people ("whales" in the vernacular) to manipulate the market to their advantage (or use bots; Gandal, Hamrick, Moore, & Oberman 2017). But for the most part, the majority of Bitcoin users simply retain their assets: 73 percent of Bitcoins are thought to be dormant (or lost) (Fry & Cheah 2016). Many cryptocurrency alternatives have similar market dynamics—for example, two-thirds of the cryptocurrency Ripple has been retained by the company (Weber 2016), making its owners billionaires, at least briefly, during an early 2018 spike in price.

Curiously, as soon as Bitcoin became valuable enough to be of possible use for actually buying things, it stopped being used to *actually* buy things. In part, this is due to the "switching costs" of using a money that so few others use (an early-user problem) (Luther 2016a; Weber 2014). While switching costs might have driven the early market's reluctance to adopt

Bitcoin for payments, since then new market dynamics have taken over. In the early days of Bitcoin there still remained a glimmer of hope that it might be used like cash. Some start-ups developed Bitcoin Automated Teller Machines (ATMs) (Wolfson 2015) and a few high-profile retailers begun accepting it for online purchases. Even for these bleeding-edge companies, however, "accepting Bitcoin" really meant installing a pre-packaged widget on an ecommerce platform that would take care of the messy transactional plumbing and instantly exchange Bitcoin for local state-issued currency. Very few companies actually held Bitcoin. This surprised few economists, since Bitcoin's extreme price volatility exposed retailers to external market shocks, conceivably wiping out a day's profit without notice. On the other hand, the skyrocketing price of Bitcoin practically guaranteed that no rational economic actor would—or should—spend it. It isn't a wise economic decision to buy a cup of coffee with Bitcoins today if you have reason to think that your money will be worth more tomorrow. Demurrage alternatives, such as "Freicoin," reverse this impulse and automatically lose value when not spent, but they have yet to catch on. Either way, people still do not use cryptocurrencies to actually buy things, as a report by Morgan Stanley concluded, noting that by 2017 the use of Bitcoin for shopping was "virtually zero and shrinking" (Chaparro 2017). Plainly, Bitcoin is too volatile to be accepted by merchants, its value appreciates too quickly to be spent (hyperdeflation), and it is difficult to use.

With the rise of speculative investment and the fall of digital money, the result is that most cryptocurrency users today do not truly own cryptocurrencies. Instead, investors trade cryptocurrencies on private exchanges, which use internal accounting systems. Only the most dedicated investors move their investments from private exchanges to cryptocurrency blockchains (which substitutes one kind of risk for another). With so much wealth stored on these centralized services, many of the larger exchanges have become a source of systemic market risk, not unlike the "too big to fail" banks of the 2008 global economic crisis. The Bitfinex cryptocurrency exchange has been the worst example of this trend in recent years, responsible for over 10 percent of global trading volume in 2017. This market concentration is not as bad as the early days, when Mt. Gox was responsible for upwards of 70 percent of trading volume, but it still causes market instabilities and makes a ripe target for hackers. Like Mt. Gox previously, Bitfinex operates without regulatory oversight and exhibits signs of financial mismanagement. Bitfinex is owned by iFinex Inc., which is registered in the tax haven British Virgin Islands and appears to be operated from China, but little else is known about this shadowy organization (Popper 2017a). Bitfinex has also been hacked in the past, but unlike the Mt. Gox hack that bankrupted the company (and caused a massive crash in the Bitcoin market), Bitfinex inexplicably weathered the storm by issuing internal "IOU" tokens. Later, after much sleuthing by critics, Bitfinex also admitted that it created the cryptocurrency Tether, which was hacked in 2017.

While there are signs of professionalization on the horizon, the early years of cryptocurrencies have been marred by chaotic governance. From software developers engaging in petty fights to inexperienced coders left to develop mission-critical software, many outsiders have wondered if there are any adults involved. The issue is not that the software is open source—there are many highly professional and well-run open-source software projects (a great deal of the Internet is run on open-source software). Rather, call it growing pains or blame it on the propensity for software that literally mints money to attract scoundrels, these early days have been pretty calamitous. Still today, many cryptocurrency startups push the bounds of legal and ethical behavior in the vein of Silicon Valley "disruption," only to discover that finance is one of the most strongly regulated environments in modern society (and for good reason: money matters).

Regulators are to blame too. As part of a widespread

tendency for governments to adopt neoliberal positions on regulation, cryptocurrencies have been largely left unregulated. Even the Canadian government, widely praised for having a sound and well-regulated banking and finance industry, early on adopted a "light touch" to regulation of this sector (Gerstein & Hervieux-Payette 2015). In practical terms, light-touch regulation meant no regulation. In recent years governments have been reasserting control and authority, but one wonders if the lack of early government guidance contributed to the current state of affairs. In the US, for example, oscillating regulation has left a piecemeal and patchwork set of inconsistent and even sometimes contradictory rules. When the US Securities and Exchange Commission (SEC) cracked down on the industry in 2018, investigating some 80 companies and individuals, it was a clear warning to the market that financial compliance was required. Yet many cryptocurrency and blockchain startups decried the SEC's punitive actions, and instead requested clear regulation capable of creating a safe and level playing field. Ultimately, bad actors continue to thrive while legitimate companies are left to navigate uncertain regulation or in some cases have simply avoided entering the market.

The communities of miners have contributed their fair share of issues too. Bitcoin miners, in particular, are becoming enormously wealthy—to the detriment of the Bitcoin ecosystem. As I discussed above, the interests of miners are strategically misaligned with users, since they are capable of providing minimum service at maximum profit despite being critical infrastructure for the network. This is because the market for miners permits private seigniorage. Once popular with kings in early modernity, seigniorage is the government's right to sell its money at a value higher than the cost of production. Today, seigniorage is usually (somewhat) offset by treasury bonds, which the government pays interest on. When the government does not fully pay for its seigniorage the result is a tax on its citizens. In a rational market, the cost of producing Bitcoins through mining (see Chapter 4) should be at equilibrium with their value (with, presumably, a small profit incentive or the existence of altruist actors). This is not the case. For example, in 2017, with the rise in price of Bitcoin and availability of cheap electricity (especially in China), Bitcoin mining was so profitable that even if the price of Bitcoin dropped by half, miners could still earn seigniorage profits. Consequently, all non-mining Bitcoin users are in effect paying a tax equivalent to the difference between the cost of production and the market price.

Many of these issues highlight the difficulty of using cryptocurrencies and blockchains. Even after ten years of development the software ecosystem has failed to provide simple and robust tools. As I mentioned above, early on Bitcoin ATMs were supposed to bring Bitcoin to the masses, but with their comical complexity and long processing wait times (upwards of 10 minutes when the network was running well), they did not catch on. Most of the Bitcoin ATMs I have seen personally were constantly managed by nearby attendants. Users also need to possess a deep understanding of computer security to safely use cryptocurrencies, and even small errors can have disastrous and irreversible consequences. There are many stories of users accidently sending Bitcoin to the wrong address or making other simple mistakes, such as mixing up the payment and fee fields during a transaction, which led one poor person in 2016 to pay a US $130,000 fee for a US $5 transfer. Of course, such transactions cannot be reversed or changed, since there are no bank errors or mulligans in Bitcoin. Even if simple errors are avoided, due to the high value of Bitcoin, user pseudonymity, and irreversible transactions, Bitcoin wallets are frequent targets for hackers. Bitcoin hacking is so widespread that many spyware tools now look specifically for locally stored Bitcoin wallets. Because of rampant hacking, recommended best practice is to only store Bitcoin on computers that are completely offline (and, ideally, have never been online). Users with large caches must go to paranoiac levels to secure their Bitcoin. For example, Cameron and Tyler Winklevoss store their Bitcoin billions on paper printouts in safe deposit boxes around the US, with each printout containing only part of the needed private key (Popper 2017b). This is not entirely dissimilar to how US nuclear launch codes are stored. As critic David Gerard (2017) points out, Bitcoin users need to be their own bank, which includes being their own chief security officer—a task few are equipped for.

The uncompromising design of Bitcoin means it is just as bad to lose Bitcoin to hackers as it is to forget the private key. In recent years a small cottage industry has emerged to help the forgetful recover their lost Bitcoins. The famous story of a man who in 2013 pitched an old hard drive containing his Bitcoin wallet had a 2017 update: with soaring Bitcoin prices he considered *excavating the landfill* with hopes of recovering his millions (Sulleyman 2017). Others who have simply forgotten the private key wrack their brains with hopes of unlocking their fortunes—even turning to hypnosis (Frauenfelder 2017). In most cases, however, it is hard to feel too sorry for these people. Many earned Bitcoins in the early days when they were effectively worthless, often by mining on a home computer. That they forgot about their Bitcoins until years later when they had increased 100 or 1,000 times in value and then were unable to access their newfound wealth is personally unfortunate but hardly a moral travesty. This also means that when Bitcoins are lost they are lost *forever*. Therefore, of the total twenty-one million Bitcoins that will be issued (a strict monetary cap programmed into the Bitcoin protocol), an estimated four million have already been permanently lost (Roberts & Rapp 2017; see also Swanson 2014).

Finally, the privacy protections of cryptocurrencies and blockchains are simultaneously too strong, too weak, and inflexible. Despite the de-anonymizing research being conducted on Bitcoin transactions, in practical terms a careful user can effectively conduct anonymous transactions that even state intelligence agencies are unable to disentangle. For example, when the US Federal Bureau of Investigation (FBI) sought the owner and operator of the infamous Silk Road dark web marketplace ("Dread Pirate Roberts") they could plainly see Bitcoin going in and out of the marketplace, but the trail of transactions left few clues. It was only in discovering an early forum post announcing the Silk Road website that led the FBI to Ross Ulbricht, who was then convicted. Access to Ulbricht's stored Bitcoin helped make the case against him, but most of the evidence that tied Ulbricht to Dread Pirate Roberts came from the laptop seized during his arrest. On the other hand, the privacy protections of Bitcoin and most cryptocurrencies are not robust or flexible enough for many legal uses, such as for use with health information or national identity schemes. In real-world use cases, considerable privacy flexibility is needed and simple privacy maximizing approaches are inappropriate. For example, in the US, the Health Insurance Portability and Accountability Act (HIPAA) permits "break the glass" procedures to allow access to health records in emergency situations but requires robust privacy otherwise. In the EU, however, the "right to be forgotten" offers privacy protections that most cryptocurrencies are unable to comply with given their all-or-nothing design for records immutability (and with the passing of the EU General Data Protection Regulation, or GDPR, many blockchain companies face stiff penalties if they cannot accommodate nuanced privacy protections; see Chapter 6). Flexible blockchain technologies designed with privacy regulation in mind may be able to accommodate these kinds of issues, but these have yet to reach widespread adoption.

Summary

This chapter introduced cryptocurrencies, focusing on Bitcoin, the first cryptocurrency. I traced the origins of Bitcoin through alternative currency projects and the cypherpunk community from which it originated. I described the context of Bitcoin as a currency system built on a distributed ledger. This description set up the next two chapters, where I complete the picture by detailing the intersection between the monetary aspirations of Bitcoin and the innovative distributed ledger that the system relies on (Chapter 3), an essential part of a network of computers that validate and secure the entire system (Chapter 4). I concluded this chapter by describing the recent turn away from monetary uses of cryptocurrencies, while recognizing that the distinction between cryptocurrencies and blockchains is fluid. Bitcoin and other cryptocurrencies have not yet been successfully adopted as money because of remaining usability issues, an uncertain regulatory climate, and the technical challenge of developing a robust and secure decentralized platform.

CHAPTER THREE

Digital Money

Perhaps you have read an online discussion about how Bitcoin is better than "fiat" money? Fiat money, Bitcoin evangelists say, is state-supported money that lacks intrinsic value (think US dollars or Euros). Worthless paper to start with, fiat money can be endlessly printed by the state or the central bank, leading to inflation (never mind that commercial banks produce most of a nation's money). Gold, on the other hand, Bitcoin evangelists say, has value because you can hold it and use it. Bitcoin is supposed to be money like gold, but for the digital age. It cannot be endlessly printed, it has real (if not quite "intrinsic") value, and its price is efficiently set by supply and demand on open markets. The problem with this narrative is that it is all ideology and little fact.

In this chapter I describe the common narratives of money as found in the cryptocurrency literature. The least plausible of these narratives is that money solves the challenges of barter exchange; this theory is neither empirically accurate nor theoretically sophisticated. More plausible, but unhelpful in its own right, is the "generic" account of money, which offers a three-pronged test. However, as a test for "moneyness," it is not clear what this theory really offers. Instead, I briefly describe a range of alternative theories of money drawn from sociologists, anthropologists, and historians. In so doing, a number of characteristics of cryptocurrencies are drawn together with the goal of spurring alternative research directions—if not quite "solving" the question of how to best characterize the monetary aspects of cryptocurrencies. My goal, therefore, is to provide groundwork for thinking beyond the typical narratives found in most cryptocurrency literature.

Before delving into the complex literature on theories of money, however, I first describe the transactional architecture of Bitcoin. I focus on the Bitcoin wallet and how transaction data are securely chained together. These chains of data are then bundled into "blocks" that are also chained together to form "blockchains," which I describe in Chapter 4.

It is important to note that while Bitcoin was the first cryptocurrency and most subsequent cryptocurrencies inherited Bitcoin's design, there are sometimes important differences among cryptocurrencies. The description offered here, therefore, should only act as a guide and point of comparison when investigating other cryptocurrencies. Some cryptocurrencies vary quite remarkably in their design and technology, such as Zcash's zero-knowledge proofs (zk-SNARKs) or Ripple's authorized gateways. Today, there is no one kind of cryptocurrency, but as this description of Bitcoin makes clear, most cryptocurrencies are cooking with the same ingredients, if not making the same recipe.

Bitcoin transactions

To use Bitcoin, you first download wallet software or register for a third-party wallet service. But the term "Bitcoin wallet" is actually a misnomer. Bitcoin wallets do not store money, and there are no coins, bills, notes, or tokens anywhere in the Bitcoin system. Rather, Bitcoin wallets store cryptographic keys that lock and unlock transactions and so, in truth, they are *keychains*. The distributed ledger, or blockchain, that stores the "money" in the Bitcoin system is a registry of transaction data (see Chapter 4). Transaction data are created by wallets as input and output values—not coins or tokens—which are then independently validated and added to the distributed ledger. Remarkably, and so thoroughly unlike any conventional wallet, the Bitcoin wallet does not even store a "balance" of money (although, for convenience, the wallet can count transaction inputs and outputs to display a virtual balance). Neither are balances recorded on the blockchain—it's all transaction inputs and outputs from wallets. So it is best to think of wallets as an important and *active* part of Bitcoin *infrastructure* rather than passive repositories for money.

Bitcoin wallets generate and store key pairs, using techniques from public key cryptography. This process is complex and I would encourage interested readers to consult Andreas Antonopoulos's excellent technical resource *Mastering Bitcoin* (2017) for further details. In brief, the key pair starts with a private key, which is a number picked at random. The private key must be kept secret, since anyone in possession of it may access the funds it protects. From the private key, a public key is generated using the elliptical curve digital signature algorithm (ECDSA, specifically, the secp256k1 standard). This algorithm has the special property of containing a mathematical "trapdoor," making it easy to derive a public key from a private one (multiplication), but not the reverse (division). This is also known as a "one way" function, because it is easy to compute the multiplication but not the division (Figure 3.1). The public key may be shared widely and is essential to the Bitcoin wallet "address," where incoming transactions (money) are sent.

A Bitcoin wallet address is derived from the public key using an algorithm known as a "hash." Hashing is an algorithmic technique for "fingerprinting" data and is used widely

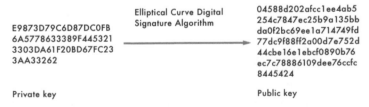

E9873D79C6D87DC0FB
6A5778633389F445321
3303DA61F20BD67FC23
3AA33262

Private key

Elliptical Curve Digital
Signature Algorithm

04588d202afcc1ee4ab5
254c7847ec25b9a135bb
da0f2bc69ee1a714749fd
77dc9f88ff2a00d7e752d
44cbe16e1ebcf0890b76
ec7c78886109dee76ccfc
8445424

Public key

Figure 3.1   Deriving a Bitcoin public key from a private key using elliptical curve multiplication

throughout cryptocurrencies and blockchains. The input of a hash algorithm is any data, and the output is a small fixed-size deterministic value or index. Hashing algorithms produce fingerprints of data because unique input data (of any size) produce unique output data (of a fixed size). If input data change, even in the tiniest amount, the output of the hash algorithm is remarkably and noticeably different. Yet, because the algorithm is deterministic, if the input data *do not change* no matter how many times the algorithm is run the output will remain the same (see Chapter 4 for more details and examples). That is, the output uniquely identifies the input, like a fingerprint identifies a person. The specific hashing algorithm used in Bitcoin is derived from cryptography (some hashing algorithms are not). Like the algorithm used to produce public and private key pairs, the hashing algorithm used to create a wallet address is a trapdoor or one-way function. Specifically, a Bitcoin wallet address is a double hash using two different algorithms: the 256 bit version of the Secure Hash Algorithm (SHA256) and the 160 bit version of the RACE Integrity Primitives Evaluation Message Digest (RIPEMD160) (Figure 3.2).

It is important to recognize that despite considerable use of cryptographic algorithms Bitcoin transaction data are not "encrypted." Transaction data are publicly accessible on the distributed ledger and stored as plain text, easily viewed by anyone. Rather, Bitcoin transactions are "signed" using

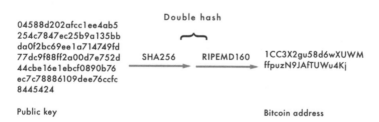

Figure 3.2   Deriving a Bitcoin address from a public key using SHA256 and RIPEMD160

another cryptographic algorithm, the Elliptical Curve Digital Signature Algorithm (ECDSA). Digital signature algorithms use techniques derived from public key cryptography to produce digital signatures that demonstrate the authenticity of digital documents. In Bitcoin, digital signatures serve important purposes: they prove that the appropriate private key authorized a transaction (described below) and ensure that transaction data cannot be modified after being signed. Best of all, digital signatures allow anyone who has access to the associated public key (in theory, everyone) to verify that a transaction was authorized and not modified. Only the person in possession of the appropriate private key can create the correct signature, but everyone can verify it.

Bitcoin wallets also monitor and record transaction data from the peer-to-peer network to help create the distributed ledger. Wallets that record transaction data are known as "full node" clients and are essential components of the peer-to-peer network. "Lightweight" clients—which are more common for average users—are wallets that store keys and create transactions but do not record the distributed ledger (for convenience, when I refer to "wallet" I mean "full node client"). Wallets perform simple validation checks on transaction data and keep a local copy of the distributed ledger. The local copy of the distributed ledger contains *all* transaction data from *all* users from the beginning of time. The local copy of the ledger is therefore very large and grows daily (currently, the Bitcoin ledger is gigabytes of data, but there are techniques to "prune" the data in some cases). Wallets must keep a full record of all transactions to ensure security and auditability, and to support the peer-to-peer network. When requested, transaction data from a wallet's local ledger are transmitted to network peers—other wallets or validating nodes called "miners." Miners collaborate extensively with wallets, and while both wallets and miners perform transaction validation, it is the miners who are ultimately responsible for transaction security (see Chapter 4).

As wallets monitor the peer-to-peer network, incoming transaction data are validated and added to the local copy of the distributed ledger. As transactions are added to the ledger, wallets watch for transactions that correspond to locally stored keys. If the wallet detects a transaction that it can unlock (using its local keys), typically, the wallet alerts the user that funds have been received and adds the value to a virtual wallet balance. Notice that the wallet does not "withdraw" funds from anywhere. Funds are "received" when the wallet detects a transaction it can unlock; the ledger remains unchanged until the wallet "spends" the received funds (by creating a new transaction using the received funds). This is an admittedly convoluted process, but it is central to how Bitcoin's ledger system functions. Since there are no coins or tokens to transfer, sending and receiving money requires careful accounting of transaction inputs and outputs.

There are privacy implications due to the open architecture of Bitcoin. The distributed ledger must be open and accessible so that wallets can monitor and validate incoming transactions and add transaction data to the ever-growing ledger. But recall that transaction data are not encrypted—sender and recipient addresses and input and output values are stored as plain text on the open ledger. Architecturally, this open design would be a privacy nightmare. In reality, however, the privacy protections for Bitcoin transactions are fairly good (but far from perfect). Bitcoin's privacy results from the fact that Bitcoin addresses (represented as hashes) are not typically associated with real identities. Anyone, including police and intelligence agencies, can inspect the distributed ledger and see *any* transaction in *complete* detail, but without knowing who is behind an address, the transactions are, in practice, private.

Bitcoin's privacy protections break down when wallet addresses are linked to real identities or when transactions are systematically de-anonymized. If an address is linked to a real identity, the complete history of transactions by that user is accessible. An address could be inadvertently linked to a real identity if, say, an ecommerce or payments platform stored Bitcoin addresses with physical addresses and was then hacked or subpoenaed. If the exposed Bitcoin address had also been reused, all transactions by that personally identified user would be traceable on the ledger, including those conducted with other companies or individuals. For this reason, it is considered best practice to create a new address after every transaction, and most wallets make it easy to store and manage multiple addresses (which can be derived from a single private key). On the other hand, de-anonymization cannot be protected against (but, depending on the method of de-anonymization, following best practices and creating new addresses may thwart such efforts). Unfortunately, Bitcoin has proven to be susceptible to de-anonymization (Biryukov et al. 2014; Dupont & Squicciarini 2015; Fanti & Viswanath 2017). One research group found that it was possible to cluster addresses for one-sixth of all Bitcoin transactions (Ermilov, Panov, & Yanovich 2017), although this is a step removed from true de-anonymization. An alternative approach to Bitcoin privacy would be to use a "mixing service." Rather than transact directly on the distributed ledger (which is visible to all), mixing services group and mix transactions internally to obfuscate the link between sender and receiver. These services, however, require users to trust that the mixing service will not abscond with the funds, keep a record of users and transactions, or do a poor job at mixing. A more reliable approach for users interested in maximum privacy would be to avoid Bitcoin entirely and use a cryptocurrency system designed with privacy in mind, such as Zcash.

Since Bitcoin is designed without coins or tokens, the transfer of Bitcoins is represented as inputs and outputs on a distributed ledger. If a transaction input is greater than an output, the difference is an implied *fee*. Fees appear innocuous—as though they are leftover change from a transaction—but they are critically important. Fees are important because they incentivize validating nodes in the peer-to-peer network to include transactions in the distributed ledger (see Chapter 4). Although fees are implied, they are, in practical terms, mandatory. Validating nodes are permitted to choose when or if a given transaction is processed, as determined by an open market of fees (based on data size for the transaction, not transferred value). There are no set rates for processing transactions, nor are there maximum bounds. This market-based approach is in keeping with the ethos of Bitcoin, but it has not been without issues. Through 2017, for example, due to network scaling issues (the "scaling debate"), miners were unable to reliably include all transactions. Users who wanted their transactions processed expediently (or in some cases, at all) had to include a fee priced on an open competitive market. Because of this unchecked market and high demand, fees soon spiraled out of control, in some cases reaching the equivalent of US $20 *per transaction*.

To transfer Bitcoin, you create a transaction with wallet software that specifies a previously unspent *output* as a new transaction's *input*. The unspent output must correspond to a key stored in your wallet, in the sense that the key can "unlock" the previous transaction (the unspent output). Notice that there is no original transaction—the output from one trans-action becomes input to the next, and so on, creating a long chain of transactions. The only truly "original" transactions are the "genesis" block from January 3, 2009 when Nakamoto turned on the Bitcoin system, and "coinbase" transactions that issue new Bitcoins with every block (see Chapter 4).

When a wallet creates a transaction, it "encumbers" unspent output data (for technical details see Antonopoulos 2017 or Shirriff 2014). To encumber a transaction, the wallet "proves" ownership of the funds to be sent. Proof of ownership is accomplished by digitally signing the hash of the transaction. This digital signature must be made by the *private key* that corresponds to the *public key* that was hashed in the *previous* transaction. Doing so allows the transaction to be indepen-dently verified, proving that the sender is in possession of the appropriate private key (this is because the user's *public key* was previously hashed and included in the transaction). By spending previously received unspent outputs the chain of transactions grows, reflecting current ownership. Or, to think about it from the other direction, to spend previously received unspent outputs the recipient encumbers the transaction by signing the *previous transaction hash* and then signing *the public key* of the *next* recipient. These two signatures (the previous transaction hash and the public key of next recipient) must be included in the transaction, which is then sent to the Bitcoin peer-to-peer network for validation. So long as the transaction is then validated, it is included in the distributed ledger.

Once a transaction is sent from a wallet to the Bitcoin network, it propagates to nearby miners in the network using a process called "flooding." Each miner then independently validates the transaction, forwards the transaction on to other miners, and adds the transaction to a list of incoming transactions. This list of incoming transactions is known as a "candidate" block. Once a candidate block of transactions is assembled, the miner then gets to work processing the block, with the hopes of earning the included transaction fees and the mining reward (the coinbase transaction). For details on these final steps—transaction validation, creating blocks, and managing a distributed network—see Chapter 4.

Money narratives

The "moneyness" of Bitcoin and cryptocurrencies has been endlessly debated in the literature (Ciaian, Rajcaniova, & Kancs 2016; Kubát 2015; Yermack 2013). In the section above, I called Bitcoin "money" as though the appellation was unproblematic. This sleight of hand, however, hides the fact that for the last few years Bitcoin has rarely been used as money and is instead, like most cryptocurrencies, traded for investment (see Chapter 5). We should not interpret this transition from money to investment as a failure for cryptocurrencies. As I suggested in Chapter 1, the decline of cryptocurrencies as money was just an experiment that has now largely run its course. Nonetheless, experiments with money are never truly complete, only dormant. New and different articulations of money are being tested today, some of which are wholly new cryptocurrencies, while some adapt features from existing ones. Many of these new money technologies, with new money narratives, have promising futures.

Typically, cryptocurrencies are said to succeed or fail as "money" if they are 1) a medium of exchange, 2) a unit of account, or 3) a store of value (sometimes a fourth property is added: means of unilateral payment). I call this the generic theory of money, which is found widely in economics textbooks and is orthodox in cryptocurrency literature (see also Ingham 2004, p. 3). It is worth noting that this definition is not usually found in the fields of sociology, anthropology, or history. This omission is likely because there are immediate and obvious problems with this generic account. Are these properties of money essential or sufficient criteria? Is it money if it functions as a medium of exchange but not a unit of account? Is two of three enough? Can unit of account and store of value be subsumed under the category of medium of exchange? Worse still, the theory fails to describe the actual history of money, how it becomes a unit of account, or how money is valued and becomes valuable.

Another popular definition of money in the cryptocurrency literature focuses on money's origins in barter exchange. This theory was described by William Stanley Jevons and Carl Menger in the nineteenth century (see Dodd 2016, p. 17; Ingham 2004, p. 17; Milkau & Bott 2015). Menger's broader political agenda, in association with Ludwig von Mises and Friedrich Hayek, was also taken up by early cryptocurrency users (Golumbia 2016). According to these theorists, money can be used to solve the problem of "double coincidence of wants"—when two people each want something but neither has what the other wants. Money might not solve either person's immediate desire for a specific good, but accepting money for payment is seemingly reasonable because, as the most salable commodity, money can be later exchanged for the good originally desired. This theory is particularly appealing to libertarians, and therefore most cryptocurrency users, because it presupposes the centrality of an open market (unlike the derided "fiat" dollars that are supposedly controlled by central banks). While it sounds plausible, this theory has been widely criticized as incompatible with the anthropological record, among other issues (Dodd 2016, p. 19; Ingham 2004, p. 22).

My goal here is not to try to settle these debates, which would imply that I have a concrete theory of money—an issue that has bedeviled some of the greatest minds of modernity, including David Hume, Immanuel Kant, Karl Marx, Max Weber, Georg Simmel, John Maynard Keynes, and Joseph Schumpeter. There is also a wealth of very good, recent (and often competing) theories to choose from (Dodd 2016; Hart 2001; Ingham 2004; Maurer 2007). Instead, my argument is that the "double coincidence of wants" theory is simply false, and that the more common and plausible "generic" account (of money's three properties) is not so much wrong as dangerous.

Literature on Bitcoin and cryptocurrencies that relies on the generic theory of money is flawed and usually misses the point. In truth, most cryptocurrency research does not seriously question the meta-theoretical issues involved and therefore assumes the veracity of the generic theory. This is not surprising since the study of money has always been something of a niche field. Even economists have never been much concerned with the role of money, despite it being a key agent of economic activity, since money is typically seen as an epiphenomenon of more basic economic behaviors (Ingham 2004). But in dismissing or confusing the dynamics of money, cryptocurrency research is liable to mistake the true essence of capitalism and therefore fail to understand the role of cryptocurrencies today. That such accounts of cryptocurrencies usually fail to say anything meaningful about modern capitalism ought to raise a cautionary flag (the notable exception is David Golumbia's critique in *The Politics of Bitcoin,* 2016).

To understand the monetary dimensions of cryptocurrencies more broadly, it is necessary to frame the narratives that support the generic theory of money. To do so, I argue that cryptocurrency's monetary theory is often not descriptively powerful but instead is socially *performative*. That is, the generic theory of money creates a *myth* that reflexively informs analysis and therefore obscures how cryptocurrencies are really used (see also Cameron 2016). This myth is often promulgated by the most active and core users of cryptocurrencies. This is why I often refer to users as evangelists—spreading the gospel of cryptocurrencies (an ecumenical thread that others have also picked up on, see Golumbia 2018). It is not important if the myth is true or false (although false myths are typically harder to maintain). Rather, the myth is either powerful or weak (Mosco 2004), and therefore capable or incapable of creating the social conditions necessary to maintain particular economic, political, and technical infrastructures.

To understand how the generic theory of money has become socially performative for cryptocurrencies, let us look at two accounts of *traditional* money narratives. In particular, Geoffrey Ingham's (2004) argument that "commodity theories of money" are critical to traditional descriptions of money, and Nigel Dodd's (2016) argument that myths give meaning and order to the economic world. According to Ingham, the commodity theories of money ideologically conceal the *social construction of money* by making it seem like money is stable and grounded in productivity and goods, which can be accurately measured and therefore controlled. In reality, Ingham argues, money is socially constructed by a complex array of infrastructures and people. Dodd characterizes the social life of money by arguing that money communities invoke "myths of origin" to explain the present and future (Dodd 2016, p. 11). These myths underpin expectations about the market and give uncertainties (such as price) a semblance of order and meaning, which they otherwise lack by nature. Ultimately, these myths emerge from the complex interplay of norms and meanings. Economic and technical theories are therefore a *precondition* of monetary value.

One way to think about cryptocurrency narratives is to imagine economic and technical theories as social products that are layered like strata. There are theories and beliefs from the bottom to the top, from permanent bedrock to changing topsoil. On this metaphor, the bedrock of cryptocurrencies would be the "mathematical" certainty of cryptographic algorithms. Should a critical error be discovered in the cryptographic algorithms underpinning cryptocurrencies the fallout would not just be economic and technical. Without trust in cryptography, the very nature of cryptocurrencies would be called into question (and with quantum code-breaking around the corner, this is a distressingly real possibility). At the next layer, cryptocurrencies require belief in a "frontier" of cyberspace. For those who believe such things, the frontier of cyberspace is a place with its own laws, rules, and norms. At this frontier, cyberspace is also believed to be a *global* market free of the impediments of national boundaries. Technologies take the place of sovereign authorities and ought to produce a monetary space free of taxation and regulation. At higher layers, the strata are more variable, with a changing "subsoil" of protocol (see also Galloway 2004). Cryptocurrency protocols are in constant change, but as I discussed in Chapter 2, changes must be carefully managed. The "topsoil" that is constantly eroding and being replenished is monetary theory and its associated definitions. The generic theory of money sits at this level—a critical component to the viability of startups, markets, and general user enthusiasm. These myths helped create confidence, trust, and a belief in the utility of cryptocurrencies, which ultimately helped drive up prices.

Alternative theories of digital money

The biggest problem facing the generic theory of money is that the theory itself does not do much work. For example, David Yermack (2013) finds that Bitcoin fails on all three accounts, leading him to conclude that Bitcoin is not a "bona fide money." On the other hand, Pavel Ciaian, Miroslava Rajcaniova, and d'Artis Kancs (2016) find that Bitcoin is partially successful on the same three-pronged test. Max Kubát (2015) finds, however, that Bitcoin fails as a "store of value." This is all very well, but what does it say about Bitcoin in a broader sense? These papers make some interesting observations along the way, but not *because* of the theory of money. The issue is that the generic theory of money is practically inconsequential for analysis, but consequential for ideology and sustaining broader social beliefs. With this issue in mind, it is clear that we need an empirically richer theory of digital money. In the following, I sample a range of alternatives. While none quite captures the full complexity of cryptocurrencies, they do chart paths towards new narratives.

Money and discourse
We often *speak* about cryptocurrencies as though they are "money," and at times we *use* cryptocurrencies like money too. This "money talk" or "money conduct" is a sign that for some communities, cryptocurrencies *are* money. This is a somewhat new way to think about money—a line of research more interested in the routines, behaviors, uses, and speech acts of money rather than, as was traditional, its material form (Agha 2017). On this conception, money is defined by its ever-changing social networks. This means that, for example, when cryptocurrency miners buy all available high-end graphics cards from retail stores, when coal is burned to

produce electricity for cryptocurrency mining, when a hacker exfiltrates Bitcoins worth millions from an online currency exchange, and when the stolen Bitcoins are permitted for use throughout the network—all stories that have been told in the last few years—these are part of the discourse of money and, in turn, define it. With its wide reach, this theory also highlights the fact that money is central to society and is intimately linked to the ways that we express and conduct ourselves.

But, as anthropologist Asif Agha (2017) points out, money media also contain the limits of their use. These limits are often inscribed in or on monetary media or are found in related artifacts such as codes and laws. Many times, these are official "utterances," as on state-issued money media, but unofficial or private usages are also common throughout history. These utterances include discussions of political and economic utopia by Bitcoin users and more conventionally, the printed statement on the British pound: "I promise to pay the bearer of demand the sum of . . ." The statements and behaviors in use are the "cultural shifters" of money and help define it (Agha 2017, p. 353). The validity of utterances is set by the boundary of the "semiotic community." The boundaries of the semiotic community also explain why, to some, Bitcoin is not "real" money—these foreigners are "unfamiliar with the metasemiotic frameworks" that enable Bitcoin's use (Agha 2017, p. 351). Indeed, the vast majority of people watching the rise of cryptocurrencies—often with horror—are strangers in a strange land, but they fail to see money use right before their eyes. In other words, for those who do not trust it, do not believe in its value, or have no context for its use, Bitcoin is not money.

Another approach characterizing money in terms of discourse is offered by Mark Coeckelbergh and Wessel Reijers, who describe cryptocurrencies as "narrative" technologies (Coeckelbergh & Reijers 2016b, 2016a; Reijers & Coeckelbergh 2016). Unlike Agha, who argues that social and cultural discourses about cryptocurrencies define their use,

Coeckelbergh and Reijers argue that the discourses about cryptocurrencies define *those who use them*. This is a somewhat subtle point, drawn from hermeneutical theory originating with Martin Heidegger and then refined by Paul Ricoeur. Ricoeur's point, according to Coeckelbergh and Reijers, is that money discourses create a hermeneutical circle—the whole can only be understood in reference to its situated and experienced parts. Ricoeur's narrative theory applies to cryptocurrencies because they are textual and therefore *programmed*. The specific way each cryptocurrency is programmed constitutes its unique "plot," in much the same way that characters and settings are described in a work of fiction. Moreover, just as the author of a work of fiction has to decide between stock elements (clichés, metaphors, and so on) and wholly new elements that require introduction to the reader, the cryptocurrency designer creates a plot through shared cultural assumptions about technology and society but is also capable of introducing new ideas (Ricoeur calls these *pre*figured and *con*figured elements). Coeckelbergh and Reijers (2016) offer the example of timestamping to explain how Ricoeur's narrative theory works. A key feature of cryptocurrencies and blockchains is the regular recording of transaction data, which, when recorded, become permanent or "immutable." This permanence, according to Coeckelbergh and Reijers, is a new narrative for how we think about time and more importantly, record-keeping (at least in an ideal sense—they recognize that technical or "real" immutability is often fictional). Ultimately, societies delegate actions and values to these new timestamping and record-keeping devices, and so activities that used to be casual or loosely monitored become rigid and non-negotiable.

Social and political realities of money
Money is a "claim upon society," wrote Georg Simmel (2004). By this, Simmel meant that money requires something from society. Just *what* money requires from society remains a

matter of debate. Nigel Dodd (2016), for example, details at least three "claims" made by money: debt, trust, and political authority. Debt is widely believed to be the oldest or original form of money (Graeber 2011), and from debt, trust and authority emerge. Debt requires higher levels of trust due to the risk of default, which must be prevented by the threat of violence, which is justified by political authority.

Cryptocurrencies make these same three claims upon society. First, cryptocurrencies claim an abstract and socialized debt to their economic communities (Dodd 2016, p. 93). This is not debt between two parties, but rather a collectivized debt upon society to accept cryptocurrencies as money. Second, with cryptocurrencies the need to trust counterparties is mitigated in a *technical* sense. Cryptocurrency transactions are final (no chargebacks, errors, and mutations of the ledger), and therefore "trustless" (akin to bearer instruments where mere possession constitutes legal ownership). But trust is reintroduced through the circularity of exchange, material scarcity, and the development of long-term "relationships" in business, among other matters (see Chapter 8). Third, and most consequentially, cryptocurrencies make a claim of authority. Money must be "authorized" by its very nature, but cryptocurrencies (so far) lack formal backing from sovereign nations and financial institutions. Instead, cryptocurrencies are authorized for use when, recalling the hermeneutical approach detailed above, authority is *delegated* from people to technology.

As cryptocurrency evangelists have long understood, however, states do not cede financial authority easily and tensions typically arise when challenged. For the state, an important aspect of money is the ability to determine acceptable forms of payment for settling tax debt. Since universal taxation was an essential component in the development of the modern state, it stands to reason that any challenge to the autonomy of state taxation is tantamount to challenging the very existence of modern statehood. Of course, other kinds of money can co-exist with state-issued money but due to the centrality of the state and its taxation policies (which includes the use of force for non-compliance) its actions are "decisive" (Knapp 1924, p. 95). So far, cryptocurrency users have had to accommodate rather than really challenge this reality. In recent years, nation states have made their sovereign authority clear by taxing earnings made from cryptocurrencies, which discounts the very possibility that cryptocurrencies could ever challenge the power of state-issued money. Instead, cryptocurrencies are treated like any other property or commodity (Fry & Cheah 2016; Weber 2016), effectively pacifying any nascent forms of challenge to political authority.

As a counterpolitical movement, one of the ways cryptocurrency users attempt to authorize their money is by forming what Brett Scott (2014) has termed a "techno-Leviathan." According to Scott, cryptocurrency users do not define their monetary relationships to the state; rather, they may try to establish novel forms of social contracts. Users agree to "contract" with cryptographic algorithms that guarantee their (financial) peace and safety. The Hobbesian parallel from which Scott's theory is drawn is that cryptocurrency users are able to exit a financial "state of nature" (pure barter) by trusting (or submitting to) cryptographic algorithms, which become a powerful Leviathan. This new world, cryptocurrency enthusiasts believe, swaps out state violence for technological equality and a set of rights and duties dictated by socio-technical protocols.

Symbols and virtual money
One of the most striking features of cryptocurrencies is their virtuality. How, nearly everyone asks when first introduced to cryptocurrencies, is some computer code *worth* anything? Of course, the same could be said of any number of software products, but cryptocurrencies get at something deeper. Cryptocurrencies, insofar as they are "true" currencies, are not priced in some other currency, in the way that the software

giant Microsoft is "worth" US $700 billion. Cryptocurrencies appear to, or at least strive to, have value without relying on some more foundational element (however, cryptocurrencies are almost exclusively priced and discussed in terms of state-issued money, such as the US dollar or the Chinese yuan). While it *is* perplexing how money becomes valued and valuable, this paradox of virtuality is far from unique to *crypto*currencies.

Many theorists have described money as a symbolic and therefore virtual medium. Talcott Parsons, Jürgen Habermas, Niklas Luhmann, and Anthony Giddens have all claimed that money is a symbolic medium without intrinsic value, which only gains value in exchange (Ingham 2004, p. 60). According to these theorists, money is a generalized medium of communication and exchange. Moreover, cryptocurrencies have symbolic properties—they are typically fungible (can be exchanged one for one without loss of value) and circulate widely, just like typical state-issued money.

So, why is a virtual thing like a cryptocurrency actually worth anything? No simple reason supplies the answer because the ontology of money is undefined, value is fugitive, price is complex and intractable, and ultimately, cryptocurrencies—in particular—do not follow common-sense explanations. Consider, for example, the blockchain fork that produced Ethereum Classic. As I describe in Chapter 8, in 2016 an ambitious funding platform built on top of the Ethereum blockchain was hacked. In the aftermath a governance challenge emerged, and a minority of miners refused to accept the majority's decision to rescue the funds lost in the hack. So, a hard fork of the Ethereum blockchain emerged and two fully independent Ethereum blockchains were produced. Rational thinking would suggest that if you take the value of one network and cut it in half, each part would be worth half the original. Or possibly the majority network would be worth proportionately more, but either way, the resulting total would be the same as the original total, or less, but *certainly not more*.

Instead, once the markets settled, the mainline Ethereum blockchain retained *all* of its original value, and the newly formed "Ethereum Classic" blockchain became fairly valuable too. The sum was greater than the parts, and value was created from nothing.

As perplexing as the Ethereum fork was, creating "value" ex nihilo is typically how money works. Leaning on a metaphorical interpretation, Jacques Derrida answers the question of value by invoking spirits and ghosts, suggesting that value is created through the stroke of the enchanter's wand (see Dodd 2016, p. 181). Elsewhere, Derrida analyzes the ephemeral distinction between true and counterfeit money, finding that their surface effects are identical, but their values are not. Therefore, Derrida concludes, the distinction must lie in faith. Yet faith is not determinate: given enough faith counterfeit and genuine money can be equally valuable, and so we are back to the paradox of value from nothing.

There are other ways to describe the virtual nature of cryptocurrencies. Simmel, for example, claims that value is a quantification of desire, in the sense that value is a measure of the distance between a subject and an object desired. Another compelling way to account for value—which resonates with the technologies behind cryptocurrencies—is to recognize that cryptocurrencies record the ephemera of time. On this theory, cryptocurrencies are an archive (Brunton 2016) or a record (Maurer 2017) as part of an information communication technology. Value arises from capturing and recording events in time. Similarly, Keith Hart (2001) claims that money is an information system and "memory bank," which, if Hart's theory is correct, would make cryptocurrencies money *par excellence*, since they never forget.

The supposed virtuality of cryptocurrencies, however, is in tension with the ideological and material origins of value for cryptocurrencies. Cryptocurrencies have long been associated with a libertarian ethos, which has a cozy relationship to metallism (Maurer et al. 2013). Metallists believe that money specie is valuable because it can be melted down and used. Therefore, cryptocurrency narratives often sound shockingly materialist and focus on "intrinsic" value. In these narratives, cryptographic algorithms take the place of metal, because, it is argued, algorithms have inherent utility (the digital version of gold). As a theory of value, however, the actual material requirements of cryptocurrencies offer a more convincing story. Cryptocurrencies (especially Bitcoin) require massive capital expenses for mining hardware and infrastructure (buildings to house mining computers, cooling facilities, and so on), and use a lot of electricity (I discuss this issue in depth in Chapter 4). Capital expenses and resource use are concrete signs of how and why cryptocurrencies participate in a wider circuit of economic activity and therefore have value.

Cryptographic algorithms provide value to cryptocurrencies in a more abstract way too. Cryptography has long been associated with depth, interiority, and symbolic polyvalence. Up until the discovery of the Rosetta Stone it was generally accepted that Egyptian hieroglyphs were cryptographic in nature, in that they were a veil for a hidden message (when in fact they are a language, prompting questions about the distinction between cryptography and language; see Eco 1995). According to the French philosopher Jean-Joseph Goux, the "symbolic charge" of money in precapitalist societies was the basis for the exchange of "meaning, libido, and commercial value" (1990, p. 125). Value in these societies was intersubjective, spiritual, and "cryptophoric." With the rise of advanced capitalism and computerized flows of finance, Goux believes we are now "far indeed from a hieroglyphic mode of signification" and that "the *power* of the symbolic has changed" (emphasis in original, p. 130). Modern currency, Goux laments, "is governed no longer by spiritual authority" (p. 130) and instead "represses . . . the cryptophoric dimension of the symbol" (p. 132). Given the rise of cryptocurrencies, then, perhaps we have returned to a precapitalist mode of value that favors the intersubjective and spiritual?

Money media

The tensions between virtual and material dimensions of cryptocurrencies point to a broader characterization of money as media. The possibility of money media also prefigures the shift from cryptocurrencies to blockchain media. For example, German philosopher Sybille Krämer analyses money to inform her media theory. With money Krämer discovers a powerful mediator capable of bringing together "those who are opposed" by "designating and assessing commonality" (2015, p. 109). Paradoxically, money unifies by remaining separate. That is, money establishes a *different* but *common* good capable of replacing barter exchange. By theorizing money in terms of media, Krämer also makes the insightful point that money, like media, is mediation between people, not goods. Wessel Reijers makes a similar point about the mediatic mechanism of money, arguing that "money . . . instantiates an inter-human component" (2016, p. 77). I return to the question of media in Chapter 4, where I chart the transition in recent years from cryptocurrencies (as "money") to blockchain technologies.

Summary

This chapter introduced the technical inner workings of Bitcoin transactions. I described how the Bitcoin wallet is an essential piece of technology in the Bitcoin ecosystem that creates and stores private keys that unlock transactions. Transactions are not encrypted, but rather are digitally signed, or "encumbered," and can then be unlocked by anyone with access to the appropriate private key.

I then described cryptocurrencies in terms of monetary theory. I described what I call the "generic" theory of money and I contextualized it within the cryptocurrency literature. I argued that the three properties of money described in the generic theory of money fail to do any real explanatory work, but that the theory is nonetheless a major contributor to the cryptocurrency narrative. In this way, I found that the generic theory was performative. Finding this orthodoxy lacking, I introduced a number of social theories of money. These social theories of money highlight the ways that we speak about and use cryptocurrencies, which take on symbolic importance. I discussed (and reconfigured) the metallist accounts that predominate discussions about cryptocurrency's value. I introduced the notion that cryptographic algorithms supply the material basis that account for cryptocurrency's value. Finally, the virtual and material origins of value of cryptocurrencies remain in tension. Therefore, cryptocurrencies can be understood in terms of media, like other forms of money.

CHAPTER FOUR

Blockchain Media

Media are what lie between. The German media theorist Friedrich Kittler argued that the origins of the term "media" (*metaxú*) are found in Aristotle's work on psychology (*De Anima*), where Kittler discovered a materialist sense of the term referring to the stuff that lies "between" a human subject and perceived object, such as air or water (Kittler 2009). Over the next two thousand years, the term morphed from matter to means (or instrument) to communication (see Guillory 2010). This genealogy highlights the ways that media often extend natural senses, such as sight or hearing, or connect distant minds, through speech, writing, and telecommunications technology. Tele-technologies bridge physical distances but also "mediate" by subtly altering the transmission. With modern media technologies such as radio or television, there is the risk that mediation completely overwhelms the meaning being conveyed, in effect substituting one for the other—as Marshall McLuhan writes, the "medium is the message" (McLuhan 2003).

In the first three chapters I discussed theories of money as media, first (in Chapters 1 and 2) with Georg Simmel's theory and then again (in Chapter 3) with Sybille Krämer's. For Simmel, money is a means or tool because it enables exchange between people who have incompatible desires. Similarly, for Krämer money is a means because it unifies while remaining separate. Significantly, money mediates objects to the point of transmutation: if I want a loaf of bread I can sell my vegetables for paper notes (money) and then exchange those for bread. In recent decades, money has undergone another transmutation, from paper to digital bits. Digital money now helps bridge distance in ways similar to more traditional media, such as radio or television. At the same time, as Mark Coeckelbergh points out, digital money also introduces new moral challenges on account of the fact that it creates ethical "distance," which in the worst cases can lead to capitalist excesses and a failure to appreciate truly human values (Coeckelbergh 2015). In the first three chapters these issues led me to conclude that cryptocurrencies are media too. In the shift from the medium of money to a generic record-keeping and computation platform we might wonder if blockchains are media too? Indeed, I think they are. Not only are blockchain technologies media, they are media *par excellence*.

Blockchain technologies are media in ways quite different from cryptocurrencies, however. Blockchain technologies are media in at least two different ways. First, blockchain technologies are media in that they sit between people, carry meaning, and transform messages. This is a medium in the familiar sense of radio, television, and the Internet. Second, blockchain technologies are media because they are saturated with cryptographic technologies. This conception of media does not draw on the practices of exchange, like money and cryptocurrencies. Instead, blockchain technologies draw on their arrangement of cryptographic algorithms to abstract away the complexity of objects and things, which makes the objects and things easily managed.

The cryptographic hash function is a key reason why blockchain technologies are media in ways unlike money and cryptocurrencies. The hash algorithm is pervasive throughout the design and operation of blockchains, and hash functions are, as I describe elsewhere, "notational technologies" (DuPont 2017). Notational technologies rely on the *shift* from a syntactic plane of reference to a semantic, or meaningful, plane of reference. This "shift" is the medium. In effect, the hash algorithm takes a complex object in the real (or ideal) world and says, by socially accepted fiat, "this string of alphanumeric data stands in for this object." In so doing, the hash algorithm does not rely on its similarity to the object (the hash does not *look* like the object). Instead, the hash algorithm has a consistent set of procedures (the algorithm) and firm social agreement that it "represents" the object. In the case of Bitcoin, blocks of transactions count as money because we "will" it into effect and because the technical system is capable of keeping up this fiction. Or, to take another example, when tracking goods through a supply chain using a blockchain (see Chapter 7), the hash representing the individual box or shipping container ignores other complexities and focuses on the item's discrete boundaries. All of the examples of blockchain technologies I discuss in this book utilize this ability to abstract complexity and make objects discrete—the key to being a medium and the reason why blockchains are generic yet potent.

This chapter details the technical components of block-chains and describes how they fit together. I describe what cryptographic hashes are, how they are used to create blocks of transactions, and how blocks are chained together to create secure records. I highlight the role of consensus protocols, focusing on the most common protocol (known as "proof of work"). The consensus protocol is responsible for keeping the distributed ledger in sync across the network of validating nodes, but in the case of the proof of work protocol, it also has the unfortunate side effect of using massive amounts of electricity (this process is known as "mining"). As the popularity of cryptocurrencies has grown, this once-niche activity has metastasized into industry-scale operations that now cause significant environmental damage. I conclude the chapter by introducing three network architectures commonly used for blockchain technologies, which offer alternatives to typical cryptocurrency mining.

Blockchains

Most cryptocurrencies use blockchains to securely record transactions, and most blockchain designs remain very similar to the one first detailed in Satoshi Nakamoto's (2008) Bitcoin whitepaper. There are many predecessors and alternative blockchain designs but none have been as successful as Nakamoto's.

A few years after the release of Bitcoin, developers started looking for ways to apply underlying technologies from Bitcoin for uses beyond money systems. Early ideas built on top of the Bitcoin system (which always had *limited* programmatic capabilities) and used the existing Bitcoin blockchain for transaction processing. By building new protocols on top of the Bitcoin blockchain, these designs extended and tailored the design to specific application areas (for example, a notable early project built on top of the Bitcoin blockchain was Mastercoin, now Omni). Gradually, systems experimented with replacing the Bitcoin blockchain—first with "side chains" that are validated independently but pegged to the original Bitcoin blockchain, then with completely independent blockchains of unique design. These early systems were variously known as Bitcoin 2.0, alt coins, and block chains.

In late 2013, the development of what was by this point called "blockchains" (as one word) started to take off. One of the earliest, most ambitious, and now most successful of these projects was Ethereum, which was founded by Vitalik Buterin, a young and active member of the Bitcoin community. In the fall of 2013, Buterin began publicly discussing his ideas for an alternative blockchain design, and then published a whitepaper in November (Buterin 2013a). On January 23, 2014, Buterin officially announced the project and published a roadmap. Soon, collaborators joined. Through 2014, a core team established the nonprofit Ethereum Foundation to guide the project, developed software in collaboration with an open-source software developer community, and released a "yellowpaper" (Wood 2014), the first of several revisions to Buterin's original whitepaper. After some of the technical parts had been developed, in mid-2014 Ethereum launched a public crowdsale of "pre-mined" tokens (Ethereum's tokens are known as Ethers, or ETH). This practice of selling pre-launch token assets (later known as "Initial Coin Offerings") would become a very popular model for startups looking to generate operating capital (see Chapter 5). With the instant success of Ethereum and the new "blockchain" branding, many existing quasi-cryptocurrency projects rebranded into blockchain companies, alongside fresh new blockchain start-ups. Closely related alternatives, in some cases preexisting the invention of blockchains altogether, found revived interest (as in, for example, R3's Corda system that was first implemented in the late 1990s). Since then, for companies large and small, "blockchain" has eclipsed cryptocurrencies as a point of interest, although in many cases the technical distinction is blurry.

At its most basic level there are three key components to a blockchain: hashes, blocks, and chains.

Hashes

Hashes are critically important to blockchains. A hash algorithm accepts an arbitrary length of data and outputs a fixed-length, deterministic but unique alphanumeric value. In Chapter 3 I described how hashes are used in Bitcoin to transform a cryptographic public key into a Bitcoin address; in this chapter I describe how hashes are used to create and identify blocks of transactions and then chain them together. In the case of systems using the "proof of work" consensus protocol, such as Bitcoin and Ethereum, hashes are used as a computational assurance of "work." This process is known as "mining." (An emerging alternative, discussed below, is known as "proof of stake," which does away with the computational work needed to keep the system secure.)

In Bitcoin, the hash algorithm creates a unique identifier (or digital "fingerprint") for transaction data that are contained within a "candidate block." The candidate block is a list of "encumbered" transactions received by the mining node from the peer-to-peer network. In comparison, the candidate block for Ethereum also contains a list of encumbered transactions, but the transactions may be either hashes of accounts (like Bitcoin) or hashes that link to executable code. This ability to execute arbitrary code is why Ethereum is a general-purpose computing environment, and, therefore, a significant techno-logical advancement over more limited cryptocurrencies such as Bitcoin.

The following are examples of the SHA256 hash, which is the specific hashing algorithm used in Bitcoin and many block-chain technologies. Ethereum uses the KECCAK-256 hash, which produces different results but is functionally similar. Interested readers may wish to consult Anders Brownworth's excellent website to interactively explore how hashes, blocks, and chains work (https://anders.com/blockchain/block.html). Most of these examples can be tested on Brownworth's website.

cryptocurrencies and blockchains = aa0c7a4477d227c-709cc35f8fe8e7a2e3bd66ed-021120f69de03107a50da02a5	cryptocurrencies and blockchain = 1d8c99804a3386efea04fbbe91f-86fe31874405936ae6fc171fcbdac-017cd2f2
cryptocurrencies & blockchains = f55120596128b745b6999b4c8e177e-4b2a2dd89f169ebb8ded-68b42550a0dc22	Cryptocurrencies and Blockchains by Quinn DuPont = f42bf9623c-8da5ce78f64f18ee26192d3f332fcb-35623375d3c47f2aa2bfbc26

Notice that no matter the length of the input, the length of the output is always the same (64 characters). The remarkable feature of hash algorithms is that if even a single character of input changes, the algorithm produces a radically different output value, as seen by the completely different hash outputs that result from similar inputs in the examples.

Producing a hash value from an input is, in computa-tional terms, quite easy and fast, but the reverse is not. Hash algorithms are deterministic, so identical inputs will always produce the same outputs, day in and day out. This means others can check the validity of a hash by re-running the algo-rithm on the original input—if the test output matches the expected output, then the hash is valid.

✓	cryptocurrencies and blockchains = aa0c7a4477d227c709c-c35f8fe8e7a2e3bd66ed-021120f69de03107a50da02a5	✗	cryptocurrencies and blockchains = 24253a6ae-75d67bc90c55605a6904d-7c528c17cd29a16459d-7855c703e6a309a

If, however, you have only the hash output and not the input, there is no easy way to discover the input. The hash algorithm is one-way. For example, this is a valid hash for *some* input: 024253a6ae75d67bc90c55605a6904d7c528c-17cd29a16459d7855c703e6a309a. We know that this hash input is *not* "cryptocurrencies and blockchains" because we already computed that hash and the output is very different. So, how would we go about discovering the input for this hash? Recall that even a tiny input change produces a completely different output (the output should be practically random but deterministic). There is in fact no simple way to discover the input for this hash (go ahead and try—it is a valid hash). The *only* way to find the input is to guess. Start at A, compute the hash, compare it, try B, compute the hash, compare it . . . Since the output is only 64 characters but the input could be any length (perhaps I calculated the hash of *War and Peace?*) guessing takes a long time (technically, the combinatorial space of the SHA256 hash is 2^{256}—an unbelievably large number). This guess→check→try again process, as I describe below, is the key to proof-of-work mining.

Blocks and mining

A block is a hashed list of transactions. In the case of Ethereum and other programmable blockchains, the list of transactions includes pointers (in the form of hashes) to executable code. A *valid block* requires a special kind of hash called a "proof of work" that securely "seals" the candidate block and chains it to the previous block. Valid blocks are produced by "mining." (This process is only applicable for proof-of-work systems, which are by far the most common. Alternatives, such as "proof of stake," use a very different mechanism to accomplish the same outcome, but it is yet to be determined if it really works.)

Hashing transaction data produces a uniquely identifiable block. This has two important consequences. First, the computed hash value serves as a helpful identifier for the block. The short alphanumeric hash creates a "summary" of transactions in the block (which could be hundreds or thousands of transactions), which can be uniquely referenced, not unlike how a URL points to a website. Second, the hash ensures that no transactions have been altered after the fact. Once a hash of transactions is created, the block can be independently verified to prove that none of the transactions have been altered. This is possible because, as I described above, any change of input for a hash algorithm produces a radically different output. Thus, if any transactions have been changed, the hash that uniquely identifies the block will also change. Verifying that no changes have been made is simple: run the hash algorithm on the transaction data and compare it to the original. If the two hashes match, then it is assured that transaction data remained unchanged. This feature, along with block chaining (discussed below) is why blockchains are "immutable" record-keeping systems.

But a simple hash of transaction data does not create a *valid* block. For most blockchains, the proof-of-work consensus protocol requires that valid blocks must be mined. A valid block that has been mined includes a proof-of-work hash (and is chained, which I describe below). Blockchain systems use different mining algorithms, but the basics are all roughly similar. Miners first validate transaction data and then compute the proof-of-work hash. Indeed, the mining process is in the first instance a validating service, but most of the complexity and effort involved in mining is spent keeping the system secure through the proof-of-work protocol.

The validation, code execution, and mining necessary for each blockchain occurs on a distributed computer network. In simple terms, this means that no single computer on the network is essential for the network's overall performance. Put another way, the system is "survivable" against isolated attack. There is, however, considerable debate and confusion about terminology and what a distributed network looks like in reality.

In the cryptocurrency and blockchain literature the terms "distributed" and "decentralized" are used interchangeably. The dictionary offers limited guidance. "Decentralized" is a relatively new word used predominantly in politics, in the sense of something that removes a center. "Distributed" is a much older word, also used in politics, and refers to spreading, bestowing, and dividing, especially in such a way that each part receives a portion. This suggests, according to the dictionary, that a blockchain network is more likely distributed than decentralized. With respect to how the term is used to describe computer networks, the canonical reference is Paul Baran's 1964 RAND report, *On Distributed Communications*, which later influenced much thinking about the architecture of the Internet. In this work, Baran sketches his vision for a network of computers that are capable of surviving physical (presumably nuclear) attack. The network is resilient because nodes are redundant and can "switch assignment" (re-route transmission) (Baran 1964, p. 13). Baran visually depicted three models for computer networks in an image that has since become famous—and widely misunderstood (Figure 4.1). Baran refers to "decentralized" networks as a common species of centralized networks, often organized hierarchically, and not requiring "complete reliance upon a single point" (p. 1). Distributed networks, on the other hand, are much rarer, and better described as "all channel" networks, highlighting the ways in which every node is connected to every other node (Arquilla & Ronfeldt 2001, p. 1).

In practice, most computer networks are at least partially hierarchical, while exhibiting some redundancy and ability to re-route. Since blockchain technologies rely on the underlying communications infrastructure of the Internet, they are in the

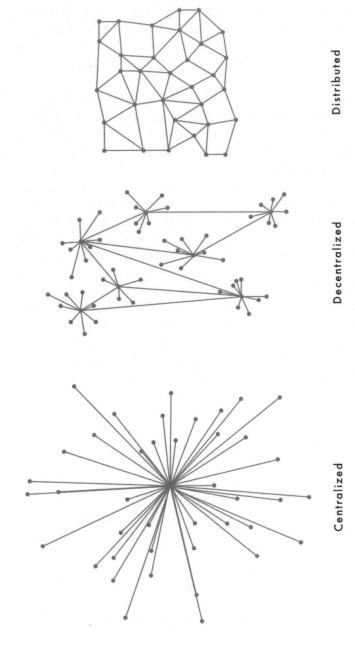

Centralized   Decentralized   Distributed

Figure 4.1   Three types of computer networks. Adapted from Baran (1964, p. 2).

first instance only as robust and distributed as the Internet, which often has localized outages but has a pretty good track record overall (the Domain Name System, however, has long been the Internet's Achilles heel and is particularly suscepti- ble to error and attack). For this reason, it is foolish to think of blockchain networks as somehow more resilient or distrib- uted than the underlying Internet infrastructure, or in any way independent from it. (It goes without saying that compar- ing the social impact of blockchain technologies to that of the Internet is equally foolhardy, despite being common in the blockchain literature.)

The distributed validation process for blockchain networks is simple: each miner independently verifies that transactions are well formed and comply with a specified set of criteria. In the case of Bitcoin, the miners validate that transactions add up correctly (ensuring that no Bitcoins go missing or are fraudulently created from nothing), that encumbered trans- actions can access the appropriate funds, and many other technical details. In the case of Ethereum, miners validate many of the same things but also check any "contract" code. If an Ethereum transaction contains references to contract code, the miner will run the code in a special environment called the Ethereum Virtual Machine (EVM). If all transactions vali- date correctly and the code runs successfully, the miner will begin the process of finding a valid proof-of-work hash.

The proof of work is a hash of transaction data that satis- fies a specific criterion set by the blockchain protocol. This criterion for hash generation is known as the "difficulty level" and is the key to proof-of-work mining. As I discussed above, the hash output of any input is effectively random, and there is no shortcut to finding a specific output. Normally, hashes are used to transform an input (e.g., transaction data) into a short, unique output. But the proof-of-work protocol requires the opposite. The proof-of-work protocol requires a miner to find the *input* from a specified output. Recall that this is virtually impossible because hash algorithms are one-way functions—it is easy to produce an output, but it is nearly impossible to find an input that corresponds to an output— and yet the proof-of-work protocol requires precisely this impossibility. To ease the burden, the blockchain protocol accepts any input that corresponds to a *range* of hash output values. By adjusting the size of the acceptable range, the protocol can adjust the difficulty level. The smaller the acceptable range the more difficult it is to find the input, and vice versa.

The acceptable range of hash outputs is defined by the number of leading zeros in the hash. For example, the protocol may require a "difficulty level" of at least four leading zeros. This might be an acceptable output hash:

```
0000fa0f4b9a687d44050019a7478812e9247e711b9eccef10odd-
3340954baa7e.
```

The input corresponding to this output is the text "cryptocurrencies and blockchains" *plus* a "nonce." A nonce is a variable that is added to transaction data to create unique hash outputs. Since hash algorithms are deterministic, if the input value does not change the output value also does not change— no matter how many times the algorithm is run. Usually, this is why hash functions are used (to ensure that data has not been altered). However, proof-of-work mining requires the miner to find an input that corresponds to a range of hash outputs. But the miner already knows the input (the list of transactions), so how does it change the output? By adding a variable number (nonce) to the transaction list.

This way, the miner can:

1. Hash the transaction data plus a nonce (a number).
2. Check to see if the output hash corresponds to the specified difficulty level (number of leading zeros).
3. If there are too few leading zeros, change the nonce, hash again.
4. Check, and continue iterating until a suitable nonce is found.

The key piece of information is the nonce: when the nonce is added to the transaction data and hashed it produces a hash value within an acceptable difficulty level. The miner keeps iterating the nonce until an acceptable nonce is found:

block #	nonce	transaction data	hash output
1	1	cryptocurrencies and blockchains	1ad3cf18d6e557729336b256425f3a93e 1e50b55e7770ebc83adedb6196681011f
1	2	cryptocurrencies and blockchains	50e33e4630eee1d2f79e7a57e5f2594 5bb3ecc60a24bbb705c3055067fb5 efbb
1	3	cryptocurrencies and blockchains	f15d3f9c50e8ae141cc69a778dec27306 0867303ec310c080daa2e2c0d7532ef
1	...		
1	8830	cryptocurrencies and blockchains	0000faof4b9a687d44050019a747881 2e9247e711b9eccef100dd3340954ba a7e

In this example, the nonce that produces a hash output within the range stipulated by the difficulty level is 8,830. If the miner starts with a nonce of 1 and increments by 1 each round, it takes 8,830 rounds until an acceptable value is found. This requires a lot of *work* and takes a lot of *time*.

Once the acceptable nonce is found the corresponding hash is broadcast to other miners in the peer-to-peer network. When a miner receives a hash from a peer that corresponds to the current block, the miner independently verifies the proof of work. Verification of proof of work is very quick because the needed ingredients are already supplied. The miner hashes the transaction data and the nonce (and other appropriate metadata) and if the result meets the stipulated difficulty level, the block is accepted. Once the block is accepted, the miner broadcasts the corresponding hash to its peers in the network, stops mining the current block, and moves on to mining the next candidate block.

Miners independently validate blocks and are in

competition to discover the correct nonce. Machines capable of running the hash algorithm quickly are imperative if the miner has any chance of discovering the correct nonce before its peers. In reality, the proof-of-work protocol is much, much more difficult than depicted in these examples, but the winner is not always the fastest computer on the network. Miners do not simply increment the nonce starting at 1. Rather, miners pick a random nonce each time, which produces a random output. So, even comparatively slow miners will occasionally find the correct nonce. But, given the enormous difficulty level required for most proof-of-work mining, an extremely powerful miner is required if one has any hope of discovering a nonce in this century, or even millennium. Mining is therefore a lottery, but those with the fastest machines will, on average, win more often (just as those who buy more lottery tickets will, on average, win more often). The fact that the lottery winner is random is important for preventing cheaters, as I discuss below.

The requirement for a proof-of-work hash is also useful for setting and adjusting the block production rate. Every blockchain has a "pulse" set by how often, on average, blocks are produced. In Bitcoin, blocks are produced about every ten minutes; in Ethereum, blocks are produced every ten to nineteen seconds. These durations are predetermined values set by the blockchain protocol and are based on a number of factors, such as desired use and a balance between fast processing and the time it takes successful blocks to propagate across the entire network. Block production in Ethereum is much faster than Bitcoin because it uses an advanced propagation technique called Greedy Heaviest Observed Subtree or "GHOST." The GHOST technique allows blocks to be counted in cases where otherwise they would fail to make it all the way across the network before the next block is processed. For example, if the block production rate was set at two seconds but due to network latency a successful block takes four seconds to reach all miners, some miners would already be

mining on the next block before the previous block was validated by the rest of the network. These missing blocks are
known as "uncles" and if there are too many the network gets
out of sync and successful blocks go unnoticed, producing an
inefficient system.

Because the proof-of-work difficulty level is adjustable, the
block production rate can be set dynamically. This is especially important for open networks like Bitcoin and Ethereum,
which have an ever-changing group of miners (this is somewhat less important for closed networks, which I discuss
below). For example, if a news story breaks or the price of
Bitcoin goes up, people might be encouraged to buy mining
hardware and contribute to the network. In doing so, the total
mining network hash rate increases, which means, on average, a suitable nonce will be found more quickly. Similarly, if
a miner goes offline for maintenance or is discouraged from
participating, the network hash rate will decrease and a suitable nonce will not be found as quickly as before. In either
case, the block production rate will not match the expected
goal—either the block will be produced too quickly or too
slowly. To compensate for these changes in network mining
power the blockchain protocol adjusts the difficulty level,
either increasing the difficulty level to slow block production
or decreasing the difficulty level to speed block production. For Bitcoin, the difficulty level is adjusted every 2,016
blocks (about every two weeks if blocks are produced every
ten minutes); for Ethereum, the difficulty level is adjusted
constantly. So if Bitcoin mining suddenly becomes popular,
for the next two weeks blocks will be produced too quickly
(each block will be produced in less than ten minutes). After
2,016 blocks the protocol will then increase the difficulty by
a suitable amount: requiring proof-of-work hashes with more
leading zeros. Since finding a proof-of-work hash with more
leading zeros is less likely to occur (the acceptable range is
smaller), miners on the network will have to iterate through
more nonces. So, on average, more hashes will need to be

produced before a suitable proof-of-work hash is found. Due to the random nature of producing proof-of-work hashes, the protocol does not know *which* miner will find the correct value, but it does know, on average, *when* the correct value will be found.

There is a final reason why the block production rate is important: for blockchains that have an underlying token, the rate of block production sets the rate of token issuance. In Bitcoin, this rate sets the monetary policy. New bitcoins are issued with every block produced, until the maximum cap (21 million) is reached. Once 21 million bitcoins have been issued (around the year 2140), the Bitcoin monetary ecosystem will transition to a fee-based model. This transition from issuing bitcoins to collecting fees for processing has significant implications for keeping the network secure and in sync, which I discuss below. Ethereum also issues tokens when blocks are created, but there is no monetary cap.

The proof-of-work hash also chains blocks together, which is important for the system's security.

Chains

Just like transactions, blocks are chained together for security. In the process of finding a hash output that satisfies the proof-of-work requirement, the miner includes the hash of the chain of transactions and the proof-of-work hash of the *previous block* (Figure 4.2). By including the previous block's proof-of-work hash, a long chain of hashes is created. If any previous block's transactions are altered the proof-of-work hash will be invalidated, and any block with a new (altered) hash will cause a ripple effect up the chain. This is an important security requirement: if a block is altered after being "sealed," the rest of the chain of hashes will be invalidated. By verifying the hash at the end of the chain, the entire chain can be validated. This is why blockchains are considered immutable and secure—even a small change to a past transaction or block breaks the rest of the chain.

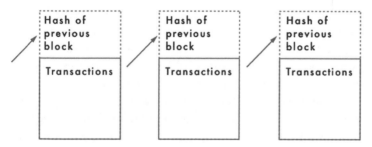

Figure 4.2   Block chaining

There is, however, a catch: given two or more perfectly well-validated chains, the miners will be unable to determine the true state of affairs. Multiple chains, known as "forks," occur in the regular course of events when blocks arrive from the network out of order and when an attacker is attempting to change previous blocks. In both cases, miners do not have enough information to determine which version of the chain is authoritative. Miners simply verify the hashes, check to see if any block contains transactions that do not correctly produce the proof-of-work hash, and if everything checks out—from the perspective of the miner—both versions of history are correct.

Consider a person who wants to change a block from yesterday—perhaps hoping to remove a large transaction or change its value. To do so, this person would need to re-create a transaction list, chain it together, and create a candidate block. The candidate block would need to include a suitable proof-of-work hash as well. If the proof-of-work hash was omitted or simply incorrect, validating miners would detect it and immediately discard it. So the only option available would be to create a new proof-of-work hash for the (altered/fraudulent) block. This is possible but difficult because it requires re-mining the block. The person looking to change the block must mine it until a valid proof-of-work hash is found (meeting the required difficulty level). This is especially hard because the difficulty level is set for the *entire network* of miners, meaning, on average, it will take the entire network ten minutes to find a proof-of-work hash. If, however, this person possessed a very powerful mining machine, perhaps equal to one-tenth of the entire network (however unlikely this would be in reality), the miner would (on average) find the proof-of-work hash for the (altered/fraudulent) block in about one hundred minutes. Only then would the person have a new block with a valid proof-of-work hash, to be submitted to the network for verification and approval. Upon doing so, the validating miners would have a conundrum: is this new block legitimate?

Consensus

To determine which chain to accept as authoritative given competing but valid options (each chain containing blocks with verified proof-of-work hashes), the proof-of-work protocol comes to *consensus* by *authorizing* (selecting) the chain with the greatest proof-of-work calculation. This is typically the longest chain, but each consensus protocol calculates this slightly differently (Bitcoin and Ethereum differ in this regard).

Returning to the example above, with the person trying to fraudulently change a previous transaction, recall that a valid proof of work was re-mined for the fraudulent block and was submitted to the network. This causes a fork in the chain. Recall also that this person had access to a *very* powerful mining machine, capable of computing a new valid proof-of-work hash in about one hundred minutes. However, once this (fraudulent) block is submitted to the network it is now one hundred minutes, or ten blocks, behind the rest of the network. The legitimate network is now working on a block ten blocks into the future. The forked chain is, therefore, shorter than the authoritative one (Figure 4.3). Seeing that this new, forked chain is shorter, the network rejects it as not authoritative.

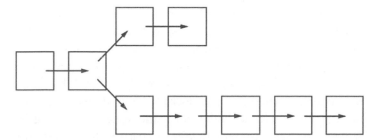

Figure 4.3   Forked chain of blocks

Suppose, however, that the person trying to fraudulently change a previous transaction is persistent and continues to mine the rest of the chain. The miner is able to produce a valid proof-of-work hash for the next block in line as well (since the previous was already created by valid means). Working this way, the person can continue to mine this fraudulent chain, making it longer and longer. However, each time the miner submits the fraudulent chain it will continue to be rejected, since it will remain the shortest. Worse still, this fraudulent chain will fall further and further behind because the miner is only able to mine at one-tenth the speed of the entire network. Within just a few hours the fraudulent chain will be hopelessly behind the main network and will never catch up. If, as I mentioned in the example, the transaction to be changed was from a block processed yesterday, the situation would be direr still—the fraudulent chain would be hundreds of blocks shorter and quickly falling behind further. Therefore, the security of the network is protected by selecting the longest chain, and all transactions remain immutable.

The consensus protocol keeps the network fair and in sync. As I mentioned above, the proof-of-work mining process is effectively a lottery—since hash outputs are random but must fall within an acceptable range (the difficulty level), it is not known *which* individual miner will be successful, but it is known (on average) *when* a miner in the network will discover the correct nonce. Once a miner wins the lottery, it is elected the leader. The winning miner propagates its valid block to the rest of the network for verification and if the proof-of-work hash checks out, the rest of the network accepts the winning miner's block (they temporarily become the "followers"). But each block is a new lottery, so when the next block is produced (in ten minutes for Bitcoin), it is unlikely that the same miner will win again. Rather, a different miner will win and become the leader until the next block, and so on. By randomly choosing the leader the lottery ensures that all miners participate in the process of constructing the authoritative chain.

This lottery system is also important to keep miners from censoring transactions. Since any one miner cannot reliably win the lottery, it cannot reliably submit doctored blocks. Only certain kinds of doctored blocks would count anyway (they are still independently verified), but is there anything preventing a miner from systematically omitting a transaction or censoring a particular address? The lottery prevents a miner from censoring transactions because a transaction skipped on one block is likely to be included in the next (by an honest miner). So long as the censoring miner does not consistently win every lottery, it is unable to reliably block a transaction.

There is, however, an important caveat about the proof-of-work consensus protocol. If a single miner is powerful enough, or if many miners collude to the extent that a majority of mining power is controlled, there is no longer any guarantee that transactions will be processed in an honest way. This is known as the "51 percent" attack. Recall, again, the example of the person trying to fraudulently change a previous transaction but suppose that instead of just 10 percent of the network's mining power, the person controlled 51 percent. By controlling a majority of the network's mining power, the person would win the lottery often and would be in control of the longest chain. Thus any block could be doctored or rejected (in fact, 51 percent of the network's mining power is required to *guarantee* control but only a much lower threshold, perhaps 30 percent, is required to reliably take control). The longest chain would therefore become the fraudulent chain. In effect, the fraudulent chain would cease to be fraudulent— it would be the authoritative chain. And until the "honest" miners on the network reclaimed a majority of mining power, the blockchain would remain fraudulent but authoritative.

In practical terms, this kind of takeover of the network is unlikely, since large open cryptocurrency networks such as Bitcoin are far too powerful for any one entity to control. The notable exceptions are mining pools. A mining pool is a group of miners who, in effect, are colluding. But, typically, a mining pool is not colluding to overtake the network. Rather, because the difficulty level of large cryptocurrency networks like Bitcoin is set so high, small miners have to wait a long time before winning the lottery. To have a better chance of winning, small miners band together and mine as a single entity. Working together, a mining pool will win the lottery more often (in proportion to the pool's total mining power). The consequence of pooling resources is that, should a mining pool control a majority of the network's mining power, it could then alter transactions as it pleases.

Controlling 51 percent of the network is not, in fact, just an academic worry. At several points in its history, the Bitcoin network (the largest by far) *has* been controlled by a mining pool with over 51 percent of the total mining power. When this has occurred, the mining pools appeared not to have acted malevolently, and soon dropped below the threshold, but this is functionally security through altruism—a worrisome prec- edent. In truth, the situation is slightly more complex: if it was discovered that the pool acted malevolently the price of Bitcoin would have cratered and the pool itself would have been worse off, thereby offering some incentive to act altruistically. But since mining pools are so prevalent on the Bitcoin network, at any point it would only take a couple of pools colluding to surpass this threshold. Since each mining pool is managed and controlled by a single person, this kind of collusion is not far-fetched. In a famous picture from the 2015 Scaling Bitcoin conference in Hong Kong, the managers of top mining pools all sat on a stage, representing a full 90 percent of the Bitcoin network's mining power. For all the rhetoric about a decentralized money system, Bitcoin is in fact *far more centralized* than any other money system.

But why do all the hard work of mining at all? This is the final piece of the puzzle and the answer to why blockchains emerged from Bitcoin, a system of money. Miners are motivated to validate transactions and not cheat because they earn valuable tokens (bitcoins, ethers, etc.). Miners earn tokens through two mechanisms: by collecting transaction fees and earning a block production reward. In Bitcoin, fees are set by a market mechanism (which has led to very high fees, as I describe in Chapter 2), and the production reward is issued through a special "coinbase" transaction. (Ethereum and other blockchains have similar mechanisms.) When a miner finds a nonce that satisfies the stipulated difficulty level, the transaction is sent to the network along with a self-awarded coinbase transaction. The number of Bitcoins issued with each coinbase transaction halves every four years until it reaches zero, when all 21 million Bitcoins have been issued. This is how money in the Bitcoin system is minted.

Economically incentivizing miners helps keep miners from spamming the network with fake blocks. Since miners earn tokens with each block successfully mined, producing fake blocks (and not receiving the reward) is not economically advantageous. In fact, in general, the economically rational behavior is to be honest up to the degree that it is profitable, which is why blockchain systems with an economic layer have an important advantage over those that do not.

Mining and waste

I started my journey with cryptocurrencies and blockchains as a Bitcoin miner in early 2013 (DuPont 2014). At the time there were few other ways to actually get Bitcoins, since online cryptocurrency exchanges were nascent and sketchy (and most proved fateful: early exchanges were hacked, bankrupted, or disappeared with customer funds). If you lived in a major city, local meetups or Craigslist hookups were an option, but these had their own kind of unsavoriness. I had an incentive to mine too. I knew that mining used electricity, but my office at the University of Toronto came with "free" electricity. So, in Marshall McLuhan's old office in the historic Coach House in downtown Toronto, I set up an aging, 2008 Mac Pro workstation on a quest to mine Bitcoins. It felt right mining Bitcoins in McLuhan's old office—doing my part to produce the new blockchain media.

With the Mac Pro at full "office heater" speed, I set off for riches. I was able to mine thirty thousand hashes per second with the central processing unit (CPU), a server-grade 3GHz quad core Intel Xeon chip. But this initial attempt was already out of date; as interest in Bitcoin had surged through 2013, CPU mining had become too slow to be practical. A few weeks later, my second attempt involved a new, midrange gaming graphics card that I bought for a few hundred dollars. Online research suggested that the AMD Radeon HD 5850 was ideal for Bitcoin mining, and a good compromise between price and performance. Plus, the card looked cool with its copper piping, edgy "gamer" graphics, and massive fan. With their 2.15 billion transistors, these cards were built for the demanding task of rendering millions of polygons for video games, but people quickly realized that they also excelled at running the SHA256 hash algorithm for Bitcoin mining. Using the graphics processing unit (GPU) on the card, with my second attempt I had transformed into a real wildcat Bitcoin miner. My machine was capable of turning out a respectable 350 million hashes per second.

Alas, my Bitcoin mining experiment did not last long. In the mining pool I had joined, I earned a half a Bitcoin, then valued at about US $10. Soon GPU mining was also too slow to be practical (even with free University of Toronto electricity). Specialized field-programmable gate array (FPGA) cards, once reserved for high-performance supercomputing tasks, were becoming commercially available. These specialized cards did more with even less—their re-programmable chips stripped computing down to the very basics of crunching through hashes. But even the era of FPGA mining was shortlived. Since Bitcoin mining was proving so lucrative, companies began fabricating tailor-made chips that were designed to do only one thing: run the SHA256 hash as fast as possible for the sole purpose of mining Bitcoin. These Application-Specific Integrated Circuits (ASICs) were soon at the cutting edge of chip design, using the smallest (and therefore most efficient) fabrication processes available and iterating the chip design dozens of times per year. Today, these are among the fastest and most efficient chips in the world.

My experience mining Bitcoin revealed that the "mining" metaphor is real. It was hot and used a lot of energy. Originally, the mining metaphor was a commentary on the metallist economic theories associated with Bitcoin (Maurer et al. 2013). Goldbugs loved that Bitcoin had a monetary cap and was scarce, so naturally the production process was called mining. But as my experience showed, it was not long before the metaphor took on a new meaning. Of course, computing has always had an important if underappreciated materiality. Reflecting on the parallels between early computing and Bitcoin mining, Finn Brunton (2015) writes, "as a practical matter, the work of computation is the work of managing heat." Brunton notes that the UNIVAC was hot and loud and that the EDVAC's 3,000 vacuum tubes required as much electricity for cooling as for operation. In hot Princeton summers the EDVAC facility resembled a ship's boiler room. Every computer since has had to deal with thermal management, from CPU bonding glue to my GPU's copper piping. Early wildcat Bitcoin miners complained about sweltering heat in the summers and the dangers of their ad hoc "fire trap" mining rigs (Gerard 2017).

In the winters, miners enjoyed their money-making heaters. Once small-scale wildcat mining became too dangerous and unprofitable, Bitcoin mining shifted to industrial-scale operations in cool locales with cheap hydroelectric power, such as Iceland, Finland, Sweden, and the American Pacific Northwest (Brunton 2015). More recently, Bitcoin mining has shifted to China, where cheap, government-subsidized electricity from imported Australian coal is plentiful—and a serious environmental issue.

Zac Zimmer (2017) makes a comparison to the environmental impact and exploitive labor practices of early modern silver mining at Potosí in colonial South America. At Potosí, wildcat surface mining using the *guayra* furnace quickly gave way to a mercury-laden process that ingested great swaths of the Cerro Rico mountain and left toxic tailings behind. The transition to industrial scale was required by Spanish colonists, who would not accept dwindling profits as the easy silver dried up; to improve profits further, the Spanish drafted indigenous laborers (*mita*). The clear parallel today can be found in China, with its massive Bitcoin mining facilities (one half of the ten largest Bitcoin mining pools are operated in China). The single dominant producer of Bitcoins in China is Bitmain, which fabricates and sells ASICs and runs its own mining facilities. At the end of 2017, Bitmain was directly responsible for 25 percent of all Bitcoin mining. The scale of Bitmain's operations are breathtaking: in a single mining facility in Ordos, China, Bitmain is responsible for 4 percent of global production. In the facility sit 21,000 mining machines in a constant state of upgrade and repair, serviced around the clock by workers who live on premises (a step up, in pay at least, from the early 2000s when young Chinese men worked long hours farming virtual gold in World of Warcraft; see Bronk, Monk, & Villasenor 2012). Each one of the 21,000 machines produce 14 trillion hashes per second from 189 ASICs. An identical story can be told at any of Bitmain's other facilities in China, or Bitfury's equally massive operations in the Republic of

Georgia, or in rentable cloud mining facilities around the globe. Zimmer (2017) argues that, just as the colonial Spanish terraformed South America, these Bitcoin mining facilities are "cryptoforming" the Internet.

There is no doubt that the environmental impact of Bitcoin mining is massive—the physical size of these facilities do not lie—but just how bad is it? In recent years the environmental impact of Bitcoin mining has become a hot-button issue within the community. With no clear way to accurately assess the electricity use or resources needed for Bitcoin mining, critics have offered measurements that highlight waste and environmental impact. It has been suggested that Bitcoin mining uses more electricity than Iceland (17 TWh), Ireland (24 TWh), or Denmark (32 TWh) (2014 figures) (T. B. Lee 2017; O'Dwyer & Malone 2014). One estimate taking into consideration a range of factors pegs Bitcoin's electricity consumption at 44 TWh in early 2018 ("Bitcoin Energy Consumption Index" n.d.). Another posits that Bitcoin might use more electricity than electric cars (Loh & Tomesco 2018), or that a *single* Bitcoin transaction uses more electricity than the average American house in a week (Malmo 2017). If Bitcoin mining continues unabated, it is speculated that by mid-2019 its electricity consumption will be greater than the total electricity consumption of the United States, and by 2020 greater than the entire global consumption today (Holthaus 2017). But supporters fire back. They point out that traditional money and payment systems use electricity too: to keep the lights on in banks, to melt coins, to run ATMs and point of sales machines, and so on. They also critique the math used by the critics. One thorough debunking pegs the lower bounds for the electricity consumption of Bitcoin at "only" 2.85 TWh in March 2017 (one-sixth of Iceland's electricity consumption). By the end the same year, however, it is likely that Bitcoin electricity consumption had already increased by a factor of four, putting it back in striking range of Iceland's consumption.

Cryptocurrencies are wasteful for two reasons: 1) the infrastructure of distributed and replicated transactions is redundant, and 2) the mining difficulty that correlates to price is an arbitrary activity and purposefully wasteful (as the price rises, miners are incentivized to increase their capital input). The first, the waste caused by redundancy in crypto-currency infrastructure, is comparatively miniscule. The second, the waste caused by mining, on the other hand, is essential to the design of proof-of-work mining and is a morally reprehensible ecological travesty. Unfortunately (for the global environment), recall that the proof-of-work consensus protocol is responsible for essential features: incentivizing transaction validation, issuing tokens, securing the network, preventing spam, and so on. For cryptocurrencies using the proof-of-work consensus protocol, wasteful mining is a *necessary* consequence.

There are, however, less wasteful alternatives. Bitcoin uses a proof-of-work mining algorithm called "scrypt," which is particularly susceptible to optimization and specialization. Even though ASICs are vastly more energy efficient than CPUs and GPUs (in terms of hashes per joule), their specialized nature has led to rapid industrialization in the cryptocurrency mining industry. Other proof-of-work mining algorithms attempt to prevent industrialization (and the centralization that comes with it) by making mining a general-purpose computing problem, which cannot be optimized. For instance, Ethereum's ethash mining algorithm requires significant memory, unlike Bitcoin's scrypt algorithm, so lean ASICs cannot compete. To mine Ethereum today, the best hardware is a beefy video card with a fast GPU and plenty of memory (until optimized hardware—already rumored to exist—is developed). Because of the diversity of alt coins that can be mined using commercially available hardware, wildcat mining has returned to the fringes of cryptocurrencies. Through 2017 and 2018 wildcat mining of alt coins became so prevalent that GPU manufactures could not produce cards quickly enough to satisfy market demand. Consequently, the gamers who traditionally purchase these high-end cards complained about empty shelves and rising prices. Gamers were being priced out by the voracious demand of cryptocurrency miners.

Ultimately, wildcat mining is still wasteful, so alternative proof-of-work mining algorithms do not fix the environmental issue. The only real solution (short of prices dropping to a level that makes mining unattractive) is a move away from the inherently wasteful proof-of-work algorithm. There are a few proposals for alternative consensus protocols that keep the network secure without wasteful mining. Intel's proof-of-elapsed-time technique skips the wasteful work requirement and focuses on the true goal of consensus mechanisms, of making computation take time. Using this consensus protocol, the lottery system relies on the secure computing environment provided by tamper-resistant Intel chips. The downside is that the protocol is vendor-specific. A more ambitious alternative consensus protocol is being developed by the Ethereum community. Instead of relying on computational work or special hardware, Ethereum is attempting to develop a game-theoretical solution known as proof of stake (dubbed "Casper"). On this model, consensus and security are achieved by requiring miners to make a "stake" in the network—by putting money (ethers) on the line, miners are disincentivized to cheat (if caught cheating they lose their stake). The challenge for the proof-of-stake consensus model is that it is not really an engineering challenge. Proof of stake requires getting right a complex set of human and social motivations and behaviors. A version of this approach has already been deployed for closed networks with known participants that have existing relationships of trust (Ripple, for example, relies on a reputational model to accomplish consensus and honesty among corporate partners), but it is not yet clear that a general solution for open networks is possible.

Network architectures

Blockchains like Bitcoin and Ethereum use open networks relying on untrusted mining participants, but this is not the only model. There are three common network architectures available for blockchain technologies, each with a specific set of benefits, drawbacks, and use cases. In many cases the boundaries between each kind of network architecture are blurry and depend on context. For instance, a network may be "open" for participation but "closed" for validation, or some other combination. Programming for each requires a new and still developing set of skills that focus on security, distributed computing, and complex social behavior. The three blockchain architectures are: private, permissioned or consortium, and open.

Private blockchains
Private blockchain architectures are ideal for organizations that want full control of data and have no need to interact with outside parties. Private blockchain architectures work within an existing trusted computing environment, such as a corporate intranet, and therefore require minimal security. Because the risk of malfeasance within a secure corporate intranet is so low, private blockchain architectures can be designed for speed and efficiency, dispensing with wasteful mining or highly distributed computing nodes. Consensus among nodes is similarly easily accomplished. There are few drawbacks for private blockchain architectures: they are externally secured, efficient, and high performant. Of course, a private blockchain is nearly indistinguishable from a database, and for this reason it is not clear why an organization would choose a private blockchain over a traditional database that already has an ecosystem of support and auxiliary tools and has been thoroughly tested for decades.

Permissioned blockchains

Permissioned or consortium blockchain architectures are ideal for organizations that want to maintain some control of data but need to work with trusted outside parties. Since outside parties are usually bound by existing legal contracts and external security measures, the risk of malfeasance is fairly low, but not nonexistent. In particular, traditional technical solutions for data sharing between business partners are at risk of internal malfeasance, such as information exfiltration or "cooking the books." Because blockchains are immutable yet distributed they are a good solution for data sharing among business partners that still require a highly secure environment. Most corporate and enterprise blockchain solutions deployed today utilize a permissioned or consortium architecture, as they are seen as a good compromise between the restrictive nature of private blockchains and the dangers of open blockchains.

Large organizations in particular tend to be conservative about data sharing and access, which makes the idea of putting potentially sensitive information on an openly accessible blockchain unappealing. In some sectors, such as healthcare or finance, government or industry regulations may forbid placing sensitive data on openly accessible blockchains (in the European Union the General Data Protection Regulation, or GRPD, is especially restrictive about access and control of private and sensitive data; see Chapter 6). This conservative approach is eminently sensible, but from a technical perspective open blockchains rarely include datastores on the blockchain and therefore avoid most privacy and security issues; rather, it is more typical to store hashes that point to data stored in off-chain encrypted environments. Nonetheless, this technical argument is rarely persuasive to companies or regulators. An additional benefit of permissioned or consortium blockchain architectures is that since the risk of malfeasance is much lower, these systems can be designed with efficiency and performance in mind, in ways that open blockchain systems cannot. Ripple's blockchain solution for consortium partners that relies on reputation instead of proof of work is a good example of a blockchain architecture appropriate for the context.

Open blockchains

Open blockchain architectures, as used in Bitcoin or Ethereum, are most common for use cases that require broad participation and cannot rely on known or trusted computing infrastructure. Bitcoin's system of money is an exemplary use case, as it requires a highly secure but decentralized network with no supervising organization and no restrictions on who can participate. Before Bitcoin, there were no known solutions to this hard problem. The disadvantage of open blockchain architectures is that satisfying security requirements in an open-participant network always involves some kind of trade-off. In the case of proof-of-work consensus protocols, performance and efficiency are traded for security; in the case of proof-of-stake consensus protocols—if they are ever successfully developed—broad and democratic participation is traded for security (the stake required for participation will almost certainly be prohibitive for all but the wealthiest participants). Open architecture and open-source blockchain technologies also require motivation for development and participation (since there are no profit-seeking corporations behind them), which is why they usually rely on an underlying monetary layer to financially support software development and improvement.

Given these different architectures, blockchain technologies require new ways of thinking about computing, as both highly distributed and constrained. For example, the programming environment of Ethereum expands considerably on what is possible with Bitcoin but compared to traditional computing environments Ethereum is complex and restrictive. For one, Ethereum is by design "open" but in many cases may be de facto permissioned (this will be especially true if Ethereum moves to a proof-of-stake model, resulting in a "public permissioned" architecture). Moreover, Ethereum is often labeled a "Turing complete" computing platform in the sense that any generally programmable application can be programmed on it, but this is not quite technically correct. Unlike with traditional software that runs in trusted, local environments, the open architecture of Ethereum introduces the possibility of an attacker deploying a "logic bomb" that has no terminal state and will continue to run until the network's resources are exhausted. To protect against such threats, Ethereum introduced a constraint called "gas." Gas is effectively a processing fee that is required to run any code on the Ethereum platform. Since gas is finite and expensive, malicious software with no terminal state cannot be run. But gas also makes many typical applications very expensive to run. What kinds of applications are suitable for the Ethereum environment is an active area of exploration.

Therefore, it is important to recognize that not all computing problems need to be or should be deployed on an open blockchain (or a blockchain at all). Open blockchain architectures have massive disadvantages in comparison to traditional computing environments but excel at certain kinds of problems. If a computing problem does not involve external, heterogeneous parties that cannot be trusted, open blockchain technologies are probably not a good fit. In such situations, a consortium or permissioned or even private blockchain may be more suitable. The security model of proof-of-work blockchain technologies is also not suitable for all situations. While no security is ever guaranteed, some traditional approaches rely on mathematically proven algorithms with formally verified code, while proof-of-work blockchain technologies are merely probabilistic. Greater or fewer security tradeoffs are available using different consensus models, such as proof-of-stake or hardware-based approaches. We do not yet know good ways to choose between the many options available.

Particular industries and use cases may also come with unique constraints that favor one approach or another. As I mentioned above, regulated environments may forbid open blockchains, at least until regulators can be convinced of the security of such systems. Today, there are a nearly endless number of industries exploring blockchains, many of which I discuss in this book. Possible applications include banking and finance, insurance, property titling, gambling, online content and social media, data storage, law and notaries, records management, Internet of Things, heavy industry and manufacturing, provenance (tracking pharmaceuticals, high-value goods, food, and raw materials), government services, identity services, prediction markets, medical records, supply chain management, voting, and charities. Many of these applications make use of smart contracts, which are also new and without guidelines for development, use, or legality (see Chapter 6).

Summary

This chapter described some of the many ways in which blockchain technologies can be configured and used, what the issues are, and how future research and development may improve upon current designs. I characterized blockchain technologies as media par excellence, being an extension of money media but far more general, abstract, and therefore powerful. I detailed the inner workings of blockchains, focusing on hashes, blocks, and chains. Hashes are widely used throughout blockchain technologies, since they fingerprint data, perform one-way transformations, and can be verified. Blocks are sets of transactions that have been sealed for security by mining a proof-of-work hash. Blocks are chained together by incorporating the previous block's hash. Miners across the network independently verify blocks and compete amongst one another in a lottery system to achieve consensus and prevent dishonesty. I detailed how the security provided by proof-of-work mining has an unfortunate side effect in that it requires massive amounts of electricity. Bitcoin mining, in particular, has grown to an industrial scale, with negative energy-use consequences comparable to the sorts of environmental disasters associated with traditional terrestrial mining. I discussed alternatives but recognized the trade-offs they bring. Finally, I concluded with a discussion of the three common blockchain architectures and why these new computing environments offer alternatives but unique challenges for software developers.

CHAPTER FIVE

Finance and Capital

One of the most unexpected developments in the history of cryptocurrencies and blockchain technologies has been the rapid acceptance of blockchain technologies in mainstream capitalism, belying cryptocurrency's roots in radical cyber-libertarianism. Cryptocurrencies were, in truth, never really "against" the capitalist mode of production. In many ways they actually reified the economic and political arguments of the right wing (Gerard 2017; Golumbia 2016). Yet the avowed goals of cryptocurrencies have always been to attack, dismantle, and render obsolete traditional capitalist systems (see Nakamoto 2008). Somewhat ironically, then, the recent shift to blockchain technologies marks a full-scale transfer to capitalist paradigms. Indeed, blockchains today are commonly used to facilitate the flow of money for banks and corporations and offer lucrative investment opportunities in their own right.

In this chapter, I explain how the early dreamers lost (Swartz 2017), and were replaced by financiers and their enterprise software applications. As we saw in Chapter 2, the hope of replacing cash vanished early on, and today the real use of cryptocurrencies lies almost exclusively in speculative investment and financial asset portfolio diversification. Along the way, the underlying blockchain technology was abstracted from "currency" and re-appropriated by banks and financial services providers, as a key part of a broader financial technology (or "fintech") moment. Highlighting the importance of this shift, and its perceived risk, the International Organization of Securities Commissions and the UK's Financial Conduct

Authority, for example, have argued that blockchains may be a significant source of systemic risk. Despite sometimes explicit political distancing and euphemistic discourse espoused by corporate blockchain users (going so far as to create the alternative term "digital ledger technology," or DLT, to avoid the taint of cryptocurrencies), fintech applications have nonetheless benefited from a halo of revolutionary spirit associated with radical cryptocurrency projects.

Blockchain technologies are proposed as a new and powerful way to increase the speed of capital flows, especially by reducing the time (and complexity) needed for interbank payments (known as settlement and clearance infrastructure). But these infrastructures are enormously complex and mission critical; their services are essential and tied to systemic financial activities. In their rush to disrupt the industry, blockchain evangelists challenging the finance and banking status quo often fail to see how existing settlement and clearance procedures add value and mitigate risk—and in many cases do so faster and cheaper than any other technology.

Cryptocurrencies and blockchain technologies have also become a new kind of risky and deeply speculative investment. To better understand these new financial opportunities, through 2017 I interviewed six hobbyist cryptocurrency traders and six professionals who manage large funds that invest exclusively in cryptocurrencies (twelve interviews in total). The results of this study suggest that this investment market presents numerous unique challenges, but that nonetheless these traders see themselves as pioneers in an exciting new investment class. I also discovered some unethical and borderline illegal activities, but for the most part I found a community of people seeking greater regulatory clarity and increased professionalization. Overall, these investors acted much like traditional venture capitalists, who make big risky bets hoping for just a few successes and big payouts. Finance and capital in the world of cryptocurrencies and blockchain technologies presents economic and social opportunity and risk, and like a gold rush in the wild West, there are fortunes to be made and lost.

Financial clearance and settlement

Blockchain technologies can facilitate the secure, relatively rapid, decentralized exchange of generic tokens. This is blockchain as decentralized ledger: an administrative utility that is being rapidly developed by technology and finance incumbents and startups alike, primarily seeking to eliminate traditional centralized clearinghouses and ad-hoc bilateral agreements across the finance sector. Businesses exploring financial blockchains include IBM, Microsoft, R3, Ripple, and SETL.io on the technology side, and NASDAQ, London Stock Exchange, Australian Stock Exchange, and T0 (Overstock. com's fintech subsidiary) on the finance side, among many others. With this much attention, there is surely a business opportunity here, and the future of these technologies will be exciting. A goal of this chapter, however, is to make it clear that efforts to replace clearance and settlement infrastructure, or even more modestly, to simply add value to the financial chain, must contend with enormous complexity and entrenched infrastructures. Decentralized ledgers may play a part in the future, but it is important to recognize that many challenges have little to do with technology, and a lot to do with business and society.

In the shift from cryptocurrencies to blockchains, finance was the first sector to explore applications beyond currency. Since then, finance has also arguably been the sector to most fully embrace the possibilities of blockchain technologies. These applications include payments (both interbank and consumer), securities trading, clearance and settlement, regulatory reporting, supply chain and trade financing (see Chapter 7), and smart contracts (see Chapter 6). Industries adjacent to banking and finance have also explored blockchain technology, including insurance, property titling (see

Chapter 6), records management, and identity services. Many of these applications take advantage of one or more features of blockchains, including their perceived efficiency, low counterparty risk, low transaction fees, security, and ledger immutability (or transaction "finality"). Despite the breadth of possibility, my description here will focus primarily on banks, which have been engaged in active research and development. In fact, several surveys indicate that over the next few years blockchain technologies will be "extensively implemented" in banks, with figures ranging from 15–60 percent penetration (Guo & Liang 2016). Two key applications for the banking sector are interbank payments and clearance and settlement procedures.

Compared to consumer bank transactions (e.g., checking, automated tellers, debit and credit transactions), which must be accomplished quickly and efficiently, interbank payments and the associated clearance and settlement procedures are slow and complicated (Buitenhek 2016). For many kinds of exchange, such as securities or currency trading, the *trades* occur very quickly (so quickly, as in the case of high-frequency trading, that they far exceed any human control), but once a trade has occurred, a slew of slow clearing processes follow until settlement, when the trade is made final.

Originally—centuries ago—clearing transactions took days or even weeks because physical money (coins, banknotes) or precious metals (silver, gold) had to be moved from one bank to another. Over time, this lag made it possible for financial services to add value in the interim gap and eventually the processes of clearance evolved into a core line of business. This "gap" is encapsulated by the central business concept of "delivery versus payment." When delivery occurs after payment, it creates risk, such as when the other party, or "counterparty," is unable or unwilling to deliver the item that has been already paid for. Today, the delay is not caused by shipping valuable materials, yet clearance processes are still necessary and have an important role in business and finance.

In many cases, faster is not always better. Clearing is necessary for mitigating risk, collecting (netting) and cancelling (novating) multiple transactions, correcting errors, and for regulatory reporting and compliance. These are significant sources of added value, and many market participants rely on these services, which all take time. Oftentimes these processes take several days, which are defined by contractual limits set according to transaction type or market (enumerated as T+0 for same-day settlement, or T+1, T+2, T+3 for one-, two-, and three-day settlements). Because of these stipulated clearing schedules, unlike familiar digital networks that are "best effort" (like the Internet), financial settlement *must* occur within these timeframes, within a tightly controlled legal framework and associated contracts.

Interbank payments are slow because there are many organizations involved and the processes of transferring value, especially with unknown or untrusted parties, are complicated and laden with regulatory requirements. These transactions are especially slow and complicated when payments cross national boundaries, and thus must deal with different currencies, legal regimes, time zones and holidays, and technical infrastructures (tied to correspondent-banking systems). This sentiment is echoed by practitioners in the field. Mark Buitenhek (2016), global head of ING Transaction Services, describes post-trade securities clearance and settlement as "slow and expensive, involving many actors including global and local/sub-custodians, central counterparties (CCPs) and central securities depositories (CSDs)." Practitioners in the field must learn and utilize a significant amount of tacit and situational knowledge.

One of the most significant challenges for interbank payment is understanding and deploying the required tacit knowledge, and, by extension, building, defining, and maintaining the necessary relationships that make the system work. For example, many systems have special market allowances, such as a "fail rule" that in some circumstances permit transactions even in the case of default. In Japan, for example, whether the fail rule is applied depends on national residency of the parties, complicating matters further (Mori 2016). Developing these relationships requires a non-technical approach. Indeed, existing clearing infrastructure is saturated with trust across central clearinghouses or between counterparties linked with bilateral agreements (Buitenhek 2016).

Although interbank payments are technically complex, clearance delays are rarely due to technical limitations. Rather, delays are caused by historical inertia, procedural inefficiencies, and regulatory requirements. Nonetheless, the mere threat of technology—blockchain-enabled fast clearing—has spurred incumbents to look at ways of speeding up settlement, while maintaining regulatory compliance and still offering a rich suite of additional services. For instance, in 2017, with obvious motivations, NACHA, responsible (with the US Federal Reserve) for Automated Clearing House (ACH) payments in the US, announced that it would be moving to shorter clearance cycles.

Typically, interbank payments occur through trusted clearinghouses (either private consortia of banks or state-backed service providers) or ad-hoc bilateral interbank agreements. Most but certainly not all payments occur through central bank systems, which are vital in lowering credit and liquidity risk at a critical point of exchange (Rosner & Kang 2015). These complex systems facilitate securities exchange (through central security depositories) and currency exchange. The latter occurs though local and international payment networks, including consumer-facing systems as well as foreign exchange markets. The major international interbank payment rails use central counterparty clearinghouses (CCPs) and real time gross settlement (RTGS) systems. Examples of CCPs are the Options Clearing Cooperation (OCC) and Depository Trust & Clearing Corporation (DTCC) in the US, and LCH.Clearnet in Europe. Examples of RTGS systems are Target2 in the Eurozone, Fedwire in the US, and CHAPS in the UK. Each organization differs with respect to technical infrastructure, scope, geographical range, market type and size, and institutional design.

To make matters *even more* complicated, interbank payments also travel through national or regional clearing systems, which might be private or state-run, and also vary in many particular ways. For instance, in the US, the Federal Reserve maintains Fedwire for large-value, time-critical payments, responsible for transferring hundreds of trillions of USD through hundreds of millions of transactions. Yet the Federal Reserve also maintains the Automated Clearing House (ACH) network, which in 2016 processed a staggering 25 billion transactions—but those transactions only accounted for a little over US $40 trillion (less than 5 percent of the value transferred by Fedwire). The discrepancy is due to the types of transactions processed by each network: Fedwire transfers high-value items like securities, while ACH processes low-value items like checks and debit transactions. On top of this, a private consortium of banks *also* maintains Clearing House Interbank Payments System (CHIPS) (under supervision of the Federal Reserve) for high-value international and domestic payments. Outside of the US, the same complex of consortia and private, public, and bilateral systems also exist: EBA Clearing and the Faster Payments Service (FPS) are two private consortia for the Eurozone and UK (respectively) that transfer high-value payments (similar to CHIPS in the US). Payments Canada maintains LVTS, a hybrid system for high-value interbank payments equivalent to other RTGS systems (but it incorporates end-of-day netting for lower costs), as well as Automated Clearing Settlement System (ACSS) for retail (small-value) transactions.

Interbank payments can also occur through bilateral and consortia agreements, which sometimes interconnect with CCPs and RTGS systems. The largest such system is the Society for Worldwide Interbank Financial Telecommunication (SWIFT), which provides standardized messaging between banks, but does not transfer funds (trans-actions occur with correspondent accounts that each bank maintains). Although SWIFT provides a secure and trusted infrastructure for interbank payments, it does not offer clear-ance and settlement facilities and thus exposes counterparties to typical forms of risk. Similarly, consumer- and retail-facing systems of interbank payment, such as ATM, credit, and debit transaction systems, are regionally or nationally coor-dinated. These systems might interconnect with major credit card providers, enabling greater cross-bank use (such as the Plus and Cirrus interbank networks managed by VISA and MasterCard, respectively), or might be grouped within bank consortia. For example, in Canada, the Interac network of debit and point-of-sale transactions works across all major Canadian banks and clears and settles transactions through Payments Canada's LVTS system. Many countries maintain similar consumer-facing interbank payment systems, such as Bacs in the UK, Groupement des Cartes Bancaires CB in France, or UnionPay in China.

As these interbank payment systems have grown in com-plexity and use they have become essential parts of modern economies. Early electronic systems for clearance and set-tlement used telegraph infrastructure and commercial code transmission (similar to Morse code). As computing tech-nologies became more widely available (in the US, around the 1960s), electronic payment networks were *decentralized* and localized (and in many cases, fragmented). Through the 1980s and 1990s many of these systems—for example, the US Fedwire—were then standardized and consolidated, creating robust, public, and efficient platforms. (A reminder to cryp-tocurrency and blockchain evangelists: decentralization isn't new, and there is good reason to sometimes prefer centralized services.) The RTGS systems that developed, in particular, quickly became a regulatory staple for central banks. The reason for this preference is that RTGS clearinghouses trade credit risk for liquidity risk, and since central banks believe they have greater control over liquidity (being responsible for money supply), the RTGS systems then became important economic levers (Kaminska 2016).

Blockchain systems compete with this complex and interconnected web of traditional clearance and settlement systems, and therefore need to match, meet, or integrate with the infrastructure of international, regional, private, and consortium partners. This means developing a technical infrastructure and social system capable of dealing with regulatory demands, global and trans-border scale, enormously high transaction and value volume, and relatively low fees. Each of these challenges requires coordination of technical and social change.

Regulatory compliance is one area that blockchain technologies are by design well suited to address. As discussed in Chapter 4, blockchain architecture is a bookkeeper's dream— the ability to inspect all transactions and be sure that none have been altered gives regulators unprecedented power and ability. Traditional interbank payments tend to operate in a black box, especially when conducted through bilateral agreements between banks. Thus, some authors have suggested that "real-time regulation" of the financial industry might be possible by moving the main capital flows to a blockchain system that eliminates the possibility of editing transaction records and is always open to inspection by regulators (Buitenhek 2016; Fanning & Centers 2016). Despite the possible benefits for regulators, due to regulatory specificity (which differs radically across the globe), no one-size-fits-all approach is feasible. Much of the work that remains for banks interested in achieving regulatory compliance with blockchain technologies is in getting the details correct.

Scale and performance of existing blockchain technologies needs to improve considerably to match existing clearance and settlement infrastructures. Blockchain technologies might be able to accommodate the relatively low transaction volume of RTGS systems but matching the high volume and high speed of consumer and retail networks is, at least today, completely unfeasible. For comparison, the Bitcoin network has struggled to process more than 300,000 transactions per day (in 2017 the system was so overburdened that transactions were frequently dropped and took hours to clear), amounting to nearly 200 million transactions in 2016. Running at capacity for the entire year, by July of 2017 the network had crossed the same threshold. Ethereum has proven somewhat more capable, able to process 500,000 transactions per day in 2017. But, as mentioned above, the ACH network reliably processed 25 billion transactions in 2016 (an average of 68 million per day), and even the relatively low-volume Fedwire cleared nearly 175 million transactions across its securities and funds services in 2016. Of course, with increased block size (a protocol limitation that was vociferously debated by the developer community through 2016–17; see De Filippi & Loveluck 2016) and newer, second-generation blockchain architectures (such as the Lightning Network), greater transaction volume is possible, but, nonetheless, in its most basic (highly redundant) design, blockchain technologies are not ideal for high-performance use cases.

With the Bitcoin network at full capacity through 2017— arguably the premier and most thoroughly battle-tested blockchain network—transaction fees rose sharply to accommodate demand. (Bitcoin fees are optional, but fees incentivize miners to include transactions, or to accept higher fee transactions first.) Traditionally, Bitcoin fees were modest but appreciable, averaging much less than US $0.10 per transaction from 2013 (when Bitcoin first caught on) until the end of 2016. Through 2017, however, fees rose to US $20.00 or more *per transaction*! For context, in the US, Fedwire charges US $0.03–$0.69 per transaction (plus additional surcharges and monthly fees) for what are often complex, multimillion-dollar transactions, and ACH charges US $0.0001 per transaction (plus US $42.00 annual fee). For all the industry talk of disrupting an ossified clearance and settlement infrastructure, in practice these networks have created a safe, secure, and competitively priced landscape.

The features that make blockchain technologies so suitable for clearance and settlement do not always match the reality of the industry. Once transactions stored on a blockchain are verified they are forever immutable and final. For record-keeping and inspection by regulators this is a boon, but, in practice, clearance is, almost by definition, a dynamic and evolving process (which is the reason there are stipulated delays, to permit adjustments). Moreover, banks rely on the fact that clearinghouses perform error checking and are able to correct mistakes (which is sometimes done by hand). Only once a transaction has settled—when it is "final"—is it considered effectively immutable. Additionally, other services offered within the existing clearance infrastructure have no parallel in the blockchain world. Far from being dumb pipes for transactions to flow through, clearinghouses often offer their clients notification services; accounts querying; transaction matching, chaining, and queuing; and the ability to net or novate transactions. Real-world blockchain solutions, it must be stressed, would need to build such features on top of basic blockchains, and add in extra "slack" to accommodate practical needs, since instant settlement is impractical and undesirable.

Many central counterparty clearinghouses also offer intraday overdraft and interest-bearing overnight credit. Having immediate access to central bank-backed credit is extremely useful for banks, but it also comes with risk (that a more decentralized system, such as a blockchain, might avoid). For example, because CCPs provide overdraft, during the 2008 global economic crisis debt became collateralized, which then had a catastrophic effect as the credit chain broke down. So, although CCPs eliminate credit exposure to counterparties, they create additional systemic risk. The lesson to be learned from the 2008 global economic crisis is that CCPs really "redistribute and transform risk," they do not eliminate it

(Pirrong 2016). Blockchain technologies do the same, but in different ways.

I discussed the complicated web of private, public, national, regional, bilateral, and consortium interbank payment systems and their plethora of services offered to illustrate the daunting task that blockchain disrupters face. According to former Bank of Tokyo–Mitsubishi UFJ employee Taketoshi Mori (2016), the traditional "procedure is very complicated," and if blockchain technologies are to compete in the market, they face many technical, legal, and social barriers. In most cases, however, companies developing potentially disruptive blockchain technologies for interbank payments do recognize the task ahead and see business value in building *on top* of a stable blockchain. The member organizations of the Hyperledger project, for example, approach the business in exactly this way: they have open-sourced the underlying blockchain technologies to provide (ideally) a stable, shared platform. Each company is then free to build additional features and services, competing with one another. It is no accident that Hyperledger is part of the Linux Foundation; the business model for Hyperledger is the same as enterprise Linux, which thrives by giving away the software for free and selling services on top.

The most established blockchain network today is Bitcoin, but it does not make a fair or practical comparison to existing clearance and settlement infrastructure. The simple reason is that Bitcoin is not used for payments or even currency exchange, due to its high volatility, lack of service providers, and high fees (see Chapter 3). Banks and blockchain technology developers instead turn to newer networks and technologies, such as Ethereum, the various Hyperledger frameworks, and in-house specialized blockchains. The transition from cryptocurrency to blockchain that we can see in the interbank payments infrastructure is part of the general shift I discussed in Chapter 1. In making the switch to generic blockchain platforms, financial service providers can more easily build additional features—which are necessary for practical adoption within the industry.

In looking at the challenges blockchain developers face, we see a clear example of the move away from cryptocurrencies and towards general-purpose blockchains, exchanging tokens of value rather than "money." In this transition, we see adoption of blockchain technologies by organizations interested in preserving traditional capital flows (but perhaps sped up, or made more secure), rather than any realization of the vision of radically decentralizing and democratizing money. Transition to privately run blockchain technologies for interbank payments does potentially curtail the role of central banks (an explicit political goal of the original cryptocurrency ideology; Golumbia 2016), and therefore possibly removes one of the levers central banks use for controlling liquidity and in turn the wider economy, but this is hardly an unprecedented development. Private consortia and bilateral agreements between banks are common, and the decision whether a payment goes through a private system or a central clearinghouse is based on a multitude of factors, not ideology or technical limitation. Clearance and settlement is an important component in the broader landscape of blockchain technologies and highlights the move towards professionalization of both cryptocurrencies and blockchains in the financial sector.

Speculative investment

Although cryptocurrencies and blockchain technologies are rarely used for commerce today, they do hold considerable economic value, and so they are actively traded. There is a vibrant and growing market for "crypto assets," which includes traditional (money-like) cryptocurrencies such as Bitcoin, Litecoin, and Neo, and (software-like) blockchain technologies such as Ethereum, Ripple, and NEM, as well as innumerable software startups launching through "Initial Coin Offerings" (ICOs) that sometimes blur the line. Either way, investors treat

cryptocurrencies and blockchain technologies like speculative
financial assets irrespective of their stated goals (it does not
matter if they are cryptocurrencies or blockchains). Market
participants tend to refer to their assets as simply "crypto."
(Despite the fact that the largely unrelated field of cryptography has long used this nomenclature, I'll adopt the term
for this chapter.) In recent years, the market for crypto has
expanded considerably, with total market capitalization sur-
passing US $600 billion in 2017 (this is, however, an entirely
fictional and unrealistic number, as I describe in Chapter 1).
Because of this hype, it is not uncommon to hear finance professionals and lay people alike discussing the wild and weird
world of investing in crypto. I've heard this myself, more than
once. Sitting in a café, a (young, white, male) individual sells
his interlocutor on this new investment opportunity, with
nary a clue about the technology or investment risks, dreaming and expectant that his investment will go "to the moon" so
that he can buy a "Lambo," as insiders say.

If it is true that high-flying financial instruments were, to
borrow a phrase, the "new exotic" of the first decade of the
millennium (Maurer 2006), then surely cryptocurrencies and
blockchains must be the new exotic for the second decade.
Cryptocurrencies and blockchain technologies are part of a
larger "fintech moment," and an important part, as they are
increasing the already ongoing algorithmization and obfuscation of financial activities (see Pasquale 2015), exemplifying
the virtual and performative nature of financial instruments
(see MacKenzie 2006, 2009), and increasing social, physical, and moral distance (see Coeckelbergh 2015 and Chapter
1). Financial technologies may have unintended effects when
they stand in for or mediate between humans, allowing us
to delegate responsibility and abnegate ethics, even in some
cases to the point of full automation (see my analysis of The
DAO in Chapter 8 for an extreme case of automation and its
risks). That is, the real risks of speculative investing in crypto
reach far beyond the individual (perhaps clueless) investor.

Neither inherently bad or good (but certainly *not neutral*), crypto is a powerful new financial engine for a broader financial technology sector, with still largely unknown social and political characteristics and implications.

Speculative investing in crypto *does* pose serious individual financial risk, and sane financial advice would be to caution against it for all but the most risk-tolerant investors. Practically, there are huge risks in every part of the investment: exchanges and wallets are frequently hacked or mismanaged (many exchanges have disappeared due to ineptitude or outright criminality, often absconding with investors' funds), investment scams are rampant, markets and prices are easily and commonly manipulated, many markets are so "thin" that trading is practically illiquid, usability and operations management are complex and error-prone (millions have been lost by simple and irreversible transaction errors; Brito & Castillo 2016; Brown 2016), and trading fees are often high (see Gerard 2017 for an extensive discussion). Part of the reason investment risk remains a worry is that the market in most jurisdictions remains largely unregulated, or is uncertain and evolving (regulating financial technologies in general is very difficult; see Douglas 2016).

Despite considerable risk, many of the early investors I have spoken with (see below) believe the investment market is a rare opportunity for "generational" wealth, akin to the 1990s' dot-com boom (and bust). Like the 1990s boom, some crypto investors have become very wealthy. As early adopters saw their holdings of nearly worthless Bitcoins rise to thousands of dollars per coin (a peak of nearly US $20,000 in late 2017), in just a few years a new class of "Bitcoin millionaires" and in some cases "Bitcoin billionaires" emerged almost by accident. Only once cryptocurrencies became somewhat more valuable (around 2013), did people start to think about cryptocurrencies as an "investment," but it was still early enough to make overnight millions. Like the 1990s bubble, as well, the crypto investment market was and remains wild and unpredictable. Of the investors I have spoken with, several reported early mistakes, but all more than recovered in the long term. It remains to be seen, however, whether the future market is going to be a massive new investment class (as the investors I spoke with believe), or something much smaller. Will the crypto market scale to the size of a mainstream financial derivative, like options (hundreds of trillions), or a subclass like the NASDAQ technology stock index (trillions)? Or perhaps crypto will emerge as a new kind of commodity, trading alongside the palm oil market (billions)? This narrative of long-term, generational wealth is a persuasive but risky one. Such rhetoric may lead investors to act on faith, rather than on realistic fundamentals about the investment market (Kaminska 2017).

Assessments of the dynamics and size of the whole crypto market have, so far, largely focused on econometric analyses. In the academic literature, most of the existing work has adopted known methods and measurements drawn from traditional investing and applied it to this new market, which in many cases has yielded incommensurable results, no doubt due to the lack of clarity about what exactly is being measured. Nonetheless, a few broad lessons do emerge: the crypto market is largely *speculative* (Briere, Oosterlinck, & Szafarz 2013; Luther & White 2014; Yermack 2013) and *volatile* (Bueno 2017; Dwyer 2015; Dyhrberg 2016a). Some analyses question these findings, but only in details and degrees, not ultimate conclusions (Hur, Jeon, & Yoo 2015). Others have found that the crypto market has gone through *bubbles* (Groshoff 2014), with prices driven by news *hype* (Kristoufek 2015; Matta, Lunesu, & Marchesi 2015) that resulted in *feedback loops* (Garcia, Tessone, Mavrodiev, & Perony 2014). The market bubbles actually brought the end to exogenous *shocks*, similar to the bursting of dot-com stocks in 2000 (Cheah & Fry 2015; Fry & Cheah 2016). The impact of these shocks, either positive or negative, influences price (Bouoiyour, Selmi, & Tiwari 2015). The wild nature of the crypto market is in part because fundamental value is zero (Cheah & Fry 2015; Hur et al. 2015; Weber 2014). Similarly, the market logic of crypto investing is both a "winner-take-all" race against other cryptocurrencies (Gandal & Halaburda 2014), and a race against other early traders (Kondor, Pósfai, Csabai, & Vattay 2014).

A summary of the existing literature on crypto investing might be as follows: the market is characterized by speculative investing and volatile dynamics, frequent market bubbles emerge and result in persistent feedback loops, and the market is subject to exogenous shocks resulting in a race against others. More succinctly: "value is based entirely on the subjective evaluation of its user community" (Weber 2016). Indeed, these econometric analyses must be taken with a grain of salt, since comparisons are made against traditional stock, commodities, or currency markets. Crypto evangelists and critics alike caution against these comparisons. David Golumbia (2017), for instance, does not believe that it makes sense to value cryptocurrencies as currencies or stocks. According to Golumbia, the crypto investment market is uglier, comparable to the practices of penny stock trading and boiler rooms—the "gross underbelly of Wall Street" that had largely been regulated out of existence but is born anew in crypto.

Since crypto investing is different from traditional investing, it has unique characteristics, with unique opportunities and risks. As anyone who has tried any crypto investing can attest to, there are significant price differences across exchanges, with opportunities for arbitrage—on average, 2 percent in the (2013–14) early market (Gandal & Halaburda 2014). Despite these opportunities, no investor I spoke with attempted to exploit exchange arbitrage, and for good reason. One analysis reports that in practice crypto arbitrage is difficult, citing issues with fiat exchanges that utilize traditional banking infrastructure (these exchanges are often the money equivalent of roach motels, where it is nearly impossible to withdraw funds), and present risks due to transaction time, transaction fees, trading fees, withdrawal time and fees, and price volatility (Brandvold, Molnár, Vagstad, & Andreas Valstad 2015). Additionally, many of these exchanges are small with very thin markets (the very reason their price discovery is so out of sync), and often fail, taking investments down with them (nearly half failed in the early market; Moore & Christin 2013). More positively, crypto investing can be useful for risk management within a traditional portfolio (Bueno 2017), in particular as a hedge against uncorrelated investment assets (Briere et al. 2013). In this way, crypto functions like gold (Dyhrberg 2016b).

Crypto investing is also a truly global market, open to all investors in all jurisdictions, without regard to whether traditional investment infrastructure is available. Optimists see this as an opportunity for emerging economies (Larios-Hernández 2017). Yet, despite being global, the crypto market is unevenly distributed and has not truly offered finance to the world's poorest people. For most of its history, the market has been predictably dominated by USD transactions and American investors. But at various times—especially in recent years—transaction volumes and values have been dominated by Chinese yuan (Brandvold et al. 2015), reflecting the significant role of Chinese investors (China also leads the cryptocurrency and blockchain mining market, see Chapter 1). However, far from satisfying the rhetoric of a fintech version of ICT4D, it is widely believed that Chinese investors are already wealthy individuals, participating in crypto in search of high-risk, high-return investments and to escape the regulated domestic investment market (a market that some believe is overregulated). But this conclusion is something of a guess, as the behaviors and motivations of Chinese investors, and investors in general, are still poorly understood.

Crypto investors

Since the crypto investment market is naturally secretive (unregulated, and hidden behind privacy-preserving blockchain technologies), and existing research has been pre-dominantly econometric, very little is known about who crypto investors are, why they invest, or even how they invest. There have been a few studies of Bitcoin users, including a bench-marking survey (Hileman & Rauchs 2017) and a single small qualitative study (Lustig & Nardi 2015), but these were limited to Bitcoin, and focused on its use as currency, not investment.

Since 2013, I have myself engaged in some crypto investing as a form of auto-ethnography. My investments were seeded from a US $120 initial investment. As this small investment grew over the years, I withdrew my position (took profits) and diversified (at no point have I held more than US $2,000 in crypto assets). I have invested in nearly a dozen different cryptocurrencies and blockchain tokens for the purposes of experimenting with technology platforms and seeking to understand investment potential. Even with my limited investment the experience was illuminating, as I felt the stress of a wildly fluctuating market and the rush of huge returns. If I had left my initial US $120 investment untouched—*which I did not*—I could have profits from the peak of the market north of US $200,000. *Impressive.* Doing this investment research also provided me with a view of the investment land-scape, and an understanding of the ways it has changed. Like many others, I lost assets in the Mt. Gox hack-and-bankruptcy, I rode out successive Bitcoin bubbles, I invested in the ill-fated The DAO (see Chapter 8), and I have participated in the rise of ICOs. Truthfully, the experience usually felt a lot like gambling, or, at best, the seedy cousin of online stock trading platforms.

Despite my relatively long involvement (in crypto terms), and the ups and downs of my investment, my auto-ethnographic methodology was limited. So to better understand the investment landscape, in late 2017 I con-ducted an exploratory qualitative study of crypto investors. This study, like my auto-ethnography, was also limited, but to date it remains the only qualitative study of crypto investors that I am aware of. I conducted semi-structured telephone interviews with six "hobby" investors and six "professional" investors. Interviews lasted between 30 and 60 minutes, and all responses have been anonymized.

The hobby participants were selected from convenience samples, recruited using online social media connections (Slack and Twitter). I use the loose designation of "hobby" to describe those participants who self-reported as "active" crypto investors, but who were not professional or full-time investors. Participants had a fairly broad range of experience with traditional investing: several participants had no previous investment experience, a few had used online stock and Forex trading platforms previously, one participant had worked in a field adjacent to the stock market, and another had traded professionally at a proprietary trading desk. Similarly, the length of involvement in crypto investing ranged widely: some had actively traded crypto for years while others had started only a few months prior to my interview. Initial investment sources were personal funds in all cases, ranging from roughly US $1,000–$30,000. Some made modest profits, while others became millionaires.

The other group, the professional investors, were selected from online searches for crypto funds, which are typically advertised as crypto "hedge funds." A traditional hedge fund is characterized by the fact that investment assets come from clients. But hedge fund managers often make personal investments as well, as a sign of confidence in their strategy, in addition to seeking additional profit for themselves. All crypto hedge funds I consulted were similar in this regard, taking in outside funds and making personal investments. The hedge funds ranged from several million to US $250 million assets under management. The hedge funds were all domiciled in tax-optimized locations (as is also typical for traditional hedge funds), either US (e.g., Delaware, Connecticut) or "offshore" locations—typically Caribbean islands (e.g., Cayman Islands, Panama). For all interviews, I spoke with fund managers who were actively responsible for trading strategy. All fund managers had at least some previous experience with traditional investing (less than 3 years), and several had significant experience (more than a decade). Those fund managers with limited traditional investment experience had domain expertise, in the sense that they were actively involved in cryptocurrencies and blockchains for several years (in this field, more than a few years of involvement is comparatively "experienced"). Most of the funds were quite new (one had yet to formally launch), but one had been in existence (in different incarnations) since the early days of Bitcoin.

All hobby and professional traders were residents of Western nations (US, Canada, and the UK), and spoke fluent English. The self-reported race and gender of all traders were overwhelmingly white and male; but, in my convenience sample of hobby traders, I purposely sought women and visible minorities, and I was able to interview one black man and one white woman. In addition to the extremely small sample size, an obvious limitation of my study was the lack of non-English participants, especially Chinese, who are known to be significant investors. Despite my limited sample and cursory methodology, the results were rich and fascinating—so much so that they can only be described in brief here.

I found that when hobbyists traded crypto, they characterized their activities in profoundly social terms; professional traders, on the other hand, characterized their activities in a more dispassionate and technical way. In a way, this is not surprising. What is remarkable is the *degree* to which hobbyists saw their "communities" as essential to their investment activities. For instance, many hobbyists reported active engagement in social media, although, importantly, they almost never made *trade decisions* based on these social interactions. Instead, hobby traders actively collaborated in an ideational way, alerting one another to new Initial Coin Offerings (ICOs), changes in software development teams, and new market opportunities. One participant had even formed a kind of "water cooler" group of like-minded individuals at her place of work, leveraging the shared interest in crypto as a way to enter into an all-male in-group. The professional traders—being fund managers at the top of the staff hierarchy—relied on a cadre of employed researchers, but largely to do the grunt work of checking on the validity of claims made by organizations and development teams. The professional traders I spoke with seemed to work in a more individualist fashion than traditional hedge fund managers, who use a kind of distributed and social cognition, according to Donald MacKenzie (2009). For the professionals, consulting and collaborating with other traders was limited, and in most cases nonexistent.

ICOs are a popular investment vehicle today, and most of the investors I spoke with focused their attention on discovering new and emerging ICOs. ICOs are the cryptocurrency version of an initial public offering (IPO). IPOs are a way for private organizations to raise capital by selling shares of stock publicly, thereby becoming a "public company." An ICO is similar in that a company wanting to raise capital sells "coins" or "tokens," which may or may not give its investors any stake in the company. Even if the ICO does not give its investors a stake in the company (which is typical), investors still stand to earn a profit if the coins go up in price. Most ICOs create a limited number of coins, which are sometimes only available during the initial ICO phase.

Prior to the frenzy of ICOs through 2017 and 2018, ICOs were originally called "token sales" or crowdfunding. The token sale of Ethereum in 2014 was one of the most influential of the early market. The next major investment opportunity came in 2016, when, building on the Ethereum blockchain, The DAO raised a then-record-breaking US $250 million in less than one month through what was at the time called a "crowdsale" (see Chapter 8). Through 2016 and early 2017, the terminology and funding landscape began to change. The discourse on these activities became increasingly financialized—changing from token sale, to crowdsale, to token fund, and then Initial Coin Offering. By mid-2017, ICOs had become extremely common, and were smashing previous records. By July 2017, ICOs had generated over US $1.3 billion across hundreds of offerings (Russo 2017).

Echoing a general and popular interest in ICOs during my interview period (late 2017), hobby and professional traders alike sought ICOs extensively. Nonetheless, I found the investment use of ICOs and post-launch "coins" to be surprisingly diverse. Hobby and professional traders sought ICOs as venture capital funds do traditional startups, even in some cases taking leadership and board roles and advising on strategy. This was not exclusive to well-capitalized hedge funds either. Several of the more committed hobby traders also expressed some participation in the leadership of ICOs and crypto companies—a surprisingly democratic financial opportunity. Hobby and professional traders also saw ICOs as relatively cheap and high-risk/high-reward investments, explaining the need to be well informed about emerging companies and upcoming ICOs. Indeed, from the outside, the distinction between insider trading, venture capital funding, and crypto trading is very blurry and problematic.

Nearly all participants characterized their engagement with ICOs as akin to an investment in venture capital. Unlike in venture capital, however, investment in ICOs, even when the investor takes an advisory or leadership role, (typically) involves no equity stake. The only opportunity for profit is the promise of rising token prices. As journalist Matt Levine explains: "for investors, it means that they are funding a risky new idea without any expectation of sharing in its profits. That seems like a wild thing to do" (Levine 2017). Despite Levine's well-placed criticism, it is important to recognize that large investors, such as the hedge funds I spoke with, receive certain other benefits that help tip the scales in favor of ICO investment. Since the pre-ICO deals often have no vesting delays or prohibitions, investors are free to cash out immediately (unlike most venture capital deals, which have specific vesting schedules). Even more significantly, these pre-ICO deals are usually offered at a discount (as was reported to me by the hedge funds I spoke with). The details of these deals are not disclosed, but there is speculation that these discounts may be very large indeed, perhaps up to 70 percent off the launch price (but more typically less than 25 percent), making the investment significantly less risky for these large institutional investors.

Most traders told me that their participation in the crypto market, despite the risks, was a once-in-a-lifetime opportunity, and a way to create "generational wealth." One professional trader expressed regret about missing the 1990s dot-com boom (apparently not concerned that the boom led to a bust that ruined many investors) and saw the crypto boom as his generation's big investment opportunity. Several traders also described the spirit of the market in terms of a "wild West," and that their roles were as "pioneers." As expected, all traders spoke of crypto investing with considerable enthusiasm and commitment—seemingly, nobody gets into this game halfway.

Before speaking with crypto traders, I had read many online discussions of crypto investing and went into the interviews with a working hypothesis that trader behavior would mirror the widespread "technical analysis" I had found online (Figure 5.1). In fact, this was not the case. Also known as "financial chartism," technical analysis tries to predict future performance based on past performance, through the analysis of price movement patterns and telltale characteristics. These patterns can be seen in ticker prices and charts, which analysts use to construct a great variety of trend lines and geometric shapes (with evocative names like "flat bottoms," "head and shoulders," and "symmetric coils") (Preda 2007). Technical analysis, however, is considered by financial economists as roughly equivalent to astrology (economists believe that price change is stochastic), despite being surprisingly popular in

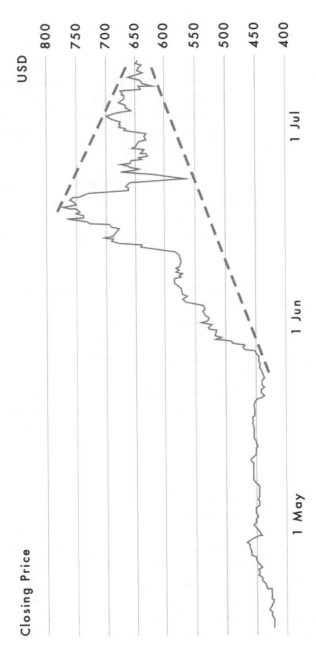

Figure 5.1 Technical analysis

traditional investing, and *rampant* in the public-facing side of crypto investing.

The traders I spoke with were all aware of widespread technical analysis in the community and would occasionally consult online charts (which are prominently displayed at most online crypto exchanges). But, despite the high visibility of technical analysis online, no traders performed any significant degree of technical analysis—certainly not the elaborate trend drawings that I had seen previously. Instead, technical analysis was used in a kind of communications frame, and, for some, as a rhetorical (that is, persuasive) device. Indeed, financial chartism appears to be a primary tool of the pump-and-dumpers, necessary to add some pseudo-scientific veneer to their schemes.

Instead, for the crypto traders I interviewed, "fundamental" analysis was the primary research and analysis method used. Fundamental analysis is distinct from technical analysis in that it attempts to derive a cause-and-effect relationship between the financial asset and its price, while technical analysis only attempts to discern correlational patterns. In mainstream economics and traditional investing, fundamental analysis is held in much higher regard than technical analysis. Fundamental analysis is believed to be a rational method of analysis, as it helps connect price and available information, which underpins the "efficient market" hypothesis. But the crypto market does not necessarily work like traditional markets. Whereas, say, when Intel releases a powerful new chip, investors expect revenues to rise, and therefore (as per the efficient market hypothesis) the stock price rises in response. In the crypto market, seasoned professional traders and hobbyists alike explained to me that they would do all kinds of deep fundamentals research before making a decision to invest: researching the reputation of development teams, assessing the quality of code, gauging a product's market size and position, determining the number of users, measuring perceived utility of the product, and so on. However, to date, very few crypto companies have robust sales, killer apps, or genuinely profitable and healthy business, which all stymies any "real" (non-speculative) fundamental analysis. ICOs are in many cases even worse, as they exist in pure potentiality, pre-selling coins for an unknown future (and in many cases, a *future product*).

But, to offer some defense of these "pioneering" investors, their investment activities are much like the gambles that venture capital funds must make (except crypto traders do not take any equity with their investments). Venture capitalists need to strike gold only every once and a while for their overall trading strategy to work. Similarly, crypto investors hope that there will, one day, be many healthy and profitable crypto companies, or even a few billion-dollar "unicorns," thereby vindicating their risky early investments in the market. At least today, many crypto investors have become rich, but only because the price of their assets has risen, not because of company sales or revenues.

The investment strategy of most of the crypto traders I interviewed makes sense in light of the risky venture capital funding model that they seem to have adopted. Nearly all crypto traders I interviewed made simple buy-and-hold investments, with occasional adjustments to diversify positions or take profits. The traders did not engage in any kind of complex or technical trading—no high-frequency trading, no arbitrage, and not even stop-loss or leverage/margin trading. (Incidentally, there is evidence that at least some high-frequency and automated trading occurs in the crypto market, as detailed by the Parasec blog; see Stubbings 2014.) The reasons given for these simple trading strategies were a combination of a belief in the long-term value of the market (buy early and cheap, wait for rise) and the difficulty and risk of executing these kinds of complex trading strategies in the crypto market (worries included automated stop-loss sniping, markets too thin to do serious arbitrage, and the unacceptably high risk of trading on leverage). The strategies of hobby traders were largely based on a combination of "gut instinct" and fundamentals research. Some professional traders reported more sophisticated strategies—deeper and more analytical kinds of fundamentals research—but ultimately tacit domain expertise and market experience seemed to be the main method.

Professional and hobby traders tended to use the same technologies for making trades. Only one trader used the application programming interface (API) offered by an exchange (citing speed of use). All other traders made their trades exclusively through the web interface of exchanges, or over-the-counter (OTC). Traders used multiple exchanges as need dictated, although each had personal preferences. In the case of ICOs, several hedge funds used legal contracts and direct exchange (through a lawyer), rather than market mechanisms. The hedge funds preferred working directly with ICO management teams, citing security of large transfers and financially preferential terms. Cryptocurrencies were held in cold storage or hardware devices, but most traders had persistent worries about security issues nonetheless. Most traders also desired and looked forward to increasing professionalization of the investment market, in terms of technical tools, market diversification, and future ("hands-off" but clear) regulation. In the time since these interviews in 2017, the demand for clear and fair regulation has grown significantly.

Summary

This chapter described a key mechanism in the shift from cryptocurrencies to blockchain technologies, focusing on the development of new financial clearance and settlement infrastructure. Clearance and settlement procedures are enormously complex, interconnected, and heavily regulated. I described some of the ways that cryptocurrency and blockchain startups have sought to challenge incumbents, but I pointed out that such visions do not always grasp the significance of the challenge that lies ahead.

In this chapter I also detailed the results of a qualitative study of cryptocurrency and blockchain investors. By interviewing hobby and professional investors alike, I found that the investment market presents numerous unique challenges, but that these traders see themselves as pioneers in an exciting new investment class. I also discovered some unethical and borderline illegal activities, but for the most part I found a community of people seeking greater regulatory clarity and increased professionalization.

CHAPTER SIX

Law and Society

Despite a decade of research and development, cryptocurrencies and blockchain technologies remain on uneasy legal and regulatory footing. Nearly everyone agrees that the law needs to catch up—banks want smart contracts with legal backing, software companies want guidance on privacy and data protection measures, and investors and startups alike want clear but unobtrusive rules for selling blockchain products. Behind these practical concerns, the widespread adoption of cryptocurrencies and blockchains prompts deeper questions about how legal experts might need to rethink some of their most foundational assumptions about finance, property, privacy, and the role of technology in society. As the latest in a long line of socially disruptive technologies, cryptocurrencies and blockchains seem to reify concerns about the encroachment of technology in society, with issues ranging from financialization to algorithmic automaticity.

In this chapter, I explore the social and legal embeddedness of cryptocurrencies and blockchains and discuss why regulators have struggled to keep pace with this rapidly advancing technology. For politicians, regulators, and attorneys, cryptocurrencies and blockchains have unsettled existing theories of jurisprudence as well as the laws and regulations that depend on these foundations. These same technologies also have potential impact on the legal profession itself. Notaries, property rights administration, insurance, and accounting are all beginning to take notice of the ways blockchain technologies can streamline and enhance their work.

Financial regulators have struggled to develop a fair and

rational regulatory climate, much to the consternation of companies developing blockchain solutions. As I discussed in Chapter 5, blockchain technologies have been speeding up capital flows. This has resulted in what Bill Maurer calls "re-risking"—a revival of excitement and risk in response to the heavily regulated and "boring" post-2008 finance landscape (Maurer 2016). However, the pendulum has swung back towards risk because cryptocurrencies and blockchain technologies have largely managed to evade the law. In this risky climate, "Initial Coin Offerings" (ICOs) have proliferated, sometimes with deleterious consequences. In the US, which is currently the most important market for these products, ICOs have to choose between "security" tokens and "utility" tokens. Given the existing laws—most importantly the "Howey test" determining what investments should come under SEC regulation as securities—many ICOs have struggled to avoid being labeled security-issuing companies, which comes with a greater compliance and reporting burden, even if (they believe) their products are simply blockchains with a value layer.

Cryptocurrency and blockchain technologies also complicate privacy and data protection regulations. The most important of these is the EU's General Data Protection Regulation (GDPR), which includes stiff penalties for non-compliance. Many worry that, despite offering many tools for strong privacy and data protection, the architecture of blockchains is on a collision course with this new regulation. Many existing blockchains, such as the Bitcoin system, are without doubt in trouble, but these systems have always been a challenge for regulators and therefore are unlikely to be much affected. On the other hand, I discuss below some of the ways that, by adopting best practices, new blockchain systems can be designed for GDPR compliance.

The key technology used by many legal professionals is the "smart contract," as deployed on blockchain technologies. The origins of the smart contract idea do, however, prompt serious questions about whether widespread use would be socially beneficial. I briefly introduce "cryptoeconomics," a peculiar and nascent field of study that, incorporating many of the possibilities and challenges described in this chapter, is an outgrowth of cryptocurrencies and blockchains.

Jurisprudence and legal technologies

Are cryptocurrencies and blockchains similar to existing forms of money, property, capital, intellectual property, insurance, and contracts—or something new? If they are in fact new, what kinds of rules, principles, and legal tests would be required to account for distributed computing, automatic and "unstoppable" systems, "smart" property, cryptoinsurance, exotic forms of finance, and obfuscated code? What were once science fictions are increasingly real, and require answers to tough questions: would or should a transfer of home ownership transacted on a blockchain be accepted? Is a marriage (or prenuptial agreement) bound by a blockchain a "legal" contract (Castillo 2016; Connell 2017)? Ultimately, these are questions of jurisprudence—the study of law, its systems, and its role in society.

As blockchain technologies are woven further into society, there is an increasing need to understand how these technologies affect traditional dimensions of life and the legal foundations it rests upon. For example, many authors have already raised the specter of algorithmic lifeworlds (Galloway & Thacker 2007; Cheney-Lippold 2011; Pasquale 2015; Saurwein, Just, & Latzer 2015). A life controlled by algorithms, these authors contend, has implicit and often unaccountable bias; it alters the relationship between humans (potentially turning us into "standing reserve," in the famous words of Martin Heidegger); it alters human relationships with other things, such as other machines or the environment; and it makes important decisions without normative rationality. For cryptocurrencies and blockchains, these pressures are even more acute. Being saturated with cryptographic technologies, crypto-currencies and blockchains are capable of producing practically unbreakable security, pervasive obfuscation and secrecy, and powerful modes of authentication and verification. Moreover, since blockchains are distributed across a heterogenous global network of computers, changing, stopping, or regulating—or even just standardizing—the technology is extremely difficult (see Brito, Shabad, & Castillo 2015; Doguet 2012; Howden 2015; Kaplanov 2012; Luther 2016b; Ly 2013; Plassaras 2013; Shcherbak 2014). Blockchains also use new and unexplored technologies, such as smart contracts, to make automatic, algorithmic decisions. These new decision-making capabilities problematize existing jurisprudence—when these systems go wrong they require answers for who (or what?) has rights, duties, and responsibilities.

The combination of algorithmic capabilities and block-chains—decentralized systems designed to resist censorship and regulation—results in autonomous law. Primavera De Fillipi and Aaron Wright capture this phenomenon with their theory of "lex cryptographia." According to De Fillipi and Wright (2018), lex cryptographia implements a "private regulatory framework" that functions according to the permissions and capabilities of software code, not existing laws. At its extreme, autonomous law is mechanical and processual, and in some cases unstoppable or unalterable. Moreover, autonomous law potentially does away with the interpretive and discretionary elements that are usually present in courts, and therefore offers little opportunity for intervention (Grimmelmann 2005). The automaticity and formalism of coded law also raises the specter of software developers as legal rulers and guardians. If blockchain technologies de facto create autonomous law, or rule by "lex cryptographia," they potentially do so in conflict with existing legal and normative claims.

Nonetheless, there are opportunities for autonomous legal mechanisms to create more efficient or fair applications of law. For instance, in many legal settings notaries do not need to be attorneys, given that the processes of notarization are often simple and mechanical. The steps required for authenticating and witnessing a digital document signature, for example, could be easily replaced by a blockchain system connected to a secure identity registry. Not only would blockchain notarization be faster, it could prevent document tampering. But, even in the simplest cases, replacing humans entirely is surprisingly difficult. Today, there are several startups seeking to disrupt this large industry, but history shows that due to entrenched incumbents, conservative and recalcitrant lawmakers, the force of tradition, and hidden complexity, these efforts are likely to be met with difficulty.

This is not the first time that technology was supposed to upend notaries. As Jean-François Blanchette (2012) describes, in the 1990s France attempted to replace notaries and other state identification services with public-key cryptography infrastructure. While obviously not identical to blockchain technologies, many of the same basic technological capabilities are possible with public-key infrastructure, and yet the effort was not a success. The take-home from this failure is the importance of social institutions, their (in)ability to change, and complexity in the face of tacit knowledges. Overcoming technological hurdles, on the other hand, is a comparatively simple task.

For a more advanced application of autonomous law, consider Joshua Fairfield's (2014) suggestion that blockchain-based "bots" might be able to negotiate for consumer protections. Fairfield argues that existing consumer protection activities are ineffective because courts are willing to uphold the legality of shrink-wrap and click-through contracts (contracts that are packaged with products and are deemed accepted when products are used), despite their obvious negative impact on consumers (this also has implications for privacy, since data-collection waivers are routinely ignored and accepted). Fairfield claims that such contracts, while notionally legal, lack the true nature of contract as "bargained-for exchange" (Fairfield 2014, p. 35). Fairfield looks to smart contracts to create semi- or fully automatic mechanisms for contractual bargaining and negotiating, alongside the creation of a market for consumer options. Rather than simply accept bad shrink-wrap contracts, automatically negotiating smart contracts working on behalf of the consumer could set minimal terms and selectively offer data (perhaps trading personal privacy for access, or negotiating payment, etc.). Smart contracts could also establish "cash-on-the-barrelhead" transactions, which would indicate to courts an *intention* by the consumer, facilitated through a smart contract (Fairfield 2014, p. 47). With a perceived intent, smart contracts would be more likely to be accepted by courts, as they would fall within traditional criteria for contract law.

Another area of application for blockchain technologies is copyright. Jurisprudence in the area of copyright has long accepted its contractual and "mechanical" nature. Typically, creators are granted automatic rights without expressly requesting copyright and, in the case of music, end-users may create derivative works from musical compositions through a mechanical license (paying a predetermined, regulated royalty). Rights could, therefore, in many cases, be disclosed and managed on blockchains without the intervention of lawyers, courts, or intermediaries. Ideally, such a system could even execute automatically; for instance, when music is purchased a portion of the sale is automatically deposited in the musician's, the agent's and the record label's wallet.

Automated peer-to-peer music download and rights management systems have, in fact, been attempted many times, with limited success in every case (with and without blockchains). Most recently, the electronic pop musician Imogen Heap collaborated with the blockchain company Mycelia to make her 2015 single "Tiny Human" available for download via a blockchain rights platform. However, the sales were modest (a year later, the track was only downloaded a few hundred times via the platform). There were also, blockchain critic David Gerard points out, a number of problems with the system. The ecommerce process was buggy and difficult and required users to make purchases with Ethereum's cryptocurrency, ETH—a daunting task for all but the most dedicated. There are also other, more systemic problems, Gerard argues: the inability for blockchains to scale appropriately for the large music download industry, worries about user surveillance and digital rights management ("smart" music downloads are a consumer blessing and curse), and industry distrust of peer-to-peer solutions.

Other kinds of blockchain rights management systems might offer more flexibility and additional features that artists could take advantage of. With the blockchain rights management system Monegraph, rights holders can operationalize their "expressions" (artworks, designs, and so on) by selling directly to consumers with fine-grained policies for use and derivation. The mechanism for fine-grained control is, principally, the hash algorithm, which can be executed on complex, changing, and amorphous objects to create uniquely identified objects that in turn are registered on a blockchain. Once registered, the blockchain can track and manage identities associated with the expression. Through the use of the hash algorithm, the digital object is, in a sense, ontologically reified—made a little more "real" in that while it can still be digitally copied, such copies lack proper "authentication" (see DuPont 2017). Through this process, the Monegraph system is able to virtually restrict digital objects, making them more like material artworks, and therefore create scarcity. By making digital objects scarce, price increases, opening up new market opportunities for digital art.

However, Martin Zeilinger (2016) argues that highly proficient blockchain rights management systems may stifle the emancipatory properties of digital art. A similar critique is offered by Laura Lotti (2016), who argues that despite efforts to create emancipatory "blockchain art," these attempts have not been successful at challenging the logic of finance. Digital art is special, argues Zeilinger, precisely because it is easy to copy, remix, and revise. If a blockchain-based rights management system takes away this ability, a digital painting, for example, becomes conceptually the same as a traditional painting, with little to recommend the former over the latter. Moreover, rather than freeing artists to earn revenue from their intellectual property, Zeilinger and Lotti each worry that such systems will further financialize artistic expressions, continuing an already worrisome trend.

Blockchain-based legal technologies are also being applied to the insurance industry. So-called "cryptoinsurance" or blockchain insurance is an emerging application of blockchain technology that utilizes smart contracts for the deployment and management of insurance. The insurance industry has in fact long been a major user of computing infrastructure. In the early years of the industry, companies like Prudential were at the cutting edge, utilizing computers for analysis and data synthesis and enriching the computing industry with heavy demand for faster and more powerful computers (Yates 1997).

Today, large insurance service providers such as Deloitte have joined blockchain startups to investigate cryptocurrencies and blockchain technologies. While there has been only modest progress so far—insurers are looking for cost reduction and efficiency boosts—there are radical ideas for the industry on the horizon. These include automatic claim processing and micro- and peer-to-peer insurance. Automatic claim processing could be triggered through smart contracts designed to provide near instant access to funds (important, for example, in the case of disasters) and on a "parametric" or partial basis until a more exhaustive (manual) claim could be made (Wang & Safavi 2016). Other ideas include micro-insurance (similar to microcredit) and peer-to-peer insurance. Peer-to-peer insurance might replace the activities of existing insurance companies with blockchain technologies, ostensibly disintermediating insureds. Interestingly, peer-to-peer insurance rekindles the historical antecedent of the very concept of insurance, as a way to pool risk by joining a collective of peers. Yet some of this "disruptive" thinking is misguided. Blockchain technologies might help reduce the dependency on (profit-seeking) intermediaries, but it is a fiction to think that the only job of a traditional insurance company is to skim cream.

Cryptocurrencies and blockchain technologies might also impact the insurance industry by enabling offshoring to evade existing regulation (Abramowicz 2015). With potentially pseudonymous and amorphous organizational structures that are operated virtually and located offshore, blockchain insurers could provide a new kind of cowboy insurance while avoiding law enforcement and regulatory bodies. Ultimately, this might help *or hurt* individuals who have been traditionally excluded from insurance markets, such as people in developing countries or with negative risk profiles. These companies might be billed as the "Ubers" of insurance, but, like Uber, there is the risk of disregard for existing laws and regulations.

Property rights administration is another industry that could be made more efficient and secure with the introduction of blockchain technologies. For example, the author and politician Hernando de Soto has long worked to eliminate dependence on illegal and black-market activities while cutting government red tape. Recently, he has turned to blockchain technologies to realize his goals. However, de Soto propagates an avowedly neoliberal and technology-focused narrative, which has its critics.

In the late 1980s and early 1990s, de Soto orchestrated changes to Peru's banking and economic system (with the tacit support of the US government) and then established legal land titles for homes and farms lacking official property rights. According to de Soto, in Peru (and elsewhere) a great deal of economic activity occurs on black markets and therefore goes unreported. Because of this, it is difficult for individuals and small companies to secure financial and legal support, such as credit, insurance, and claims of property ownership. His reforms have focused on the advantages of legal land ownership to enable the use of legal land assets for collateral, which can then be used to grow businesses. De Soto's narrative, however, propagates IMF-style neoliberal reforms, which critics argue do not actually benefit the poor and instead open new markets for exploitation by economic service providers (see Gilbert 2002).

More recently, de Soto has turned to blockchain technologies as a high-tech solution to land registry. In the Republic of Georgia, with the help of the government and industry partner BitFury, de Soto launched a pilot project using blockchain technologies to provide legal land titles for unregistered land (Shin 2016). De Soto hopes that blockchain technologies will be effective in facilitating his twin goals of reducing red tape and providing access to legal and economic systems. The blockchain solution, however, does not address existing critiques of de Soto's political agenda. For example, Alan Gilbert (2002) found that de Soto's reforms in Bogotá did not create the secondary housing markets that were hoped for. Worse still, blockchain technology potentially adds other technology-based issues. Implementing a large land registry is a socially and politically complex problem and is likely to require expensive devices at a grassroots level. De Soto's goal of solving poverty through a simple technological fix appears to be a variant of solutionism (Morozov 2014).

The blockchain-based land registry being piloted in the Republic of Georgia also aims to create a profound change in the legal status of property. When paired with smart contracts, a property regime could add programmatic features to the otherwise inert concept of property, enabling a form of "smart property." In his article "Secure Property Titles with Owner Authority" (1998), Nick Szabo introduces this idea. Szabo echoes (and references) de Soto's claim that land registry is key to overcoming poverty. Szabo argues that early de Soto-style efforts were insufficient or worse, because "straightforward transcription of written records into a centralized online repository would make these problems . . . worse" on account of records being lost or forged (Szabo 1998). Writing presciently, nearly a decade before the invention of blockchains, Szabo suggested that emerging concepts in cryptography and distributed computing might offer one way to create a secure, tamper-proof land registry system.

For Szabo, land registration was only the tip of the iceberg for the reform of property regimes. He argued that "all such agreements of control . . . to be made across . . . trust boundaries are problems of agreeing on and maintaining property rights" (Szabo 1998). In other words, his idea for a proto-blockchain had general application to all systems of property and ownership (similar ideas were explored around the same time by Joseph M. Reagle Jr. (1996)). He imagined a system where people trade access to property (symbolic or otherwise) by holding private/public key-pairs that are registered in a distributed system with "automated . . . rules and an unforgeable audit trail" (Szabo 1998). The description is— not incidentally—similar to the later blockchain systems that actually did develop.

Szabo's beliefs about the political economy of property, however, are unorthodox and resemble implicitly right-wing and libertarian politics. In a blog post on the security of property to enable "productive" use of land, Szabo references David Friedman's work on the origins of law and markets in tenth to thirteenth century Iceland (Szabo 2005). Friedman explores the case of Iceland because in it he sees an example of "the lengths to which market systems could supplant government in its most fundamental functions" (Friedman 1979), an explicitly small-government, libertarian analysis. Szabo takes from Friedman the argument that private property arises from the ability to secure it: "forms of government and property law . . . [arise from] interaction between the security and the productivity of property" (Szabo 2005). Where early people might have had to secure property through established armies and navies, however, Szabo believes that today "information technology . . . [can] revolutionize the security of goods," and therefore produce new property regimes and even barebones (libertarian) "microgovernments," based solely around voting and private property ownership (Szabo 1998). For critics, the risk of blockchain technologies for property rights management, therefore, is that anti-regulation, small-government, laissez-faire economics and politics might be smuggled in under the guise of efficiency and security.

Financial regulation

In the years following the 2008 global economic crisis, the financial industry faced significant threats in the form of tough new regulations. Internationally, the Basel Committee on Banking Supervision released Basel III reforms that required banks to hold higher quality capital with lower rates of leverage, and improved risk management, transparency, and disclosure practices. Notably, these reforms included significant changes to bank clearance and settlement procedures (see Chapter 5), which were identified as areas of systemic destabilization during the crisis. Intraday lending, for example, previously relied on two large clearing banks providing huge amounts of credit that had become collateralized during the crisis (Dudley 2016), and was therefore a target for reform. Banks were also encouraged to move away from riskier over-the-counter (OTC) transactions, and instead were to make greater use of central counterparties (CCPs) to structure exposure and therefore reduce counterparty risk (this occurred alongside an attempt to create more resilient CCPs).

Although many critics believed that the reforms were piecemeal (Davies 2010) and insufficiently strong or decisive to create real change (Helleiner 2014), the banks were nonetheless fearful that reform might stifle existing business lines. So banks sought ways to optimize, strategically diversify, and end-run regulation. This included paying greater attention to back-office technologies to optimize business (and achieve regulatory risk compliance), which had been growing in sophistication over the previous decade (I worked at a risk-management software company prior to and during the crisis, and I can confirm that Basel reforms were a major business generator). At the same time, banks were having an image problem (seen as both boring and corrupt), and worried they might lose top employees to Silicon Valley (Desai 2015). Banks responded by pouring resources into information technologies, and subsequently those employees who did leave for Silicon Valley often returned—with new financial technology products for sale. In was after 2008 when financial technologies really took off, and cryptocurrencies and blockchain technologies are a small but growing part of this.

Not only did engagement with cryptocurrencies and blockchain technologies signal that banks were hip places to work on challenging new problems (many banks created new startup-like divisions just to work on fintech), the solutions that emerged helped create new business opportunities. Bill Maurer (2016) details how cryptocurrencies and blockchain technologies seek to create higher velocity capital flows by decreasing the time needed for clearance and settlement. In so doing, banks have created new opportunities for risk (what Maurer calls "re-risking") that are positioned to be highly lucrative. Money can be made because as the time needed to clear and settle transactions decreases capital is freed up and can be put to productive use. Additionally, since the post-2008 regulatory climate forced banks towards "boring" fees-based profit models, the prospect of working on new technologies capable of creating new sources of revenue was for many in the industry, quite frankly, exciting.

This increased velocity of capital flows is, as Maurer identified, a much riskier financial environment. As the architecture of capital flows changes in response to new technologies, banks are also better positioned to get around existing regulations, which are often far too slow to keep up with Silicon Valley-paced innovation. Internationally, the fintech applications of cryptocurrencies and blockchain technologies has really caught on. For instance, to contend with the "new normal" of decelerating economic growth in China (Guo & Liang 2016), fintech is being vigorously adopted there (one estimate puts the number of fintech startups in the Asian region at 2,500, compared to 4,000 in the US and UK) (Desai 2015). What cryptocurrency and blockchain enthusiasts potentially miss in the race for high-speed capital flows, however, is that existing infrastructure is often slow on purpose. Slow clearance and settlement procedures, for instance, function as a speedbump, to lower overall velocity and give actors time to react, fix mistakes, and make rational decisions. In other words, slowness itself is a form of regulation.

One of the fastest moving and seemingly most difficult to regulate areas of fintech has been the emergence of Initial Coin Offerings (ICOs). ICOs create new architectures of financialization that rely on blockchain technologies. The reason these new financialization techniques emerged with blockchains is that the blockchain design enables coins, or tokens, to be securely and transparently tracked after they have been issued. Unlike traditional private money solutions (e.g., PayPal or Alipay), blockchains can create wholly new tokens that cannot be "double spent" and can be managed without a central clearinghouse. The blockchain can also achieve consensus that purports to represent "one version of the truth" among multiple parties. In Chapter 2, I characterized the blockchain as a distributed version of traditional double-entry bookkeeping.

But, then as now, as much as double-entry bookkeeping has in some ways worked to keep companies honest to regulators, tax officials, and business partners, it has also in many cases obfuscated economic realities. The perception of honesty and mercantile virtue that resulted from careful bookkeeping was in reality less accurate than outsiders were led to believe. Traditionally, by "opening the books" merchants could make their virtue visible and available to inspection. Token sales and ICOs seem to work on the same logic as mercantile double-entry bookkeeping, in that they rhetorically demonstrate fair and equitable financing but contain layers of truth. For example, it is an open secret that ICOs offer preferential terms for pre-mined coin purchases to large institutional investors. ICOs also come without the traditional legal protections of equity investments, nor any of the investor disclosures that are otherwise common.

Due to the lack of appropriate disclosure and the largely unregulated landscape, investing in ICOs is risky. In many cases ICOs are issued for pre-revenue companies. ICOs also rely on artificial scarcity to promote investment, which heavily favors early investors and creates potentially volatile markets where "pump and dump" schemes run rampant. (A "pump and dump" is when one or more individuals generate excitement about a company to raise share prices, and then once the price has risen the "pumpers" become "dumpers" and sell at a profit.) There are also new kinds of outright criminal opportunities associated with ICOs, such as impersonating ICO developers and then bilking potential investors by posting fake wallet addresses (Gerard 2017; J. Russell 2017).

The regulatory landscape for ICOs is beginning to shape up, however, and with any luck will chase out bad actors. Previously, regulators and law enforcement agencies debated how to best control cryptocurrencies and blockchain startups. For example, in March 2013, US FinCEN announced it would regulate Bitcoin exchanges like money transmitters (Wolfson 2015). However, showing that regulators were starting to catch up with the fast-paced nature of cryptocurrencies and blockchain technologies, on July 25, 2017, the US Securities and Exchange Commission (SEC) released an investment bulletin about ICOs, noting that they "can be used improperly to entice investors with the promise of high returns" (Office of Investor Education and Advocacy 2017). The bulletin did not sanction such investment, but it made it clear that ICOs were on notice.

The investor bulletin was released by the SEC alongside an analysis of the earlier The DAO crowdsale (see Chapter 8). Between these two documents, the US government gestured towards regulation of an overheated market but stopped short of full regulation. Similarly, around the same time a warning was issued by the UK's Financial Conduct Authority (2017) regarding investment in cryptocurrencies in general. These actions can be compared, however, to the largely positive regulatory report (advocating a "light touch") issued in Canada just two years prior, when the market was still nascent, and its real regulatory risks were not as pronounced (Gerstein & Hervieux-Payette 2015). Regulators have become more active in recent years, but much work remains if they are to create consistent rules that promote new financial and technological innovation, rather than simply penalize the market.

The central question being undertaken in the SEC's analyses was whether ICOs and related activities that use cryptocurrency sales to raise capital funds should be interpreted as securities, and therefore be subject to regulatory oversight. In the US, this question has often come down to an interpretation of the "Howey Test." In *SEC v. W. J. Howey Co.*, an "investment contract" (as per the Securities Act of 1933) is defined as "investment of money in a common enterprise with profits to come solely from the efforts of others" (US Supreme Court 1946, p. 327). However, relying solely on the Howey Test, in the words of the attorney Marco Santori (2016), is some "bush league" lawyering. In the SEC's analysis of The DAO crowdsale, the Howey Test does make an appearance, alongside other decisions, such as *SEC v. Edwards*, and *United Housing Found., Inc. v. Forman*. According to the SEC, the key to interpretation is that a security should be defined broadly with disregard to form, and with an emphasis placed on the "economic realities underlying a transaction" (Office of Investor Education and Advocacy 2017, p. 11). Regulators have adopted a broad interpretation because they worry that narrow interpretations potentially skirt existing regulation designed to create a fair and safe investment market.

The SEC and other regulators are also worried about ICOs and cryptocurrencies because, by their very design, they tend to resist Anti-Money Laundering (AML) and Know Your Customer (KYC) regulations. Here, too, regulators have shown a willingness to use existing laws to address infringements. For example, in 2015 the blockchain company Ripple was fined US $700,000 by FinCEN for failure to comply with AML rules. As I discussed in Chapters 2 and 3, the uncertain ontological status of cryptocurrencies had previously caused confusion in the investment market (are they money, capital, representations of value, or something else?). Since then, regulators have favored the interpretation that, if tokens are being used to generate capital, they are considered a security. The guidance being offered by the SEC suggests that investors ought to look to the underlying economic realities to determine regulatory status, and not the form of the investment (i.e., "tokens"). In other words, the fact that an ICO uses virtual tokens does not preclude it from being a security and therefore falling under the purview of securities regulations.

Privacy and data protection regulation

It is with considerable irony that financial regulators worry about the ways that cryptocurrency and blockchain users potentially evade regulation using strong security and privacy techniques, while privacy and data protection regulators worry about the ways that the same users might lack data security and privacy. Nowhere is this clearer than in the European Union (EU), where new privacy and data protection rules impose stiff penalties for any company found to be operating in the region without appropriate measures in place. First adopted in 2016 and enforceable since 2018, the EU General Data Protection Regulations (GDPR) replace the

1996 Data Protection Directive. This complex set of require-ments has wide scope and detailed rules and on the face of it many blockchain technologies appear to be in contravention (see also Finck 2017).

The issues facing most blockchain technologies affected by the GDPR are that 1) transactions are immutable, 2) data can be de-anonymized (or "re-linked"), and 3) all (potentially private) data is "controlled" and/or "processed" publicly by validator nodes (miners). Because most blockchains are (by design) immutable, stored private data are impossible to remove or erase. The GDPR creates a "right to erasure" (Article 17), replacing the previous and broader "right to be forgotten." The right to erasure guarantees that any request to remove private data (within stipulated limits) must be com-plied with, but obviously such a request would be impossible for a system explicitly designed to frustrate attempts to change records. In reality, however, the right to erasure is of limited concern since it only applies to *private* data. Because of the distributed (i.e., redundant) design, many blockchain systems (such as Bitcoin) offer very limited data storage capabilities. Those designs such as Ethereum that do provide greater data storage capabilities do so at incredible cost (depending on the price of ETH, data storage costs US $1 million or more *per gigabyte*). Except for a few specialized blockchain systems designed with replicated storage in mind (such as Filecoin), due to price and performance costs it is rare to store much data "on-chain." Rather, data are usually "linked" through a hash (see Chapter 3). Private data *could* still be stored on-chain, in much the same way as pornography (including illegal child pornography) *has* been immutably stored on public blockchains (introducing other legal and ethical con-cerns; see Matzutt et al. 2018), but best practices dictate that private data are encrypted and stored in access-restricted databases off-chain.

What, however, if the designers of a blockchain system ignore best practices and store private data on-chain (perhaps small but important data, such as national identity numbers)? This introduces the possibility that private data are handled by public controllers and processors and can be de-anonymized or re-linked. Typically, in such a scenario private data would be hashed and only the hash value would be stored on-chain (otherwise, if stored as plain text, it would be an *obvious* privacy infringement). Would hashing private data nullify the privacy and data protection risk, according to the GDPR? It appears that it would not.

According to the guidance offered by Working Party 216 on Article 29 (Working Party 216 2014), hash algorithms are merely pseudonymous. In Chapter 1, I implicitly addressed this point by characterizing Bitcoin as pseudonymous and not anonymous because there are sophisticated techniques for de-anonymizing blockchain data. The Working Party 216 opinion explicitly references hashing techniques under the category of pseudonymization techniques, arguing that salted-hash and keyed-hashes with a stored key do not sufficiently transform data to count as anonymized. For blockchains, the most relevant and important example discussed in the opinion is for "deterministic encryption or keyed-hash function with the deletion of the key," which roughly corresponds to wallet best practices. As I discussed in Chapter 3, best practice for wallets is to create a new address for *every* transaction, otherwise (as is the concern of the GDPR), de-anonymization techniques may be able to re-link or single out users. Here, assuming wallet best practices are *strictly* adhered to, the Working Party 216 opinion cautiously accepts this approach, writing "this solution allows diminishing the risk of linkability" (2014, p. 21). Strict adherence would only be possible by making it *impossible* for users to choose otherwise (implemented at the protocol level), so systems such as Bitcoin and Ethereum are likely not compliant with the GDPR. It *does* seem possible, however, to design a blockchain system that is compliant. While this brief discussion of the EU's GDPR only touches on the complexities of making blockchain systems compliant with privacy regulations, it does at least offer one tentative path forward.

Smart contracts

A smart contract is the automated version of a traditional contract (wherein a traditional contract is an agreement between people that is sometimes formalized in a written document). But, this description undersells the complexity and potential impact of smart contracts on society. The term "smart contract" was invented by Nick Szabo in "Smart Contracts: Building Blocks for Digital Free Markets," written for the transhumanist magazine *Extropy* (1996). During 1996 and 1997, Szabo reworked his idea of smart contracts, which eventually led to the academic publication "Formalizing and Securing Relationships on Public Networks" (1997). In his earlier work, Szabo defined a smart contract as "a set of promises, specified in digital form, including protocols within which the parties perform on these promises" (1996), which, crucially, can be automated. In his later work, he extended the concept of smart contract to include traditional contracts that can be "embedded in hardware and software" to make breach of contract expensive (1997). This embeddedness requires a "meeting of the minds" (1997). Yet this meeting of the minds seems to be precisely the characteristic that automated, smart contracts strive to do away with.

Szabo uses the example of a car with a "smart lien" to illustrate how smart contracts might work in the real world. Consider, he writes, a contract to purchase a car on credit. Traditionally, the bank would need to carefully assess the risk of lending because if the loan holder defaults on the loan, the bank would either lose the value of the unpaid loan or would need to engage in expensive and time-consuming loan and property recovery. With a smart contract, however, the moment the loan holder defaults the bank can activate the contract enforcement mechanisms. Since the concept of a smart contract is, for Szabo, tied to the security of property, the car with a smart contract already has the "desired characteristics of ownership embedded into [it]" (Szabo 1996). So a loan default might automatically trigger financial redress (if, say, tied into the loan holder's digital wallet), or simply stop the car from operating (remotely engaging a kill switch). The smart contract ensures that compliance occurs *automatically* and cannot be tampered with—it is, in a word, "unstoppable." However, an unstoppable contract does not necessarily mean a static contract. Updating, correcting, and revising are essential and necessary parts of the contract lifecycle and developers have only begun to explore how change mechanisms can be implemented equitably and securely, either through a contractual change, forced change, or consensus-led mechanism.

Since the concept of security is essential to property rights, according to Szabo, he sees the possibility for a shift from the security of property to a negotiated and ultimately smart contract—as he writes, "from a crude security system to a reified contact" (Szabo 1997). In being "smart," the performance of a contract shifts from traditional after-the-fact enforcement ("reactive" enforcement, such as deterrence, physical enforcement, loss of reputation, and so on), to preventative enforcement ("proactive" or "dynamic" enforcement) (Szabo 1997). In the example of the car with a smart lien, enforcement is not proactive, but being nearly instant the effect is practically the same.

When contracts become conceptually (and not just practically) proactive, however, they potentially sidestep more foundational rights and duties. This is the context that led Lawrence Lessig (1999, 2006) to craft his slogan "code is law." Lessig realized that as private contracts shift from the letter of the law to self-enforcing code, some rights and legal exemptions will get eliminated. In traditional written contracts, parties are unable to legally enter into contracts that contravene other, more fundamental rights (e.g., one cannot enter into slavery by contract). With smart contracts, it is more difficult for legal and state apparatuses to determine who is responsible for "illegal" contracts (imagine the difficulty of tracking down the pseudonymous parties bound in a smart contract on a global blockchain). Moreover, there are certain rights and legal exemptions that do not activate until particular actions have occurred—actions that might be proactively barred through the instant activation of smart contracts. Lessig (1999, 2006) points to copyright and digital rights management for an example of this behavior: if you are prevented from making a copy in the first instance (through proactive code), then legal exemptions cannot occur (exemptions that, for instance, permit libraries to legally make copies). The fact that you are legally permitted to act in a certain way but prevented from doing so by the execution of code does not mean that the code is "illegal"—rather, the code is antecedent to, or executed *prior* to, law.

Smart contracts with "dual integration" offer a richer context than smart contracts operating solely in the paradigm of code. A dual integration system has the automatically enforcing capabilities of a typical smart contract, but is bundled with a more conventional, black-letter of the law, written contract (Christidis & Devetsikiotis 2016). One example of a dual integration blockchain system is Monax (formerly Eris). The developers of Monax envision the system as a practical stopgap measure because "legal systems are unlikely to resolve disputes stemming from smart contracts solely on the basis of their code" (Monax 2017). Another system, and perhaps the first ever dual integration smart contract, is Ian Grigg and Gary Howland's Ricardian contract, which they developed as part of their proto-cryptocurrency system, the Ricardo Payment System (Grigg 2004). The Ricardian contract is human *and* computer readable and digitally signed (using public-key infrastructure). Ricardian contracts start life as legalese, stipulating the who, what, when, and where of the contract. From the legal document, a surrogate document containing key-value pairs of the salient information is produced.

Both documents are at least somewhat human-readable, but the key-value version is encoded with the semantics of the legal document such that it can be executed algorithmically. Should an issue arise with the coded version, a court could fall back to the legal, black-letter version as the ultimate source of truth. Although Ricardian contracts lack the excitement of autonomous, unstoppable, and exact blockchain smart contracts, they are an effective transitional technology until the utopia (or dystopia) of fully automated smart contracts arrives.

If smart contracts curtail necessary forms of contractual "meeting of the minds," the theory of Schelling points or focal points can potentially enrich negotiations in the absence of trust or information (Szabo 1997). Schelling points, in the context of blockchain technologies, have typically been discussed in terms of the emerging field of rationalized economic thinking called "cryptoeconomics." Schelling points or focal points are a game theory concept developed by Thomas Schelling in *The Strategy of Conflict* (1960). The coordination strategy allows two or more parties to reach agreement in an environment with little information and no possibility of communication. The key insight of Schelling's theory is that coordination is easier when attention is drawn to prominent or "focal" points. Schelling offers the example of two people in New York who need to meet in an undetermined location without having prior communication. According to Schelling, on game theory assumptions, each party will likely pick Grand Central Station because in a world where many possibilities are equally likely, humans look for patterns or unusual focal points of reference. The assumption made by each party is, "if I think Grand Central Station is a good meeting spot, the other person may think the same."

Similarly, in his descriptions of cryptoeconomics, Vitalik Buterin offers the example of picking matching numbers from a list without coordination or communication (*Vitalik Buterin: Cryptoeconomic Protocols In the Context of Wider Society* 2014). People will, according to the theory, look for something—anything—that makes one number stand out—perhaps an even number, or a number with many zeros, or a well-known lucky number. Thus, given the following numbers: 2349 65 22 100 932, both parties will likely choose "100." In Western, decimal-based numeracy, 100 "stands out" from the rest of the numbers, and therefore, lacking any other way to coordinate, the rational choice is to assume a common set of beliefs. Of course, these choices are specific to culture and context—with numbers, other patterns might be significant (such as "lucky" numbers). The same specifics of context change for focal points in New York: as times, people, and places change there might be other possible focal points—Times Square, One World Trade Center, Brooklyn Bridge, or the New York Public Library.

In many scenarios, available options may be either too hard or too weak to facilitate contractual meeting of the minds. Consider the scenario where a workers' union and a business owner are unable to satisfactorily negotiate. Using the theory of Schelling points, one way of describing the situation is that the terms of the proposed contract are insufficiently strong—with too few shared interests and values—which inevitably leads to a breakdown of communication. Until some stronger focal points can be found, coordination will not be effective. On the other hand, some focal points are very hard, to the point that they curtail negotiation altogether. Consider the scenario in a typical North American grocery store. The presence of a price tag is usually a signal that the grocery store has a very hard focal point in mind and that haggling will not be accepted (Szabo 1997). The price tag, therefore, is a hard focal point that communicates the context and the parameters of the contract with little opportunity for negotiation.

With this game-theoretical logic in place, it is possible to create flexible smart contracts that dynamically adjust to shared values and individual preferences. Unlike all-or-nothing contracts that fail to facilitate a meeting of the minds, a dynamically adjusting smart contract would enrich the contracting process. There are many ways a "cryptoeconomics" solution might be implemented on a blockchain, including markets (prediction markets are one popular mechanism), or, as described above, negotiating "bots" that work on your behalf behind the scenes. In these cases, however, contracting would no longer be absolute and would need to operate within acceptable bounds for each party. Figuring out precisely what these bounds are, and what a sufficiently strong focal point might be, is no trivial task.

Summary

This chapter detailed a host of issues facing law and the legal profession. I discussed possible ways to understand the jurisprudence of cryptocurrencies and blockchains. Despite changing legal foundations, cryptocurrencies and blockchain tokens are often considered, in the US at least, a financial security and therefore involve greater regulatory scrutiny. In this context, I discussed how a 2017 Securities and Exchange Commission investor bulletin interpreted the "Howey test" and other rulings. The SEC argued for a broad interpretation, noting that securities can take any form. Given the recent prevalence of ICOs, regulatory interpretation has become very important but remains complex. I also discussed the regulatory landscape of financial technologies after the 2008 global economic crisis. In the burgeoning "fintech moment" today, cryptocurrencies and blockchain technologies are being adopted as practical solutions (especially for disrupting the clearance and settlement industry) and used to "re-risk" markets in light of post-2008 regulatory reforms.

In this chapter I also detailed the concept of "smart property." The origins of smart property are to be found in Nick Szabo's work from the late 1990s, which is implicitly based on libertarian and right-wing thinking. Hernando de Soto, in particular, was later responsible for setting up a pilot project using blockchain technologies to issue property titles in the Republic of Georgia. Szabo also invented the idea of smart contracts, which were based on his particular—and peculiar—theory of property. I discussed how smart contracts potentially change the enforcement of contracts, from reactive to proactive, which might cause issues. One way around some of these issues is to use "dual integration" smart contracts that are both "smart" and traditional. Another way is to create richer negotiations using smart contracts that negotiate using Schelling or focal points, as commonly discussed in the emerging field of cryptoeconomics.

CHAPTER SEVEN

Internet of Things, Logistics, and Smart Manufacturing

Cryptocurrencies and blockchain technologies are increasingly part of the world and yet we do not see them. They are not in products that end up in consumers' homes and are unlikely to be anytime soon because of high power and performance requirements. Rather, ubiquitous devices and small industrial sensors are the invisible endpoints that feed data into logistical networks powered by blockchains.

This blockchain vanishing act is already well under way. In recent years, many blockchain technologies transformed from high-profile proofs of concept into infrastructural products and services. This transformation has been especially rapid in logistics and manufacturing, which has strong market demand for blockchain solutions. The future for blockchain technologies likely involves one that unifies the entire supply chain through sensor networks and Internet of Things (IoT) devices. These devices will be capable of communicating with control and management platforms interlinked with blockchain technologies. Companies developing these new solutions imagine a set of blockchain technologies that tie consumer endpoints to household management hubs to supply chain systems to smart manufacturing, and thereby unite everything from everywhere.

The story of infrastructural blockchain technologies starts with logistics. Logistics is the field of research, development, and operation concerned with the transformation and circulation of things, particularly in the form of supply chains. Logistics has become an influential but largely hidden actor in modern society and is responsible for key activities that are commonly taken for granted—from the production and delivery of food to gasoline at the pump. In recent years, IoT devices in shipping containers and transport vehicles have become an important part of robust supply chain systems. This has resulted in more efficient transport mechanisms, detailed material and product tracking, and supply and demand analytics. Today, most of these systems make use of networked and Internet-connected sensors, embedded micro-controllers, robotic actuators, and cloud computing. Now that proofs of concepts have started to become productized, over the next few years these systems will increasingly be connected through blockchain technologies on the back end. This chapter discusses the intersections between these technologies and explains how and why blockchain technologies have been taken up with such vigor in these powerful yet invisible ways.

As I have stressed throughout this book, it is largely the *social* and not technological dimensions of blockchain technologies that are so important. For the logistics ecosystem, the social aspects drive business value. Companies use blockchain technologies to work with partners and to exchange information in granular ways. Blockchain technologies are also able to shore up existing conservative models of trust and risk because they provide secure and immutable platforms. Rather than disrupting the industry by opening up new vistas of business, the business case for blockchain technologies for logistics is actually quite modest and simple, yet influential.

The blockchain technologies being deployed for logistics today are conservative in design. Most blockchain platforms in development are simple permissioned blockchains that are built for robustness and security and do not add fancy new features. In many cases, these blockchain systems look a lot like existing database-driven systems. However, as I learned from speaking with IBM about their proofs of concept (they are currently the leaders in this space), organizations are often encouraged by blockchain technologies precisely because they are made up of traditional technologies, with known and tested capabilities. In many cases, it is the simple efficiencies of blockchain technologies that are driving business decisions in the logistics industry. This includes motivation for digitization and the use of open-source software. Blockchain technologies are not directly responsible for the digitization of existing systems, but they are a powerful motivator to update old-fashioned systems. Open-source software, on the other hand, is typical in many industrial contexts, but somewhat rare in logistics (rather famously, companies like SAP sell closed-source products for prodigious profits). But, experts tell me, the simple fact that blockchain technologies are being developed using open-source methodologies is reason for excitement. The barrier to adoption is lowered because open-source software is less likely to silo information and avoids the risks of buying into a single technology provider. In many cases, blockchain technologies function as efficient middleware—*boring middleware*, yes. Nonetheless, this is an important role, since the digital interconnector between parties is the path through which information flows in an organization.

Logistics has always been a technology and information industry. Over the last few decades, logistics technology solutions have improved transport efficiency, reduced manufacturing volumes and made them more accurate, enabled leaner stock holdings, improved operational risk management, and created financial flexibility. These are also important possible application areas for blockchain technologies. Perhaps the most significant change in logistics technology in recent years has been the widespread availability and low cost of sensors, many of which are now connected to the global Internet. When combined with IoT devices, these sensors enable the tracking and management of the physical environment of logistics—from manufacturing, warehousing, and transport, to consumer-goods servicing and monitoring market demand. Here, too, blockchain technologies are potentially useful. Blockchains can ensure sensor data is made available in a secure and auditable fashion to all approved parties. With smart contracts running on blockchain platforms, these data inputs could also be used to automate processes that might have otherwise required costly manual intervention.

Most of this technology still lies in the future. Therefore, some of this chapter is speculative and anticipatory, but small-scale proofs of concept have already demonstrated the technology's potential and the business opportunity. In writing this chapter, I spoke with numerous market players and heard predictable stories of hype and hope, but also, surprisingly, successful real-world tests bootstrapped from little more than a year of software development. These are encouraging results, even for the cynic. As these tests mature into full-scale products, in a decade's time it is hard to imagine a future where blockchain technologies have not significantly altered the logistics industry and in turn affected society. These changes have important, far-reaching effects that require critical attention.

This chapter introduces the history of information technologies for logistics; provides details of how emerging IoT and sensor networks and other "smart" devices work on blockchain platforms; anticipates the shift to blockchain technology solutions for "Industry 4.0" applications; and concludes with a critique of blockchain technologies that are part of emerging logistical media.

New logistical systems

In 2017, the focus of anti-G20 protests in Hamburg, Germany were directed at logistics. In their blockades and harbor actions—seeking to bring "hell" to the harbors—protestors realized an essential truth about global capital: that logistics are the "central discipline of the contemporary world" (Thrift 2008, p. 95). By some reckonings, logistics account for 9 percent of US gross domestic productivity (GDP) (Rogers &

Tibben-Lembke 2001), or possibly 10 to 15 percent of global GDP (Hesse & Rodrigue 2009). In the context of globalization and its critique, Hesse and Rodrigue note, "logistics includes the set of operations required for goods *to be made available* on markets or to specific destinations" (my emphasis, 2009, p. 277). That is, logistics encompasses more than just moving things—it also includes control and analysis of production, financing, location, and time. Ideally, logistics also interfaces with business partners, systems design, marketing, sales, and service. In this most advanced form, logistics is meant to be integrated across the supply (or value) chain. In theory, an integrated supply chain would include every part of the process from raw material to consumer reuse and repair.

The harbor activities that aimed to disrupt logistical movement in Hamburg were also a part of a new environment of risk (Yu & Goh 2014). According to Christopher and Holweg (2011), most supply chain management (SCM) techniques and theories that developed over the last thirty years were done in an era of stability that, by their analysis, is largely coming to an end (post-2008 shocks in critical variables are at volumes and speeds not seen since the 1973 oil crisis). Adapting to new logistical turbulence means moving beyond efficiency-squeezing optimizations (exemplified by huge economies of scale enabled by far offshore production, with single points of failure), and embracing risk and flexibility. Traditional models of resilience (excess stock for cushion against demand surges) and control (simple cost accounting such as discounted cash flow) may lead to amplification of risk in this new environment (Christopher & Holweg 2011). Multidimensional solutions, including flexible financing, end-to-end physical and information connectivity, and the establishment of markets for services are important components for avoiding logistics risk. To this end, Calatayud (2017) argues that emerging technologies such as IoT, blockchain technologies, advanced sensor systems, self-thinking/"smart" and autonomous supply chains may help mitigate risk.

Through 2017 several proofs of concept and small-scale trials of blockchain technologies for supply chains were completed and have begun to be productized. To see where blockchain technologies might fit within the breadth and history of information technology in logistics, consider Stenger's (1986) classic typology of logistics technology. According to Stenger, in logistics there are transaction systems, short-term scheduling and inventory replenishment systems, flow planning systems, and network planning and design systems. Transaction systems automate the flow of information for daily business, including customer orders, purchase orders, bills of lading, freight bills, and master databases. Short-term scheduling and inventory replenishment includes automatic scheduling of production and transport, vehicle routing, and picking lists in warehouses and distribution centers. Flow planning systems plan the flow of materials, including raw materials and supplies, and respond to demand and capacity changes. Network planning and design systems are used to develop optimal networks of supply sources, including modes and sizes of transportation vehicles and optimization of service levels. Given this typology, where might blockchain systems fit in? A likely role would be as *transactions systems*. For the technologist, this is good news, since this is a strategic position within business information systems. Transactions systems are, in fact, the key component of the logistics technology stack, necessary for day-to-day operations *and* the supply of data for other systems (Stenger 1986).

To date, the most successful transaction systems have utilized Electronic Data Interchange (EDI) standards. Although many of the components and standards of EDI predate widespread Internet connectivity, it is precisely because of global Internet access that EDI has become pervasive and powerful and is now a key driver of internal communication and inter-firm partnerships. Despite the success of EDI, however, many companies still suffer from problematic bullwhip effects (small fluctuations in demand or downstream changes that lead to large upstream fluctuations) due to lack of efficient and comprehensive information sharing (Ouyang 2007).

This information sharing deficient suggests a number of places for integration of blockchain technologies. Daniel Wilson of the shipping company Maersk told me that their interest in blockchain technology in large part stemmed from the perceived benefit of blockchains as *digital* information solutions (D. Wilson 2017). That is, for the shipping industry, simply moving beyond paper-based bills of lading (sometimes thousands of pages high), would be a significant cost and time saver. According to Wilson, blockchains might provide the shipping industry a trusted and decentralized solution to entice conservative organizations to upgrade their systems. In their collaborations with Maersk and others, IBM sees the use of blockchain technologies in the logistics industry in much the same way. Brigid McDermott of IBM described to me how, despite efforts to upgrade technologies over the decades, much of the logistics industry remains pre-digital or tied to outmoded EDI systems (McDermott 2017). McDermott believes that while EDI was successful in many regards (and it intended to solve many of the challenges of enterprise information sharing), the EDI messaging layer has become complex and outdated. Blockchain technologies might take the place of EDI messaging, as a transactions system. Nonetheless, it remains to be seen how blockchain technologies will integrate with existing EDI messaging systems since the systems and designs are not immediately compatible. Despite these impediments, blockchain technologies come at a good time for the industry, since organizations increasingly see the need for increased security, an inherent feature of blockchain technologies. Finally, the hype driving blockchain technologies may spur otherwise conservative organizations to make long-needed technology upgrades.

Optimists studying blockchain technologies believe this toolset may be able to address some of the top issues facing logistics technology today (English & Nezhadian 2017).

Two key issues are 1) the lack of access to appropriate and timely finance and 2) security and privacy (Calatayud 2017). Cryptocurrencies or peer-exchanged tokens could be used to create capital and credit markets among parties (in much the same way that banks use tokens for settlement and clearance; see Chapter 5). Blockchain technologies could also add much-needed security to networks and data. Specifically, blockchain technologies provide robust transaction verification and data non-repudiation, with network transparency and resilience.

Traditionally, most EDI messages pass through Enterprise Resource Planning (ERP) platforms, which facilitate multiple business goals in an integrated fashion. ERP platforms often integrate product and production planning, inventory management, finance, and many other aspects, sometimes in real or close to real time. Here, the likely integration point for prospective blockchain technologies is to facilitate transactions through ERP platforms, rather than replacing existing suites of technology, many of which are sold by large, entrenched incumbents, including Oracle and SAP.

We might also consider the ways that blockchain technologies would alter relationships between people and their labor in the supply chain. Michael J. Casey and Pindar Wong (2017) argue for workplace surveillance systems tied to blockchain identities to create complex permissions-based management of workforces. They cite the example of workers in a beef slaughterhouse who perform sterilization and disinfection activities that are then logged in a blockchain platform. Of course, workplace surveillance is nothing new for workers (especially the low-waged), and traditionally this kind of surveillance only requires a database and logging interface. However, one might argue, rather optimistically, that blockchain-based surveillance could permit greater *global* transparency. For example, efforts to hide malfeasance or frustrate scrutiny by outside regulators (who often act in the interest of fair labor) would be thwarted, since logged data on a blockchain are immutable, even by managers running the system itself. Rather obviously, an immutable, total workplace surveillance system has numerous possible benefits and risks and introduces ethical issues (much like the debate about police "body cams").

Many believe that the future of supply chains will be the integration of blockchains and IoT for logistics systems. In particular, these systems offer the possibility for cyber-physical representations, which makes possible advanced applications in logistics, such as "Industry 4.0" initiatives and reverse logistics. There is a considerable business opportunity here too: a double-digit percentage of the logistics industry is responsible for the flow of goods *back to suppliers* for returns, repair, servicing, and recycling. Indeed, when multiple IoT platforms are able to communicate with one another through a blockchain, for example, in "smart cities" or "smart factories," there is a potential multiplier effect. The hope (and hype) within the industry is that when inexpensive and ubiquitous IoT is combined with blockchains the complete supply chain will be decentralized, immutable, secure, and verifiable.

Logistics and IoT

To better understand how logistics, IoT, and blockchain all work together, let's consider two high-profile proofs of concept of blockchain logistics: IBM's 2016–17 tests using the Fabric blockchain technology running custom logistics software. In one proof of concept, IBM partnered with the shipping company Maersk to transport a container of perishable flowers from Kenya to Holland (later, experiments with pineapples from Columbia and oranges from California). In another proof of concept, IBM partnered with Walmart to track and monitor perishable foodstuffs (pork) through the supply chain in China (and in a later experiment, from Latin America to the United States). In both cases, the proofs of concept were considered "shadow" processes: complex and real-world experiments, but ultimately surrogate to the existing processes already in place. Another limitation of the test, relevant here, was that while environmental sensors to monitor the cold chain were considered critical components for product quality and safety, they were not part of the proofs of concept. According to Ramesh Gopinath of IBM, additional features and integrations will occur later, when the system is expanded and fully productized (from 2018 onwards). Likely, this will include integration of IoT and sensor devices (storing environmental sensor data on the blockchain is an obvious opportunity), as well as other value-added features.

Both proofs of concept start with perishable goods being loaded into refrigerated containers (known as "reefers"). Integrated or attached sensors in the container monitor physical conditions. Typical data are temperature, humidity, geographical location, shock, and anti-theft measures. Using ruggedized tablet devices, transport workers manually inputted the containers into the system, which were then automatically added to the IBM Fabric blockchain and made available for monitoring and analysis. In future versions, sensor data would be captured and all data would be inputted automatically through wireless transmission.

Once the container is registered with the system, data are onboarded to the blockchain. On a typical (public) blockchain, data would be sent to a node, collected into blocks, and then distributed and validated across the peer-to-peer network to achieve blockchain consensus (see Chapter 4). In the case of the two proofs of concept, however, IBM's Fabric blockchain uses a highly permissioned blockchain architecture with its own validation mechanisms. Rather than sending data to public validator nodes (typically, the "mining" process), IBM's Fabric uses private nodes. This process, as used for the proofs of concept, begins with data sent to an "endorsing peer." Then, an "ordering" or block-making service collects and organizes the endorsed data, which is followed by a validation of policies (ensuring compliance with a set of stipulated rules associated with the particular item). Finally, with data endorsed, ordered into blocks, and validated against stipulated policies, data are permanently committed to the ledger, where it remains unalterable.

While there remains considerable debate about whether an open, permissioned, or private architecture is best in general, for the logistics industry—like most enterprise applications—the private or permissioned model is the most common. In fact, an open architecture is probably both redundant and risky. Since logistics and shipping partners are already known entities that are bound through legal and fiduciary ties, there is little need to guard against a network-scale attack. Most of the advantages of an open architecture, such as solving the "double spending" problem for cryptocurrencies, are of little business value in enterprise settings (see Chapters 3 and 4). Rather, most enterprises are interested in blockchain technologies as a technical solution to provide one version of the truth—a distributed model of trust and data assurance.

When a container passes from one transport party to another it passes through a critical stage. During this hand-off, the container becomes the responsibility of the receiving party, which has a set of contracted rights and duties. The contracts that bind each party might stipulate service-level agreements, various prohibitions and penalties, as well as incentives and of course the terms of payment for services rendered. Conceivably, blockchains using input from IoT devices could automate much of this contractual process. Through self-executing "smart contracts" that satisfy programmed rules, the blockchain might automate or even take the place of written contracts and other implicit agreements (however, this contractual automaticity is mired in social and institutional challenges; see Chapters 6 and 8). As these automation technologies mature, perhaps, the supply chain could even become "self-thinking" or autonomous (Calatayud 2017).

The idea that a company could immediately, programmatically, and securely track a container in the supply chain is an exciting proposition for the logistics industry. For one, should an issue in the supply chain arise, the time-stamped, immutable sensor data could be retrospectively audited to see who, what, when, and where in the supply chain the issue arose. Or, one better: even before the container arrived at its terminus, the receiver could access real-time information about the location, status, and environmental parameters within the container. With real-time data feeds, reports would be immediate, enabling anticipatory business decisions and mid-chain changes. When connected to smart contracts, programmatic responses might also autonomously take action, such as triggering other transport activities or sending invoices. This process could also offer greater data assurance and in turn make records management and business operations more efficient and robust.

Blockchain technologies also help solve the digitization issue. The traditional supply chain generates considerable paperwork and requires extensive hand-off and communication. In their research on typical supply chains, IBM and Maersk found that the paperwork accompanying a container might pass between 30 people and organizations and require over 200 interactions. Digitizing these communications and data processing steps creates a more efficient process (and is therefore a major motivator for the industry, as mentioned above).

Blockchain technologies might also allow organizations that have been traditionally external to the supply chain to make quicker and better decisions about supply chain activities. For instance, being able to inspect a tamper-proof record of transport conditions (including whether a container has been opened, or where it originated from), would let customs and border agents more quickly and accurately assess whether the container requires further inspection. Blockchain data thus might work in conjunction with existing border risk modelling analysis with the goal of increasing border safety and the overall speed of transport, which in turn lowers cost. The same verification of origins and transport conditions might also benefit the consumer. For instance, giving consumers access to the logistics blockchain would allow for more informed shopping decisions. Being able to verify that lettuce in a grocery store is in fact organic or that the coffee beans were fairly traded is something that has always required consumers to trust self-regulating inspection organizations. The ability to verify data at the consumer level (as the blockchain startup Provenance is exploring), is a step well beyond traditional labelling assurances, which have sometimes been accused of lacking transparency and doing little to engage the consumer. As consumer concerns about origins and trade practices continue to rise, access to a product's supply chain data might become an important product differentiator and therefore a business opportunity.

Because most blockchains are also a store of value, the underlying tokens might open up new opportunities for supply chain finance. Supply chain finance is the process of optimizing cash flow through integration with invoicing and payments for suppliers and receivers and the offering of credit that frees capital otherwise tied up for funding transport and logistics activities. Supply chain finance also—ideally—links buyer, seller, and financing institution in one efficient market. Because most blockchain technologies are dual-use in that they have tokens pegged to tradable cryptocurrencies, there are a number of opportunities for supply chain finance. For example, blockchains could be used to create and enhance markets for logistical activities, offer credit, incentivize payments, free up cash flow, improve payment and invoicing, and generally reduce financial risk.

Supply chain finance has become an increasingly important aspect of logistics as offshoring has led to extended transport times and as production partners have become more varied in their geography and economic context. These geopolitical changes have also impacted regulation and the availability of capital markets, further prompting the demand for available supply chain finance. Indeed, Peter Drucker noted this convergence of logistics and finance nearly 20 years ago: arguing that the "systems approach embeds the physical process of making things, that is, manufacturing, in the economic process of business" (Drucker 1990).

Cryptocurrencies and blockchain technologies offer an interesting approach to solving the needs of supply chain financing. For one thing, blockchains are able to create more seamless connections between operational systems and accounting. With smart contracts, invoicing and payment processing could be automated and by escrowing funds held in a smart contract, counterparty risk would be lowered (ensuring payment occurs even when companies default or lack liquidity). Additionally, credit markets could be set up using cryptocurrencies rather than fiat currencies, freeing traditional capital from this burden. Other kinds of marketplaces are possible as well, such as those that directly sell services between businesses, which might be negotiated automatically through smart contracts, on behalf of companies interested in finding the best price or supplier.

Blockchain logistics are not limited to the transport phase of logistics. As products themselves become "smarter"—endpoints and peers in the IoT—interaction with the whole supply chain will become increasingly important and complex, necessitating next-generation management technologies. For example, an IoT device might be remotely serviceable (through secure firmware updates), pseudonymously monitored for performance, or tracked back to its manufacturer (reverse logistics). For very high-value goods (such as aircraft parts), IoT capabilities might enable more efficient servicing and repair (and individual audit trails in the event of malfunction). In some cases, products might become a form of "smart property" (see Chapter 6), which conceivably also interface with large IoT and sensor networks in a "smart city." Of course, behind this vision are myriad social, ethical, and political issues (labor, privacy, and regulation, to start). Nonetheless, blockchain evangelists see the possibility for leaner and "just-in-time" supply chains, which include advanced security and safety capabilities.

The blockchain's decentralized model of information flow might also be effective for logistics and supply chains. Based on empirical analysis of manufacturing companies, Frohlich and Westbrook (2001) found that those organizations with the widest "arc of integration" will achieve the highest performance. A wide arc of integration occurs when the supplier, manufacturer, and customers are joined by a system that combines planning, control, and information exchange. Companies with a narrow arc of integration (inward-looking entities) have the lowest performance. Moreover, if an organization focuses solely on one side of the supply chain (either the supplier or customer side), there are few integration performance advantages (Frohlich & Westbrook 2001, p. 195). Their analysis suggests that a weak link in the chain can undo many of the performance gains of system integration. Thus, decentralized blockchain solutions that are tightly coupled to existing systems (such as EDI and ERP) may achieve a wide arc of integration, tying together the entire supply chain. This might lead to improved business performance (see also Mattila, Seppälä, & Holmström 2016).

Industry 4.0

The buzzy, emerging idea of an "Industry 4.0" (in the original German, "Industrie 4.0") is predicated on the existence of widespread IoT and "smart factories." In recent decades, advanced manufacturing has become highly computerized (e.g., CAD/CAM, shop-floor robotic arms), but these systems tend to be preprogrammed, repetitive labor-savers. The goal of Industry 4.0 is to add "smarts" to every device and to interconnect previously disparate systems (Hermann, Pentek, & Otto 2016). When equipped with sensors and IoT capabilities, smart factories become context aware and capable of making algorithmic decisions. A secure, decentralized, and tamper-proof blockchain might therefore lend itself to applications in Industry 4.0 (Hofmann & Rüsch 2017).

Hermann, Pentek, and Otto (2016) identify four design principles for Industry 4.0: information and physical interconnection, information transparency, decentralized decision-making, and human–computer technical assistance. Similarly, Hofmann and Rüsch (2017) characterize Industry 4.0 as composed of "autonomous, knowledge- and sensor-based, self-regulating production systems." In both cases, as machines and devices become more interconnected, more decentralized, and more aware of their cyber-physical environment, they increasingly interact with complex human decision-making and their environment. The goal is a more flexible manufacturing process that is better able to respond to changes in supply chain and market conditions.

In an Industry 4.0 manufacturing future (should such a reality ever emerge), market dynamics and production are more tightly coupled than ever before. By tying market supply and demand more closely to the mode of production, in theory integrating vendor-managed inventory (Hofmann & Rüsch 2017), manufacturing lead times and excess volumes would be lower (this is called just-in-time, Kanban, or lean manufacturing). At the extreme, production systems could be linked to point-of-sale terminals for more accurate and near-instant market demand responses. Through cyber-physical representations of the supply chain, alongside automated modelling and analysis tools, Industry 4.0 might reduce bullwhip effects.

"Smart" manufacturing environments respond to supply-and-demand issues and enable product customization and rapid revision. Since manufacturing must rely on suppliers and distributors, rapid and "smart" production responses would need to rely on extensive collaboration and partnership, third-party logistics, and possibly "Internet of services" marketplaces (Christidis & Devetsikiotis 2016; Mentzer, Min, & Zacharia 2000). Networking manufacturing, supply, and consumer markets requires a connected supply chain. Indeed, this comprehensive production, supply, and value chain would need to account for materials well before they entered the manufacturing shop floor and would extend management and analysis beyond the point of sale. Blockchains, especially when paired with smart contracts, might provide a suitable platform for integration across these industries. Blockchain technologies might offer a smart factory greater security, decentralized decision-making through peer-to-peer system interconnectivity, and clear audit trails that can be shared with supply chain members.

In the same way that blockchain technologies help to create trust in supply chains, blockchains for smart manufacturing might also create trust. Having trusted data and verifiable processes is especially important for highly regulated environments, such as the pharmaceutical industry. For example, knowing the origin, production method, and supply chain—all stored in tamper-proof blockchains—would help regulators ensure safe end products (Apte & Petrovsky 2016). Of course, it is simpler to state a goal than to realize it. Having a manufacturing environment capable of building broad trust that is also secure and smart enough to track its many inputs and outputs remains a significant social and technical challenge. Blockchain technologies might offer one approach to reaching this goal.

Logistical media

The logistics landscape I introduced above is largely speculative and anticipatory and oriented towards creating business value in logistics and supply chain industries. Other characterizations of the industry and its adoption of technology, however, are possible. In Chapter 4, I discussed how blockchains can be seen as an information and communication medium. The adoption of blockchain technologies for logistics, by extension, can be seen as a tacit consequence of "logistical media." The remainder of this chapter is a reflection on logistical media and the modalities of blockchain technologies—the ways mediation, disintermediation, and social impact occur.

The modern version of logistics stems from its roots in the military. In the 1940s, during and after World War II, logistics was critical to solving problems of inventory and distribution—feeding, housing, and equipping war efforts, and supplying postwar building booms. By the 1960s, logistics was the proving ground for new forms of technical analysis, such as flow charts, lifecycle analysis, network analysis, and new forms of scheduling labor and the movement of goods (Thrift 2005, p. 219). New forms of advanced technical analysis often made use of computers supplied by the military and were put to work by military-associated organizations such as RAND (nicknamed by the Soviets "the academy of science and death and destruction"). Since these early days, logistics has become privatized and commercialized, but it remains tied to computing, analysis, and information communication. Most recently, logistics has become an integral element of production itself (Thrift 2005, p. 219), reaching its zenith with efforts such as Industry 4.0, which are predicated on very tight coupling of production and logistical flow.

Contemporary supply chains have become so well integrated that they are commonly modelled in cybernetic terms as feedback loops, or in computer terms as networks—both also military inventions of the twentieth century (DeLanda 1991, p. 107). The idea that a supply chain operates like a feedback loop is by now quite traditional, often adopted as an uncritical assumption in trade literature and introductory textbooks. As a feedback loop, the supply chain provides the circulatory mechanism that connects the supplier, market, consumer, and so forth—a never-ending chain. The chain does not end, however, until disaster strikes. For example, the September 11, 2001, terrorist attacks in the US caused widespread stoppages and critical issues for the entire logistics industry, requiring human intervention and creative solutions to keep goods moving (D. M. Russell & Saldanha 2003). The obvious problem with a single looping chain is that disruptions and slow-downs do occur, and with some frequency. More robust supply chains resemble networks rather than feedback loops. Decentralized networks, however, require sufficient "local intelligence" or autonomy for items to be routed appropriately (DeLanda 1991, p. 107). This is why, through competition and coordination, a *supply network* is significantly more resilient than a chain. The decentralized and autonomous nature of blockchain technologies have obvious applications here, and, as such, can trace their lineage to these distant cybernetic and computing origins.

Contemporary logistics networks are media, and therefore cause "media effects." John Durham Peters (2015) first developed the term "logistical media" to describe this phenomenon, which he believes is an omnipresent feature of contemporary life, even beyond the formal logistics industry. According to Peters, logistical media function as the zero point upon which everything is built, including technical artifacts but also natural objects and social properties. Ned Rossiter (2016) develops Peters's concept by focusing specifically on the logistics industry and its technologies. As such, Rossiter argues that logistics is a form of software infrastructure. This software infrastructure—what Deborah Cowen (2014) calls "soft infrastructure"—mediates the flow of goods. Foremost among these technologies are locative media used in the logistics industry. For Rossiter, these "software-driven systems generate protocols and standards that shape social, economic, and cross-institutional relationships" (2016, p. 4) and to the extent that they are invisible, secret, or otherwise obfuscated, they are cause for concern.

The social shaping of logistical media is in large part due to the ways that they calibrate and control space and time. Traditionally, we think about logistics in terms of space, and the geographies that are intersected. Cargo airplanes transport pineapples from Hawaii, ships transport iPhones from

Shenzhen, and now—using IBM's Fabric blockchain—Walmart tracks the intermodal movement of pork across China. However, through these logistical media, time also changes. Sometimes time is shortened (Amazon Prime offers *same day* shipping in many US cities), but just as often, time is lengthened. There are many reasons to strategically delay or extend transportation time: a cheaper mode of transportation is available, stock levelling across distribution centers is required, or customer orders can be strategically bundled using this delay. These movements lend themselves to the belief that we live on an ever-shrinking planet, what in previous eras was thought to be a "global village" (McLuhan 2011). This "annihilation" of time and space, however, is largely a fiction (DuPont & Takhteyev 2016). Instead, what these logistical media have produced is a *different* geography. To adopt Nigel Thrift's characterization, with logistical media the world becomes a "geography of calculation" (Thrift 2005, p. 219).

Consider the ways that Walmart—a pioneer in the field—has strategically used logistical media to its business advantage, sometimes to the detriment of its partners, competitors, consumers, and labor force. Walmart was among the first companies to develop a comprehensive supply chain and is still one of the best at it. Rather than develop a top-down, micromanaged supply chain like those of Ford Motor Company (famous for sourcing raw pig iron on one end of the factory floor and producing finished vehicles on the other end), Walmart created a heterogeneous model. This version of logistical media permits a great deal of local variation, and is therefore highly flexible, decentralized, and organic (Tsing 2009).

Walmart also pioneered the use of universal product codes (UPCs), leveraging the processes of governance and standardization to their explicit benefit. Rather famously, Walmart requires all suppliers to use UPCs if they want the "option" of participating in Walmart's huge market presence. By setting the rules of engagement, Walmart is able to accommodate a large and diverse supply chain, with internal freedom for its suppliers. The benefit of a diverse supply chain is that complexity is difficult to control entirely, so supplier relationships can be strategically structured: requiring UPCs but having no explicit requirement about "externalities" such as local wages. This is made possible by granular control of a complex supply chain.

Governance and control by large companies like Walmart are managed by ERP software. This software is extremely flexible, unlike the Fordist and Taylorist modes of control developed in the twentieth century. According to Rossiter (2016, p. 128), ERP software is also a key tool in the financialization of daily life. As cryptocurrencies and blockchain technologies further integrate into ERP platforms, geographies and cultures are financialized, producing a form of neoliberalism that shifts power to private organizations.

Nowhere in logistics is the trend towards neoliberal governmentality clearer than with supply chain security, which will be significantly enhanced and sped up as blockchain technologies are adopted. Today, supply chain security is a heavily privatized domain that operates with minimal regulation or self-regulation. It is common for companies to set the terms of their own security compliance, and to be measured against economic criteria. Even most state border controls have adopted a neoliberal compliance structure, evaluating risk through an economic lens (high-volume shippers are subject to less scrutiny). Proponents of light regulation and market-based solutions, of course, see this as a fair and efficient solution—preferring (as Michel Foucault pointed out long ago) markets over violence and ideology. Deborah Cowen argues that the privatized supply chain industry shifted from sovereign (state) power to disciplinary power to today: biopolitical power focusing on the "circulation" rather than localization of power (Cowen 2014, p. 192). This shift traces Walmart's growing embrace of complex supply chains, which favors self-censorship, self-exploitation, and docility through technological apparatuses. As blockchain technologies become entrenched within these logics, old-fashioned linear and looping supply chain architectures may become replaced by a new form of protocological power (Galloway 2004). In logistics, protocological power (in which institutions are networked information infrastructures) may utilize the decentralized architecture of blockchain technologies to redraw the neoliberal subject, through her labor, her consumption, and her patterns of daily life.

Summary

This chapter introduced the possibility that blockchain technologies may become a new infrastructural layer for logistics. I argued that cheap and ubiquitous IoT for logistics systems can be managed by blockchain technologies. Traditionally, technologies such as Electronic Data Interchange (EDI) and Enterprise Resource Management (ERP) systems are used to efficiently move goods across the globe. Drawing on the two proofs of concept of blockchain technologies by IBM and its partners Maersk and Walmart, I considered the ways that the added security (tamper-proof ledgers and audit trails) and architectural decentralization resulting from blockchains might benefit the industry. Additionally, cryptocurrencies can be used to create interesting new kinds of markets, especially for the increasingly important industry of supply chain financing. I also considered the ways that when a supply chain is fully integrated—across supplier, manufacturer, and retailer—a new model for manufacturing is possible. This advanced form of manufacturing is called "Industry 4.0" and is anticipated to make use of blockchains, especially for automated smart contract capabilities.

I concluded this chapter with a critique of blockchain technologies' impact on society, as a type of "logistical media." I argued that logistical media change the topology of geographical and temporal realities. Returning to the example of Walmart, a pioneer in the field of logistics, I critiqued Walmart's supply chain flexibility. By using logistical technologies such as blockchains to capture messy local conditions within a flexible supra- or global system, Walmart is able to create neoliberal forms of private power. Neoliberal power is also present in the ways that the logistics industry handles security, which is modeled on economic terms that create biopolitical subjects controlled by protocol.

CHAPTER EIGHT

The Promise of New Organizations

Cryptocurrencies and blockchains offer the promise of a new kind of organization. We have already seen the building blocks: high-velocity financial flows and new ways of raising capital (Chapter 5); self-executing smart contracts and "cryptoeconomic" markets (Chapter 6); and deep integration of blockchain infrastructure into smart products, smart supply chains, and advanced manufacturing (Chapter 7). According to many, blockchain technologies promise not just new ways of doing business—they promise to overhaul how decisions are made, activities are coordinated, and relationships are formed. The grand idea that is supposed to realize this promise is called a Decentralized Autonomous Organization, or DAO.

Decentralized autonomous organizations are blockchain and smart contract systems for human and machine coordination and decision-making. DAOs rely on blockchain technologies to execute code and record transactions and use smart contracts to tie together people, information sources, and algorithmic agents. Since blockchains are decentralized and persistent, DAOs are too. Smart contracts work autonomously by making decisions based on inputs and programmed responses (see Chapter 6), and DAOs take action through the output of smart contracts. In many cases, DAOs control and manage participants (rather than the other way around) through economic incentives and prohibitions. DAOs, it is believed, are a radical new mechanism for organizational behavior and social interaction, capable of doing away with the messiness of human relationships, legal contracts, and leaky information flows. Moreover, as governments increasingly function like businesses, they too service their constituents with smart contracts, new voting mechanisms, and strong identity services and authentication. DAOs are, in important ways, the culmination of everything I have discussed in this book, which is why they are one of the most difficult and exciting areas of cryptocurrencies and blockchains today.

The designers of DAOs have focused on an important aspect of modern organizations: contracts, which are both the glue that binds relationships and a useful conduit to consumers. Smart contracts, however, are thought to operate without any need for social trust among parties. Instead of trust, contracting parties delegate their personal authority to the smart contract system, which operates algorithmically. The result is that DAOs operate, in important ways, through algorithmic authority, which I introduced in Chapter 6. However, DAOs are complex, network-scale systems that service inter-relationships between people and are ultimately governed by people who participate in, fund, and develop the system. This assemblage of human and algorithmic authority is new and therefore there are few guides or existing examples for how to govern these systems. As such, governance *of* algorithmic authority and governance *by* algorithmic authority is, as with the theme of this book, a grand experiment. DAOs are fundamentally complex because they are social tools acting through algorithmic means.

The most famous real-world example of a DAO was "The DAO." With its unfortunate name, "The DAO" was a DAO platform that would spawn further child DAOs and invest in proposed projects and startups. In essence, The DAO was part investment fund and part infrastructure to support DAOs. To participate in The DAO, organizations would submit proposals that would be voted on by the community of investors and developers through direct token funding mechanisms. The DAO was a test of society's ability to manage these new organizations. As I describe below, we failed this test, and spectacularly.

The most exciting part of The DAO was its audacity and willingness to experiment with hallowed social and political mechanisms. With The DAO, we really went for it: new kinds of voting, new kinds of capital, new kinds of human–computer interface, and new kinds of business. During its brief existence in 2016, I went for it too. I experimented with a radical idea that, had it been successful, would have upended our inherited beliefs about human–computer relationships and the limits of socio-technical responsibility. The DAO was, in retrospect, perfectly representative of the liveliness of young technologies and the community's heady ideals.

This chapter introduces the idea of Decentralized Autonomous Organizations, frames their operation in the context of trust and relationships, and then details a case study for evaluation. I discuss the origins of DAOs, which predate the Ethereum platform but find their clearest expression there. I discuss how contracts are a traditional and key technology for developing trust, which the advent of smart contracts running autonomously on blockchain platforms seeks to displace. I offer a brief analysis of The DAO, describe my attempt to create an extreme version of a charity organization running on it, and introduce some of the ways that DAOs make governance difficult. I conclude with a discussion about how the governance of DAOs is at the cutting edge of research on blockchain technologies.

Collective action and decision-making

Like many aspects of blockchain technologies, decentralized autonomous organizations try to solve collective action and decision-making problems. Many of the proposed solutions originated from thinking about peer production and crowdsourcing, collective intelligence, and voting. Often, however, these new and disruptive "discoveries" are little more than re-inventions. Consequently, DAOs are now also re-discovering the complexities and pitfalls associated with attempts to change society, sometimes without fully appreciating how these issues were tackled in the past.

DAOs combine financial investment, decision-making, and production. This amalgam of social mechanisms is closely related to cryptoeconomics and the ideology of efficient markets (see also Chapter 6). For DAOs, decision-making is roughly equivalent to financial investment; voting is "staking" or funding; and production is economically incentivized. Ideally, since money and markets saturate DAOs, this activity is dynamic and collective, which in turn makes the configuration of market participation quite different from traditional investment contexts where participants are comparatively passive. An apt comparison can be made to "activist investors" who, in traditional settings, are (troublesome) investors using their large holdings in a company to sway decision-making. For DAOs, practically everyone is an activist, at least to the extent that correlates with token investment (there are, as I discuss below, many ways to fine-tune how investment stake correlates to authority and control). DAOs have discovered that active engagement in social, political, and commercial institutions is an ideal of democracy but also sometimes its curse.

There is a long history of decentralized organizations (e.g., Roman Catholic Church) and autonomous organizations (e.g., blind trusts), but the conjunction—decentralized autonomous organizations—appears to be wholly original to cryptocurrencies and blockchain technologies. Writing in the context of Bitcoin and nascent cryptoeconomics, in 2013 Daniel Larimer and Vitalik Buterin each began articulating their vision for DAOs. Larimer soon explored some of his ideas for DAOs through his decentralized cryptocurrency exchange, BitShares. With BitShares, Larimer developed an alternative consensus model (called Delegated Proof of Stake), prediction markets for intelligent decision-making, and robust incentive mechanisms. A year later, Buterin created Ethereum, his ambitious platform for distributed computing. Even before its formal launch, Buterin saw the possibility of DAOs as a crowning achievement for Ethereum (2013b). For Buterin, DAOs were a step towards replacing the messy and acrimonious realities of business and democracy with a computational platform capable of incentivizing good behaviors and making intelligent decisions.

A DAO is any organization that is capable of running autonomously and has a decentralized (or really, distributed) organizational structure. Being decentralized and autonomous, DAOs are designed to be institutionally resilient but also flexible, so they are equally suitable for small clubs, projects with specific goals, and large corporations. Decentralized Autonomous Corporations (DACs) are DAOs with an explicitly commercial goal. Most DAOs and DACs are, in practice, an assemblage of Decentralized Applications (Dapps) that implement programmed management decisions (aka "business logic") and are governed through collective action. Dapps are software code—principally smart contracts—that either run on blockchain infrastructure or interface with it. Dapps often replace management activities, largely leaving human decision-making to questions of governance.

Governance is *the* buzzword in blockchains today, and experiments with DAOs are at the cutting edge of this discussion (see also Davidson, De Filippi, & Potts 2016; Levy 2017). However, governance is notoriously difficult to define, let alone operationalize. A definition for governance might be: stewardship, a mechanism that sets institutional rules and incentives, or the strategic exercise of power. Governance, therefore, takes many forms. Political structures have particular forms of governance, such as, for example, the US federal republic with its division of powers and shared sovereignty with states. Corporate governance is similar to political governance but is responsible for a corporation's financial success. Corporate governance might be accomplished with

sets of rules or policies, a board of directors that wields ultimate authority, or a union of workers who collectively make
decisions. Other kinds of governance are possible too, such as
nonprofit governance, environmental governance, and global
governance.

Typically, governance is distinct from the practices of management, which is responsible for the execution of rules set
by governance mechanisms. However, DAOs complicate
the division between management and governance because
robust decision-making can be programmed into DAOs. For
example, routine business decisions can be automatically executed by an algorithm reading a data feed just as easily as the
algorithm decides to terminate operation. Since autonomy is
inversely correlate to governance, if *all* management and governance decisions were programmed into a DAO (a practical
impossibility) it would become truly autonomous.

The most important steps in designing a DAO are to determine how it will be governed and what processes will be
implemented "on-chain" or "off-chain." On-chain governance
is a set of mechanisms for change that has been programmed
into the blockchain. Voting through a blockchain Dapp would
be an example of an on-chain governance technique. On-chain
governance tends to be more conservative and limited because
it works within the existing governance model. Off-chain
governance is any technique for change that occurs external
to the blockchain. In some cases, off-chain governance is
revolutionary—e.g., the decision to fork a blockchain system—
but in other cases off-chain governance is simply how the
system was designed to work. Indeed, while it will continue to
be debated, there is no one right approach to DAO governance.
As I describe below, there are risks and opportunities for each.

While there is no one best model for governance, DAOs
usually have ideals dictated by the cultural norms of their
communities. In practice, this means DAOs are often
designed to be operated transparently. Blockchains offers
many opportunities for transparent systems, since even very

small decisions can be programmed into Dapps, which can be verified by both insiders and outsiders (such as regulators). In many cases, radically transparent operation is a real boon for organizations. For example, charities must traditionally rely a lot on trust—or brand recognition as a stand-in for trust. Were a charity to be run as a DAO, it could program its finances and organizational bylaws into a series of Dapps that could be independently verified. Donors would no longer need to trust that the charity is acting appropriately. Moreover, big questions about vision and organizational purpose could be decided through robust governance mechanisms, ensuring that the original purpose of the charity is not corrupted. The result—if it were to be perfected—would be a highly efficient organization that is stable and long-lasting. In 2016, I explored this idea with my own attempt at a DAO charity, which I discuss below.

DAOs are also capable of supporting collective action and decision-making at a tremendous range of scales—from the smallest company to nation states. Within corporations, for example, small-scale voting about daily business decisions or important corporate changes could be conducted on a DAO in a fair and transparent way. By putting corporate decision-making in the hands of many employees, corporations running as DAOs could support bottom-up decision-making—long a dream of many equitably minded organizations. At the largest scale, DAOs can be set up to support national democratic activities, including implementing difficult and time-consuming democratic mechanisms, such as direct, ranked-choice, and delegated voting.

Proofs of concept for blockchain-based state and municipal voting are already underway. In theory, blockchain voting is attractive because it offers a safer and more secure version of centralized e-voting. The benefit of e-voting is that it dispenses with the fuss of paper votes, but in doing so it also eliminates the paper trail that is necessary to verify votes and to investigate counting irregularities. In recent years, scandals about e-voting machines have become common, including accusations that the voting machine manufacturer Diebold surreptitiously altered voting machine software leading up to an election and the possibility of malfeasance by the foreign-owned voting machine company Smartmatic. Voting on a blockchain, however, solves many of these problems by combining the best of both worlds: efficient electronic records and a virtual paper trail in the form of an immutable ledger. Advanced voting capabilities, such as secret verifiable voting or interactive and weighted voting, are also possible with a blockchain. However, strong technical security for blockchain-based voting, let alone best practices for voting system governance, have yet to be truly tested. Until blockchain-based voting can solve the many real-world issues that persist, these experiments will remain at the fringe.

Voting is a core feature of DAOs. DAOs typically use cryptocurrency tokens to represent "votes," so the process of "voting" is, from a different perspective, investment and funding. Ideas are directly funded and since voters are investors, they are economically incentivized to make intelligent decisions. Many DAOs are in fact designed to be little more than decentralized crowdfunding systems, improving on Kickstarter and GoFundMe by cutting out the intermediary. Similarly, ICOs and blockchain startups (Chapter 5) are often financed this way, even if their operational design does not resemble a DAO.

DAOs also potentially improve on traditional voting schemes. Direct voting, where each person has one vote, is the simplest form. Another common form of voting is representative voting, where each person votes for a representative who, if elected, is authorized to make decisions on behalf of the voter. Direct and representative voting in digital environments, however, have many obstacles. For one, e-voting replaces the flesh-and-blood voter with a digital doppelgänger. This means that, because digital tokens are easily duplicated, it is possible for one person to vote many times, as though there are many digital pseudonyms. This is known as a Sybil attack (Sybil attacks also potentially affect cryptocurrencies by generating spam pseudonyms). Another challenge for direct voting is that it can become time-consuming and onerous, especially when decisions are very granular (this is one of the reasons why direct democracy is so rare). Because of the time commitment needed to vote, direct voting often suffers from lack of engagement. Representative voting solves the problem of lack of engagement, but trades ease of voting for lack of transparency and accountability (see Hardt & Lopes 2015). DAOs, however, are not limited to simple direct or representative voting schemes. DAOs can facilitate exotic forms of voting that can only practically be implemented in digital environments. One of the more popular forms of blockchain-based voting is delegated voting, as used in "liquid democracies." Delegated voting predates DAOs but has since become popular among blockchain enthusiasts given the ease of implementation on blockchain technologies and the promise of a high-tech solution to an old, thorny problem.

Delegated voting is a type of direct voting where voters can vote on every topic under consideration but also have the possibility to delegate or proxy votes to others instead. With delegated voting, individual authority is divided among many decision-makers, sometimes in complex ways that bisect and intersect over and over. Delegated voting can be contrasted with representative voting in that voters do not elect leaders to stand in for the authority of the voter. Delegated voting is also typically dynamic, in that voters can rescind delegations at any time. Delegates are voters themselves and have the same opportunity to vote directly or further delegate. When delegates delegate, the original vote transfers onwards (and is optionally weighted as it is subdivided upwards). Delegates, therefore, are similar to representatives (in representative voting), but have the possibility of further delegating. It is also believed, although not empirically demonstrated, that as delegates demonstrate their expertise or ability to make good decisions, they will become more trusted and valued and will therefore become important social hubs. In this way, delegated voting tends to favor meritocracies, which can also be enhanced with (economic) incentives for good decision-making. Because of all these complexities—votes that shift about, can be weighted, incentivized, and so forth—implementing delegated voting requires fairly sophisticated computing systems.

Blockchain technologies offer an ideal platform for delegated voting. The open and immutable distributed ledger with verifiable transactions lets voters monitor their delegations and voting performance. With transparent voting, voters can hold delegates accountable for their decisions (and dynamically change delegation if needed). The ability to conduct secret yet transparent votes (using David Chaum's Blind Signatures or pseudonyms in the same way as Bitcoin transactions) is a critical feature of blockchain-based delegated voting. This ensures transparency, and transparency is needed to maintain trust and accountability in the democratic system (Hardt & Lopes 2015).

The most exotic, and also most hyped, application of delegated voting is known as liquid democracy. According to one influential manifesto, liquid democracy is more than a voting system—it is a "distributed, scalable, question-answering algorithm" (*Liquid Democracy In Context, or, An Infrastructuralist Manifesto* n.d.). Insofar as this vision is true, liquid democracy is a significant reconfiguration of traditional social and political structures. Where traditional democracy is largely passive, liquid democracy is energized and active, and therefore capable of creating collective intelligence that far outperforms the "wisdom of crowds" (which typically degenerates into groupthink and mob rule). Implied in this socio-technical infrastructure, however, is also a particular kind of technocratic ideal where experts have authority to make decisions, are relatively aware of their epistemic limitations, and are assumed to be rational. In many cases, leveraging the collective intelligence of heterogeneous experts is optimal, but there is also a robust and now quite well-established field of research that questions the efficacy of experts (see, e.g., Kaplan, Skogstad, & Girshick 1950). Those racing to find new technological solutions often ignore these criticisms, only to find that the issues previously identified in the literature re-emerge.

Voting is a mechanism that produces collective intelligence, but betting, as it turns out, might be even more effective for making correct decisions, especially when the topic is speculative and not well bounded. Known as "prediction markets," these betting environments are simply markets where information is the traded commodity (economists will tell you that all free and open markets are, in reality, information markets). Empirical literature suggests that prediction markets are quite effective (Smith, Paton, & Williams 2006; Wolfers & Zitzewitz 2004). The key insights behind prediction markets are that unlike typical decision-making scenarios, markets reward seeking information, telling the truth, and aggregating diverse opinions. Markets are "efficient," advocates say, because prices capture information—the "price" of a given datum is the market's belief in the likelihood it will come true. Basically, money is a strong motivator for making smart choices.

Given how well prediction markets appear to work, economists have long advocated for their use, but regulators and lawmakers have resisted. Regulators worry that prediction markets amount to little more than betting, which is associated with social problems and is therefore usually controlled and taxed. Blockchain technologies, already at the fringe of regulatory compliance, often implement prediction markets to solve challenging decision-making problems.

Prediction markets and other techniques can also be used as a tamper-resistant mechanism to get off-chain information into DAOs. DAOs use secure, decentralized techniques known as "oracles" to query data, which is used as input for Dapps and smart contracts. Getting access to external information is tricky but important for DAOs because by design DAOs do not rely on trusted sources of information. DAO designers worry about trusted sources, such as NASDAQ stock price feeds, *New York Times* news headlines, and so on, because if the source can be manipulated, The DAO becomes vulnerable to attack. Unlike traditional organizations, The DAO has no way of determining trust or seeing when it has been cheated.

Trust and business

Trust is an important and prevalent social bond that underpins organizational behaviors and business interactions. Trust is also the battleground of cryptocurrencies and blockchains, since these systems purport to eliminate trust, or seek to replace interpersonal trust with various kinds of technical trust (Davidson et al. 2016; De Filippi & Hassan 2016; De Filippi & Wright 2018). The slogan "trust in numbers" is often used to describe how cryptocurrencies and blockchain technologies reconfigure trust. The belief is that the trust required for exchange between people or businesses can be wholly replaced by a simpler kind of technological or mathematical trust. According to the slogan, trust in the security of cryptographic protocols is all that is required for new organizations running on secure blockchain platforms. Ultimately, "trust in numbers" is not wrong—the cryptographic protocols *are* extremely robust—but the slogan mistakes the part for the whole.

Traditionally, exchange involves risk for the participating parties. These "counterparties" risk receiving goods that are of poor quality or counterfeit, or receiving no goods at all. Consider the typical exchange of money for goods: you want to trade an item with a person who has promised to pay upon receipt. The other person, the counterparty, may refuse to pay upon receipt or the payment may be counterfeit. Consider the same example when the length of distance, time, or number of parties increases, as often happens with transactions conducted on the Internet. As the distance increases the risk increases because the available options for redress decrease (due to transactional anonymity, legal jurisdictions, etc.). If there is a gap of time between payment and fulfillment, as is common with real business agreements, the risk that the counterparty is unable to fulfil the agreement increases further still.

Despite these counterparty risks, businesses are able to interact and exchange because relationships are mediated by trust. Trust is the glue that binds people together. Over time, entire social institutions have emerged to help reduce the need for trust and to improve risky relationships. Contracts are designed to clarify obligations, lower the need for trust, and mediate counterparty risk. Laws, courts, and police all play social roles to incentivize good behavior and execute redress when issues arise. Similarly, a profitable line of business has emerged to help mediate relationships with insufficient trust. These intermediaries are *mutually trusted third parties* that facilitate exchange. So long as each party can trust the mediator, there is no need for trust between the interacting parties. Mutually trusted third parties, such as PricewaterhouseCoopers or KPMG, have become enormously important in modern society and consequently have also become a staple of modern business, as needed to provide reliable, on-demand trust to mediate business relationships. But with the emergence of blockchain technologies, some commentators have suggested that these "trust" companies are potentially susceptible to disruption or even obsolescence ("The Trust Machine" 2015).

Blockchain technologies potentially challenge those in the trust business by mediating exchange with smart contracts running on blockchains that take the place of mutually trusted third parties and eliminate the need for trust between the parties. Since smart contracts automatically execute the terms of agreement when specified conditions are met there is little opportunity for malfeasance. Smart contracts running on blockchain technologies are "atomic" (all or nothing) and difficult to censor or defraud. Moreover, transactions occur relatively quickly, further reducing counterparty risk. Optimistically, the operations of smart contracts are so transparent that they "disintermediate" rather than mediate transactions. Given that the terms of contracts must be programmed into the smart contract, contractual obligations must also be made clear and unambiguous, thereby eliminating another potential source of risk. Finally, smart contracts can also run algorithmic operations, potentially enabling complex forms of exchange that would otherwise be highly risky.

Smart contracts, and DAOs more generally, practically eliminate counterparty risk, but counterparty risk is a comparatively tiny part of business. Moreover, mutually trusted third parties provide many additional services beyond facilitating contracts, such as managing logistical activities, providing security, and creating forecasts and business analytics. In reality, contracts are complex and negotiated in ways that smart contracts will necessarily struggle to replace. In fact, contracts are often used *strategically*, as part of a complex political economy that is essential to business.

Stewart Macaulay's (1963) classic study of "non-contractual relations" in business highlights some of the ways that contracts are used to create exchange relationships. By empirically studying business relationships, Macaulay found that contracts were often used for planning, coordinating mutual understandings, and expressing assumptions. Even when a formal contract existed and was upheld, Macaulay found that if a party was in breach of contract the contract was rarely used for enforcement. Macaulay described the ways that businesses would speak of simply "cancelling orders," when in reality they were in breach of contract (Macaulay 1963, p. 61). Both sides were likely to accept the consequences of a "cancelled order" because to enforce terms or seek redress would strain or destroy business relations, thereby curtailing future business. In these cases, the contract was really a tool for *adjusting the relationship* to reach an acceptable result. That is, the contract was a means and not an end for a business relationship. Such relationships did not establish or enforce trust and honesty, rather they worked as a mechanism to coordinate business for reaching agreement (Macaulay 1963, p. 58).

Smart contracts, unlike traditional contracts, seek to defer trust to machines, even if, according to Macaulay, this deferral of trust often misses the point of contractual relations. The premise and promise of new organizations built on blockchains is that trust relationships are concrete rather than, in truth, fluid and social mechanisms. This is, I argue, a serious mistake and a blinkered view of business. As efficient and useful as smart contacts might be—capable of automating and streamlining business—the wholesale replacement of trust with technical apparatuses risks eliminating the very fabric of business. Indeed, trust is not a binary to be turned on or off. Rather, it is negotiated and developed. Traditional contracts, either formal or informal, smart or dumb, are a key site of negotiation where these values of trust are built.

Trans-human organizations

In the original thinking about DAOs, Larimer and Buterin gestured towards a new kind of organization devoid of the foibles of humans. This vision implied a blueprint for society where human labor is managed by algorithms that produce reliable results, humans are encouraged to act intelligently, and malfeasance is nearly impossible. In 2016, a loose group of developers and enthusiasts launched an ambitious DAO with the hopes of bringing about this society.

"The DAO" was a DAO platform built on the Ethereum blockchain with the goal of funding and managing startups, much like how Kickstarter funds the development of consumer goods. The DAO launched in 2016 and at the time was the highest crowdfunded project ever, reaching a peak valuation of 11,944,260.98 ETH, worth US $251,665,578 at launch.

(This valuation is often misreported as much lower; my valuation comes from internal accounting by Slock.it and is based on the spot price at a major exchange.) The DAO accepted proposals from community members for projects, which in many cases would themselves be DAOs or blockchain products. Once a proposal was submitted it would be voted on by the stakeholders of The DAO and if successful the proposal would be funded through the money raised in the initial sale (the US $251 million total fund). But the success of The DAO was short-lived, as it was hacked within weeks of its launch, drained of nearly 3.7 million Ethereum tokens (which were later recovered), shuttered by the Ethereum community, and then in the ensuing chaos precipitated a hard fork of the Ethereum blockchain (for a full analysis see DuPont 2018).

Seeing the launch of The DAO as a rare opportunity to experiment with these technologies, I planned to launch a charity DAO with unusual ambitions. I believed it was possible to create a decentralized autonomous organization that would fully realize The DAO's *post- or trans-human ambitions*. To do so, I imagined an environmental charity called "The DAO of Whales," which would be funded by humans, be run by machines, and protect whales. Yes, an actual pod of whales.

Running on The DAO platform, the charity sought to directly and *autonomously* care for a pod of orca whales in the Pacific Northwest. The charity would run in a transparent fashion on the blockchain and through a series of smart contracts it would disburse funds to a scientific research group studying the adopted pod of orcas. Being a DAO, all decisions, including the choice of research group receiving funds, would also be decided through The DAO's voting mechanisms. Payments from the charity would also be automated through the blockchain, and therefore verifiable and immune to censorship. In effect, the charity would be unstoppable, short of a radical change in the platform.

I began to pitch the charity organization to the community, arguing that it would be the ideal setting to experiment with radical blockchain ideas, and especially to test if it is possible to create an organization that is unstoppable even in the face of social or political resistance. With efficient and transparent controls and funding by a large, decentralized group, an environmental charity seemed like a perfect fit for The DAO.

As if the design was not already radical enough, I wanted to see if DAOs could be used to experiment with the boundaries between humans, the environment, and machines—in effect, realizing the trans-human rhetoric of The DAO's inception. To do so, I proposed reviving the concept of a "deodand" to create a human-robot-whale hybrid organization. A deodand is a medieval legal concept in which, according to medieval laws, all created things have legal status and therefore have rights and duties. This strange idea has led to legal cases in the past where animals have stood trial for their crimes, including, for example, a pig dressed in appropriate clothing and sitting in the courtroom—presumably unable to make a convincing case for its innocence. For my human-robot-whale hybrid, The DAO would legitimize the identity of the human-robot-whale hybrid in the same way that the pig in the courtroom had its legal rights *prima facie* respected. The human-robot-whale hybrid, I hoped, would fare somewhat better than a pig facing the gallows, or at the very least would be much more powerful and capable of defending itself from outside attack.

Why whales? I was inspired by a science-fiction idea mooted in the Ethereum community (Schroeder 2014), which imagined that a DAO might work as a kind of legal counsel on behalf of a pod of whales. So, for example, to ensure its own safety, the human-robot-whale hybrid could automatically and irrevocably disburse funds if programmed criteria were met, such as if an oil spill occurred in the region (perhaps as detected by sensors or a secure oracle). In this way, The DAO (funded by humans, working on behalf of the whales) could automatically hold *humans* financially responsible for their actions and redress harmful activities through financial countermeasures. As the original author of the idea stated, "This is not 'save the whales,' it's 'give the whales the tools to save themselves'" (Schroeder 2014).

Unfortunately, my vision of creating a radical charity was cut short when The DAO was hacked and subsequently shut down. Nonetheless, the idea introduced interesting opportunities to provoke critical thinking. For instance, The DAO of Whales highlighted the potential role of DAOs in accelerating "cognitive capitalism." Cognitive capitalism is a theory that describes societies that have developed beyond industrial modes of production and instead produce creative and intellectual labor as capital. The DAO of Whales challenged simple thinking about the benefits and risks of cognitive capitalism and its alienating forms of labor. One way of looking at The DAO of Whales was that it strove to create a new kind of "triple bottom line" or socially responsible capitalism by holding humans accountable—the capitalist version of deep ecology activism.

The DAO was a social experiment. My DAO of Whales proposal played up the provocative and experimental side of DAOs, hoping to explore new dimensions of social coordination and to test the limits of social acceptability for autonomous agents. This playfulness invites comparisons to other autonomous technologies that are much less fun, such as autonomous cars, autonomous weapons, and algorithmic financial technologies. This provocation allowed me to question the role of cognitive labor and the boundaries of human activity in the digital future. The DAO of Whales also highlighted how DAOs problematize assumptions about who (or what) are the agents of change in contemporary society.

Governance challenges

What went wrong with The DAO? It is tempting to think that the issue was a technical one—if only The DAO framework was coded better or more thoroughly tested then the bug that led to the exploit would have been caught and the platform would not have been hacked. But this line of thinking is too simple. First, The DAO was developed and vetted by some of the best software developers in the business. Christoph Jentzsch, core Ethereum Foundation member and Lead Tester, wrote most of the open-source code for the platform; Christian Reitwießner, creator of the Solidity programming language used to program The DAO, analyzed and vetted the code; and Vitalik Buterin, among many others in the open-source community, inspected and tested the code rigorously. Second, software code always has errors and can always be hacked. The best bet today is formal software verification. But this security utopia has been a dream since the first software compilers were developed in the mid-twentieth century. Since then, every effort to develop a "secure kernel" for operating systems has proven unsuccessful (MacKenzie 1996). Formal verification is improving, but ultimately the real issue is not technical—it's human.

Returning to the theme introduced above, cryptocurrencies, blockchains, and DAOs will have to increasingly contend with governance issues as they mature. In the aftermath of the attack on The DAO, I am encouraged to see ways that blockchains and DAOs are being rigorously explored as platforms for solving tough governance problems. The attack on The DAO was sobering for the community, but it does not appear to have drained the spirit of experimentation. The task that remains for the community of developers, researchers, and entrepreneurs is to critically evaluate blockchain governance and create best practices. Then, and only then, will cryptocurrencies and blockchains be able to change society in the ways that have been imagined.

Blockchain technologies have many opportunities for governance that can be explored. Blockchain technologies support highly granular decision-making and make it relatively easy to create complex management and governance frameworks (for example, delegated voting). Tokens can be used as a powerful motivator to incentivize and discourage behaviors, which can create long-lasting institutions by being highly resilient. Finally, blockchain technologies can automate many activities, making efficient and secure decisions that are flexible to their contexts.

Blockchain technologies also introduce governance risks. Governing mechanisms that motivate and prohibit behaviors require the ability to understand and operationalize how individual and community interests are aligned. Misaligned community interests between miners and software developers, for example, is why Bitcoin has been undergoing governance issues for years and has been unable to scale the network. Similarly, having the ability to automate everything also means that when errors do occur they can quickly escape control. It is often difficult (or impossible) to fix mistakes once they have been committed to the blockchain. Finally, blockchain technologies provide access to the levers of society, but direct governance—the actualization of algorithmic authority—is risky. As I mentioned in Chapter 6, algorithmic authority provides the ability to govern by algorithms, but also introduces the challenge of governing algorithms themselves.

DAOs are complex social experiments that rely on the technical and legal affordances of smart contracts, the finances of cryptocurrencies, and the security of blockchain technologies. As a social experiment the stakes are high, for potential social good and harm. The danger of these experiments has already been seen. The DAO barely recovered the hacked funds, which could easily have been permanently lost. Such a loss would have affected an estimated 10,000 funders, many of whom were unsophisticated investors with little comprehension of the risks involved.

Navigating this complex and uncharted territory means investing in the development of a "new science" of blockchains (see DuPont 2018). This new science may take inspiration from the emerging field of cryptoeconomics (see Chapter 6) in an attempt to understand how governance can be managed with economic and technical tools. Alternatively, rather than re-discovering so many of the pitfalls that have plagued traditional organizations and institutions, we would be wise to look at the rich social science and humanities literatures, some of which I have highlighted throughout this book. Whichever path is taken, developing good governance models that accommodate new forms of collective action, decision-making, and authority remains a task for the future.

Summary

This chapter detailed the ways that cryptocurrencies and blockchain technologies promise to create new kinds of organizations. The central technologies for this vision are smart contracts combined with blockchain platforms. The most ambitious of these technologies is the decentralized autonomous organization, which offers a new way of controlling labor, managing assets, and exchanging information. In traditional organizations, collective action and decision-making is accomplished by a hierarchy of management classes, but DAOs provide opportunities to radically reimagine this. I explored some of these challenges through an attempt to launch a charity DAO on The DAO platform. Specifically, I proposed a human-robot-whale hybrid that would complicate existing notions of human and machine interaction. While this proposal was never given the opportunity to launch, it did provide insight for thinking through trans-human conceptions of society and ethics. The hack on The DAO highlighted the challenges of governing a technology that is by design unstoppable and difficult to govern. The DAO was a complex bit of technology, but ultimately it was difficult to manage because of its social embeddedness. In particular, The DAO showcased the difficulties of algorithmic authority. Unfortunately, there are no clear paths for the governance of algorithms, nor a clear picture of what life governed by algorithms might look like. I conclude with some optimism that a new science is needed to deal with these emerging challenges and that cryptocurrencies and blockchains are the laboratories for this new science.

I can scarcely think of another platform as vibrant and suitable for learning how technologies can be responsibly embedded in society.

References

Abramowicz, M. (2015). Cryptoinsurance. *Wake Forest L. Rev., 50,* 671.

Agha, A. (2017). Money Talk and Conduct from Cowries to Bitcoin. *Signs and Society, 5*(2), 293–355. https://doi.org/10.1086/693775

Ammous, S. (2015). Economics beyond Financial Intermediation: Digital Currencies' Possibilities for Growth, Poverty Alleviation, and International Development. *Journal of Private Enterprise, 30*(3), 19.

Antonopoulos, A. M. (2017). *Mastering Bitcoin: Programming the Open Blockchain* (Second edition). Boston: O'Reilly.

Apte, S., & Petrovsky, N. (2016). Will Blockchain Technology Revolutionize Excipient Supply Chain Management? *Journal of Excipients and Food Chemicals, 7*(3), 76–78.

Arquilla, J., & Ronfeldt, D. (2001). *Networks and Netwars: The Future of Terror, Crime, and Militancy.* Santa Monica, CA: Rand Corporation.

Athey, S., Catalini, C., & Tucker, C. (2017). *The Digital Privacy Paradox: Small Money, Small Costs, Small Talk* (Working Paper No. 23488). Cambridge, MA: National Bureau of Economic Research.

Baran, P. (1964). *On Distributed Communications: I. Introduction to Distributed Communications Networks* (No. RM-3420-PR). Santa Monica, CA: The Rand Corporation.

Biryukov, A., Khovratovich, D., & Pustogarov, I. (2014). Deanonymisation of Clients in Bitcoin P2P network. *CCS '14 Proceedings of the 2014 ACM SIGSAC Conference on Computer and Communications Security,* 15–29. https://doi.org/10.1145/26602 67.2660379

Bitcoin Energy Consumption Index. (n.d.). Retrieved June 14, 2017, from http://digiconomist.net/bitcoin-energy-consumption

Blanchette, J.-F. (2012). *Burdens of Proof: Cryptographic Culture and Evidence Law in the Age of Electronic Documents.* Cambridge, MA: MIT Press.

Böhme, R., Christin, N., Edelman, B., & Moore, T. (2015). Bitcoin: Economics, Technology, and Governance. *Journal of Economic Perspectives, 29*(2), 213–238. https://doi.org/10.1257/jep.29.2.213

Bohr, J., & Bashir, M. (2014). Who Uses Bitcoin? An Exploration of the

Bitcoin Community. In 2014 *Twelfth Annual International Conference on Privacy, Security and Trust (PST)* (pp. 94–101). https://doi.org/10.1109/PST.2014.6890928

Bouoiyour, J., Selmi, R., & Tiwari, A. K. (2015). Is Bitcoin Business Income or Speculative Foolery? New Ideas through an Improved Frequency Domain Analysis. *Annals of Financial Economics, 10*(01), 1550002.

Brandvold, M., Molnár, P., Vagstad, K., & Andreas Valstad, O. C. (2015). Price Discovery on Bitcoin Exchanges. *Journal of International Financial Markets, Institutions and Money, 36*, 18–35. https://doi.org/10.1016/j.intfin.2015.02.010

Briere, M., Oosterlinck, K., & Szafarz, A. (2013, September 12). *Virtual Currency, Tangible Return: Portfolio Diversification with Bitcoins.* Retrieved from https://papers.ssrn.com/abstract=2324780

Brito, J., & Castillo, A. (2016). *Bitcoin: A Primer for Policymakers* (2nd edition). Arlington, VA: Mercatus Center at George Mason University.

Brito, J., Shabad, H., & Castillo, A. (2015). Bitcoin Financial Regulation: Securities, Derivatives, Prediction Markets, and Gambling. *Columbia Science and Technology Law Review, 16*(144). Retrieved from http://www.stlr.org/cite.cgi?volume=16&article=4

Bronk, C., Monk, C., & Villasenor, J. (2012). The Dark Side of Cyber Finance. *Survival,* 54(2), 129–142. https://doi.org/10.1080/00396338.2012.672794

Brown, S. D. (2016). Cryptocurrency and Criminality: The Bitcoin Opportunity. *The Police Journal, 89*(4), 327–339.

Brunton, F. (2013). *Spam: A Shadow History of the Internet.* Cambridge, MA: The MIT Press.

Brunton, F. (2015). Heat Exchanges. In G. Lovink, N. Tkacz, & P. de Vries (Eds.), *MoneyLab Reader: An Intervention in Digital Economy* (pp. 158–172). Amsterdam: Institute of Network Cultures.

Brunton, F. (2016). Keeping the Books. *Limn,* (6). Retrieved from http://limn.it/keeping-the-books/

Brunton, F. (2018). *Digital Cash: A Cultural History.* Princeton, NJ: Princeton University Press.

Bueno, P. B. (2017). Speculative Investment, Heavy-tailed Distribution and Risk Management of Bitcoin Exchange Rate Returns. *Journal of Progressive Research in Social Sciences, 5*(1), 347–355.

Buitenhek, M. (2016). Understanding and Applying Blockchain Technology in Banking: Evolution or Revolution? *Journal of Digital Banking, 1*(2), 111–119.

Buterin, V. (2013a). *Ethereum White Paper: A Next-generation Smart*

Contract and Decentralized Application Platform. Retrieved from https://github.com/ethereum/wiki/wiki/White-Paper

Buterin, V. (2013b, September 20). Bootstrapping a Decentralized Autonomous Corporation: Part I. Retrieved April 29, 2016, from https://bitcoinmagazine.com/articles/bootstrapping-a-decentral ized-autonomous-corporation-part-i-1379644274

Calatayud, A. (2017). *The Connected Supply Chain: Enhancing Risk Management in a Changing World*. Inter-American Development Bank. Retrieved from https://publications.iadb.org/handle/11319/ 8204

Cameron, A. (2016). Money's Unholy Trinity: Devil, Trickster, Fool. *Culture & Organization*, 22(1), 4–19. https://doi.org/10.1080/ 14759551.2015.1035721

Casey, M. J., & Wong, P. (2017, March 13). Global Supply Chains Are About to Get Better, Thanks to Blockchain. *Harvard Business Review*. Retrieved from https://hbr.org/2017/03/global-supply-chains-are-about-to-get-better-thanks-to-blockchain

Castillo, M. del. (2016, June 1). Prenup Built in Ethereum Smart Contract Rethinks Marriage Obligations. Retrieved from https:// www.coindesk.com/prenup-ethereum-marriage-obligations/

Catalini, C., & Tucker, C. (2016). *Seeding the S-Curve? The Role of Early Adopters in Diffusion* (No. 22596). National Bureau of Economic Research.

Chaparro, F. (2017, July 12). MORGAN STANLEY: "Bitcoin acceptance is virtually zero and shrinking." *Business Insider*. Retrieved from http://www.businessinsider.com/bitcoin-price-rises-but-retailers-wont-accept-it-7-2017

Chaum, D. (1982). Blind Signatures for Untraceable Payments. In R. L. Rivest, D. Chaum, & A. T. Sherman (Eds.) (pp. 199–203). Presented at the Advances in Cryptology Proceedings of Crypto 82, Plenum.

Cheah, E.-T., & Fry, J. (2015). Speculative Bubbles in Bitcoin Markets? An Empirical Investigation into the Fundamental Value of Bitcoin. *Economics Letters*, 130, 32–36. https://doi.org/10.1016/ j.econlet.2015.02.029

Cheney-Lippold, J. (2011). A New Algorithmic Identity. *Theory, Culture & Society*, 28(6), 164–181. https://doi.org/10.1177/ 0263276411424420

Christidis, K., & Devetsikiotis, M. (2016). Blockchains and Smart Contracts for the Internet of Things. *IEEE Access*, 4, 2,292–2,303.

Christopher, M., & Holweg, M. (2011). "Supply Chain 2.0": Managing Supply Chains in the Era of Turbulence. *International Journal of Physical Distribution & Logistics Management*, 41(1), 63–82.

Ciaian, P., Rajcaniova, M., & Kancs, d'Artis. (2016). The Economics of BitCoin Price Formation. *Applied Economics*, 48(19), 1,799–1,815.

Clark, J. (2016). The Long Road to Bitcoin. In *Bitcoin and Cryptocurrency Technologies: A Comprehensive Introduction*. Princeton: Princeton University Press.

Coeckelbergh, M. (2015). *Money Machines: Electronic Financial Technologies, Distancing, and Responsibility in Global Finance*. Burlington, VT: Ashgate.

Coeckelbergh, M., & Reijers, W. (2016a). Cryptocurrencies as Narrative Technologies. *ACM SIGCAS Computers and Society*, 45(3), 172–178.

Coeckelbergh, M., & Reijers, W. (2016b). Narrative Technologies: A Philosophical Investigation of the Narrative Capacities of Technologies by Using Ricoeur's Narrative Theory. *Human Studies*. https://doi.org/10.1007/s10746-016-9383-7

Connell, J. (2017, February 14). How Humans Now Use the Blockchain to Declare Love and Marriage. Retrieved from https://news.bitcoin.com/cross-border-love-on-the-blockchain/

Cowen, D. (2014). *The Deadly Life of Logistics*. Minneapolis: University of Minnesota Press.

Davidson, S., De Filippi, P., & Potts, J. (2016). *Disrupting Governance: The New Institutional Economics of Distributed Ledger Technology*. Retrieved from https://papers.ssrn.com/sol3/papers.cfm?abstract_id=2811995

Davies, H. (2010). Global Financial Regulation after the Credit Crisis. *Global Policy*, 1(2), 185–190.

De Filippi, P., & Loveluck, B. (2016). The Invisible Politics of Bitcoin: Governance Crisis of a Decentralized Infrastructure. *Internet Policy Review*, 5(4).

De Filippi, P. D., & Hassan, S. (2016). Blockchain Technology as a Regulatory Technology: From Code is Law to Law is Code. *First Monday*, 21(12). https://doi.org/10.5210/fm.v21i12.7113

De Filippi, P. D., & Wright, A. (2018). *Blockchain and the Law: The Rule of Code*. Cambridge, MA: Harvard University Press.

DeLanda, M. (1991). *War in the Age of Intelligent Machines*. New York: Zone Books.

Desai, F. (2015, December 14). The Fintech Boom and Bank Innovation. *Forbes*. Retrieved from https://www.forbes.com/sites/falgunidesai/2015/12/14/the-fintech-revolution/

Dodd, N. (2016). *The Social Life of Money*. Princeton, NJ: Princeton University Press.

Dodd, N. (2017). The Social Life of Bitcoin. *Theory, Culture & Society*.

Doguet, J. J. (2012). The Nature of the Form: Legal and Regulatory Issues Surrounding the Bitcoin Digital Currency System. *La. L. Rev.*, *73*, 1,119.

Douglas, J. L. (2016). New Wine Into Old Bottles: Fintech Meets the Bank Regulatory World. *NC Banking Inst.*, *20*, 17.

Drucker, P. F. (1990, May 1). The Emerging Theory of Manufacturing. *Harvard Business Review*, (May–June). Retrieved from https://hbr.org/1990/05/the-emerging-theory-of-manufacturing

Dudley, W. C. (2016, December 9). Financial Regulation Nine Years On from the Global Financial Crisis—Where Do We Stand? Retrieved January 31, 2018, from https://corpgov.law.harvard.edu/2016/12/09/financial-regulation-nine-years-on-from-the-gfc-where-do-we-stand/

Dupont, J., & Squicciarini, A. C. (2015). Toward De-Anonymizing Bitcoin by Mapping Users Location. In *Proceedings of the 5th ACM Conference on Data and Application Security and Privacy* (pp. 139–141). San Antonio, Texas: ACM. Retrieved from http://dl.acm.org/citation.cfm?id=2699128

DuPont, Q. (2014). The Politics of Cryptography: Bitcoin and the Ordering Machines. *The Journal of Peer Production, 1*(4), 1–29.

DuPont, Q. (2017). Blockchain Identities: Notational Technologies for Control and Management of Abstracted Entities. *Metaphilosophy, 48*(5), 634–653. https://doi.org/10.1111/meta.12267

DuPont, Q. (2018). Experiments in Algorithmic Governance: An Ethnography of "The DAO," a Failed Decentralized Autonomous Organization. In M. Campbell-Verduyn (Ed.), *Bitcoin and Beyond: The Challenges and Opportunities of Blockchains for Global Governance*. New York: Routledge.

DuPont, Q., & Takhteyev, Y. (2016). Ordering Space: Alternative Views of ICT and Geography. *First Monday, 21*(8). https://doi.org/10.5210/fm.v21i8.6724

Dwyer, G. P. (2015). The Economics of Bitcoin and Similar Private Digital Currencies. *Journal of Financial Stability, 17*, 81–91.

Dyhrberg, A. H. (2016a). Bitcoin, Gold and the Dollar—A GARCH Volatility Analysis. *Finance Research Letters, 16*, 85–92. https://doi.org/10.1016/j.frl.2015.10.008

Dyhrberg, A. H. (2016b). Hedging Capabilities of Bitcoin. Is It the Virtual Gold? *Finance Research Letters, 16*, 139–144.

Eco, U. (1995). *The Search for the Perfect Language*. (J. Fentress, Trans.). Cambridge, MA: Blackwell.

English, S. M., & Nezhadian, E. (2017). *Application of Bitcoin*

Data-Structures & Design Principles to Supply Chain Management. Retrieved from https://arxiv.org/abs/1703.04206

Ermilov, D., Panov, M., & Yanovich, Y. (2017). Automatic Bitcoin Address Clustering. Presented at the IEEE International Conference on Machine Learning and Applications, Cancun, Mexico. Retrieved from http://bitfury.com/content/5-white-papers-research/clusterin g_whitepaper.pdf

Fairfield, J. (2014). Smart Contracts, Bitcoin Bots, and Consumer Protection. *Wash. & Lee L. Rev. Online, 71*(2), 35–299.

Fanning, K., & Centers, D. P. (2016). Blockchain and Its Coming Impact on Financial Services. *Journal of Corporate Accounting & Finance, 27*(5), 53–57. https://doi.org/10.1002/jcaf.22179

Fanti, G., & Viswanath, P. (2017). Deanonymization in the Bitcoin P2P Network. In *Advances in Neural Information Processing Systems* (pp. 1,364–1,373).

Ferguson, N. (2009). *The Ascent of Money: A Financial History of the World*. New York: Penguin Books.

Financial Conduct Authority. (2017). *Discussion Paper on Distributed Ledger Technology* (No. DP17/3). London: Financial Conduct Authority.

Finck, M. (2017). *Blockchains and Data Protection in the European Union* (Max Planck Institute for Innovation & Competition Research Paper No. 18–01). Oxford: University of Oxford. Retrieved from https://papers.ssrn.com/abstract=3080322

Frauenfelder, M. (2017, October 29). "I Forgot My PIN": An Epic Tale of Losing $30,000 in Bitcoin. *WIRED*. Retrieved from https://www.wired.com/story/i-forgot-my-pin-an-epic-tale-of-losing-dollar 30000-in-bitcoin/

Friedman, D. (1979). Private Creation and Enforcement of Law: A Historical Case. *The Journal of Legal Studies, 8*(2), 399–415.

Frohlich, M. T., & Westbrook, R. (2001). Arcs of Integration: An International Study of Supply Chain Strategies. *Journal of Operations Management, 19*(2), 185–200.

Fry, J., & Cheah, E.-T. (2016). Negative Bubbles and Shocks in Cryptocurrency Markets. *International Review of Financial Analysis, 47*, 343–352.

Fuchs, C. (2007). *Internet and Society: Social Theory in the Information Age*. New York: Routledge.

Galloway, A. R. (2004). *Protocol: How Control Exists After Decentralization*. Cambridge, MA: MIT Press.

Galloway, A. R., & Thacker, E. (2007). *The Exploit: A Theory of Networks*. Minneapolis: University of Minnesota Press.

Gandal, N., & Halaburda, H. (2014, September). *Competition in the Cryptocurrency Market*. Working Paper. Retrieved from http://econ papers.repec.org/paper/cesceswps/_5f4980.htm

Gandal, N., Hamrick, J. T., Moore, T., & Oberman, T. (2017). Price Manipulation in the Bitcoin Ecosystem. Presented at the Workshop on the Economics of Information Security (WEIS) 2017. Retrieved from http://weis2017.econinfosec.org/wp-content/uploads/sites/3/2017/05/WEIS_2017_paper_21.pdf

Garcia, D., Tessone, C. J., Mavrodiev, P., & Perony, N. (2014). The Digital Traces of Bubbles: Feedback Cycles Between Socio-Economic Signals in the Bitcoin Economy. *Journal of the Royal Society Interface*, *11*(99), 20140623.

Gencer, A. E., Basu, S., Eyal, I., van Renesse, R., & Sirer, E. G. (2018). Decentralization in Bitcoin and Ethereum Networks. Retrieved from http://arxiv.org/abs/1801.03998

Gerard, D. (2017). *Attack of the 50 Foot Blockchain: Bitcoin, Blockchain, Ethereum and Smart Contracts*.

Gerstein, I. R., & Hervieux-Payette, C. (2015). *Digital Currency: You Can't Flip This Coin! Report of the Standing Senate Committee on Banking, Trade and Commerce*. Ottawa, ON: Senate Committee on Banking, Trade and Commerce.

Gilbert, A. (2002). On the mystery of capital and the myths of Hernando de Soto: What difference does legal title make? *International Development Planning Review*, *24*(1), 1–19. https://doi.org/10.3828/idpr.24.1.1

Golumbia, D. (2016). *The Politics of Bitcoin: Software as Right-Wing Extremism*. Minneapolis, MN: University of Minnesota Press.

Golumbia, D. (2017, August 22). Cryptocurrencies Aren't Currencies. They Aren't Stocks, Either. Retrieved August 26, 2017, from https://motherboard.vice.com/en_us/article/xwwv83/cryptocurrencies-are nt-currencies-they-arent-stocks-either

Golumbia, D. (2018, March 4). Zealots of the Blockchain | David Golumbia. *The Baffler*, *38*. Retrieved from https://thebaffler.com/salvos/zealots-of-the-blockchain-golumbia

Goux, J.-J. (1990). *Symbolic Economies: After Marx and Freud*. (J. C. Gage, Trans. Ithaca, NY: Cornell University Press.

Graeber, D. (2011). *Debt: The First 5,000 Years*. Brooklyn, NY: Melville House.

Grigg, I. (2004, July 6). The Ricardian Contract. Retrieved April 27, 2017, from http://iang.org/papers/ricardian_contract.html

Grimmelmann, J. (2005). Regulation By Software. *The Yale Law Journal*, *114*, 1,719–1,758.

Groshoff, D. (2014). Kickstarter My Heart: Extraordinary Popular Delusions and the Madness of Crowdfunding Constraints and Bitcoin Bubbles. *William & Mary Business Law Review*, 5(2), 489.

Guillory, J. (2010). Genesis of the Media Concept. *Critical Inquiry*, 36(2), 321–362. https://doi.org/10.1086/648528

Guo, Y., & Liang, C. (2016). Blockchain Application and Outlook in the Banking Industry. *Financial Innovation*, 2(1), 24. https://doi.org/10.1186/s40854-016-0034-9

Hardt, S., & Lopes, L. (2015). Google Votes: A Liquid Democracy Experiment on a Corporate Social Network. *Defensive Publications Series*. Retrieved from https://www.tdcommons.org/dpubs_series/79

Harris, A., Goodman, S., & Traynor, P. (2012). Privacy and Security Concerns Associated with Mobile Money Applications in Africa. *Wash. JL Tech. & Arts*, 8, 245.

Hart, K. (2001). *Money in an Unequal World: Keith Hart and His Memory Bank*. London: Texere.

Heidegger, M. (1993). The Question Concerning Technology. In *Basic Writings* (Revised and Expanded, pp. 306–341). New York: HarperCollins Publishers.

Helleiner, E. (2014). *The Status Quo Crisis: Global Financial Governance After the 2008 Meltdown*. Oxford University Press.

Hermann, M., Pentek, T., & Otto, B. (2016). Design Principles for Industrie 4.0 Scenarios. In *2016 49th Hawaii International Conference on System Sciences (HICSS)* (pp. 3,928–3,937). https://doi.org/10.1109/HICSS.2016.488

Hernandez, I., Bashir, M., Jeon, G., & Bohr, J. (2014). Are Bitcoin Users Less Sociable? An Analysis of Users' Language and Social Connections on Twitter. In *International Conference on Human-Computer Interaction* (pp. 26–31). Springer. Retrieved from http://link.springer.com/10.1007/978-3-319-07854-0_5

Hesse, M., & Rodrigue, J. P. (2009). Logistics. In *International Encyclopedia of Human Geography*. Amsterdam: Elsevier B.V. Retrieved from http://www.sciencedirect.com/science/reference works/9780080449104

Hileman, G., & Rauchs, M. (2017). *Global Cryptocurrency Benchmarking Study*. Cambridge, England: University of Cambridge.

Hobbes, M. (2017). Generation Screwed. *The Huffington Post*. Retrieved from http://highline.huffingtonpost.com/articles/en/poor-millennials/

Hofmann, E., & Rüsch, M. (2017). Industry 4.0 and the Current Status as Well as Future Prospects on Logistics. *Computers in Industry, 89,* 23–34.

Holthaus, E. (2017, December 5). Bitcoin Could Cost Us Our Clean-Energy Future. Retrieved January 26, 2018, from https://grist.org/article/bitcoin-could-cost-us-our-clean-energy-future/

Howden, E. (2015). The Crypto-Currency Conundrum: Regulating An Uncertain Future. *Emory International Law Review, 29,* 741–742.

Hur, Y., Jeon, S., & Yoo, B. (2015). *Is Bitcoin a Viable E-Business?: Empirical Analysis of the Digital Currency's Speculative Nature.* Retrieved from http://aisel.aisnet.org/icis2015/proceedings/eBize Gov/18/

Ingham, G. (2004). *The Nature of Money.* Cambridge, UK: Polity.

InterPARES Trust Terminology Project. (2017). ITrust Terminology: Blockchain Terminology. Retrieved January 8, 2018, from http://arstweb.clayton.edu/interlex/blockchain/

Kaminska, I. (2016, February 1). RTGS, and the Story of Collateralised Risk instead of Credit Risk. Retrieved August 29, 2017, from http://ftalphaville.ft.com/2016/02/01/2151882/rtgs-and-the-story-of-collateralised-risk-instead-of-credit-risk/

Kaminska, I. (2017, September 12). Cultish Long-Termism Can Hobble Investors. *Financial Times.* Retrieved from https://www.ft.com/content/d5cbb4ee-9708-11e7-a652-cde3f882dd7b

Kaplan, A., Skogstad, A. L., & Girshick, M. A. (1950). The Prediction of Social and Technological Events. *The Public Opinion Quarterly, 14(1),* 93–110.

Kaplanov, N. (2012). Nerdy Money: Bitcoin, the Private Digital Currency, and the Case against its Regulation. *Loyola Consumer Law Review, 25,* 111.

Kazerani, A., Rosati, D., & Lesser, B. (2017). Determining the Usability of Bitcoin for Beginners Using Change Tip and Coinbase. In *Proceedings of the 35th ACM International Conference on the Design of Communication* (pp. 51–55). New York: ACM. https://doi.org/10.1145/3121113.3121125

Kharif, O. (2017, December 8). 1,000 People Own 40% of the Bitcoin Market. *Bloomberg Businessweek.* Retrieved from https://www.bloomberg.com/news/articles/2017-12-08/the-bitcoin-whales-1-000-people-who-own-40-percent-of-the-market

Kittler, F. (2009). Towards an Ontology of Media. *Theory, Culture & Society, 26(2–3),* 23–31. https://doi.org/10.1177/0263276409010 3106

Knapp, G. (1924). *The State Theory of Money.* London: Macmillan & Company Limited.

Kondor, D., Pósfai, M., Csabai, I., & Vattay, G. (2014). Do the Rich Get Richer? An Empirical Analysis of the Bitcoin Transaction Network. *PLOS ONE, 9*(2). https://doi.org/10.1371/journal.pone.0086197

Konings, M. (2017, December 28). The Time of Finance. *Los Angeles Review of Books*. Retrieved from https://lareviewofbooks.org/article/the-time-of-finance/

Krämer, S. (2015). *Medium, Messenger, Transmission: An Approach to Media Philosophy*. (A. Enns, Trans.). Amsterdam: Amsterdam University Press.

Kristoufek, L. (2015). What Are the Main Drivers of the Bitcoin Price? Evidence from Wavelet Coherence Analysis. *PLOS ONE, 10*(4). https://doi.org/10.1371/journal.pone.0123923

Kubát, M. (2015). Virtual Currency Bitcoin in the Scope of Money Definition and Store of Value. *Procedia Economics and Finance, 30*, 409–416. https://doi.org/10.1016/S2212-5671(15)01308-8

Lamport, L., Shostak, R., & Pease, M. (1982). The Byzantine Generals Problem. *ACM Transactions on Programming Languages and Systems (TOPLAS), 4*(3), 382–401.

Larios-Hernández, G. J. (2017). Blockchain Entrepreneurship Opportunity in the Practices of the Unbanked. *Business Horizons*. https://doi.org/10.1016/j.bushor.2017.07.012

Latour, B., & Woolgar, S. (1986). *Laboratory Life: The Construction of Scientific Facts* (Reprint). Princeton, NJ: Princeton University Press.

Lee, T. B. (2017, December 6). Bitcoin's Insane Energy Consumption, Explained. Retrieved January 27, 2018, from https://arstechnica.com/tech-policy/2017/12/bitcoins-insane-energy-consumption-explained/

Lee, Y. N. (2017, December 22). Bitcoin: China, Singapore, Japan Issue Cryptocurrency Warnings. *CNBC*. Retrieved from https://www.cnbc.com/2017/12/22/bitcoin-china-singapore-japan-issue-cryptocurrency-warnings.html

Lessig, L. (1999). *Code and Other Laws of Cyberspace*. New York: Basic Books.

Lessig, L. (2006). *Code v2*. New York: Basic Books.

Levine, M. (2017, September 15). ICOs, VCs, IPOs and SPACs. *Bloomberg.Com*. Retrieved from https://www.bloomberg.com/view/articles/2017-09-15/icos-vcs-ipos-and-spacs

Levy, K. E. C. (2017). Book-Smart, Not Street-Smart: Blockchain-Based Smart Contracts and The Social Workings of Law. *Engaging Science, Technology, and Society, 3*(0), 1–15. https://doi.org/10.17351/ests2017.107

Liao, S. (2017, October 31). Inside Russia's Love-Hate Relationship with Bitcoin. Retrieved January 3, 2018, from https://www.theverge.com/2017/10/31/16387042/russia-putin-bitcoin-regulation-ethereum-blockchain-technology

Liquid Democracy In Context, or, An Infrastructuralist Manifesto. (n.d.). Retrieved from http://seed.sourceforge.net/ld_k5_article_004.html

Loh, T., & Tomesco, F. (2018, January 10). Bitcoin Could End Up Using More Power Than Electric Cars. *Bloomberg.Com*. Retrieved from https://www.bloomberg.com/news/articles/2018-01-10/bitco in-outshines-electric-cars-as-driver-of-global-power-use

Loon, V. P. (2018, January 4). ethereum/research. Retrieved January 7, 2018, from https://gitter.im/ethereum/research?source=orgpage

Lotti, L. (2016). Contemporary Art, Capitalization and the Blockchain: On the Autonomy and Automation of Art's Value. *Finance and Society*, *2*(2), 96–110.

Lustig, C., & Nardi, B. (2015). Algorithmic Authority: The Case of Bitcoin (pp. 743–752). IEEE. https://doi.org/10.1109/HICSS.20 15.95

Luther, W. J. (2016a). Cryptocurrencies, Network Effects, and Switching Costs. *Contemporary Economic Policy*, *34*(3), 553–571.

Luther, W. J. (2016b, May 13). *Regulating Bitcoin: On What Grounds?* Retrieved from https://papers.ssrn.com/abstract=2631307

Luther, W. J., & White, L. H. (2014). Can Bitcoin Become a Major Currency? *GMU Working Paper in Economics*, *14–17*. Retrieved from https://papers.ssrn.com/abstract=2446604

Ly, M. K.-M. (2013). Coining Bitcoin's Legal-Bits: Examining the Regulatory Framework for Bitcoin and Virtual Currencies. *Harv. JL & Tech.*, *27*, 587.

Macaulay, S. (1963). Non-Contractual Relations in Business: A Preliminary Study. *American Sociological Review*, *28*(1), 55–67.

MacKenzie, D. A. (1996). *Knowing Machines: Essays on Technical Change*. Cambridge, MA: MIT Press.

MacKenzie, D. A. (2006). *An Engine, Not a Camera: How Financial Models Shape Markets*. Cambridge, MA: MIT Press.

MacKenzie, D. A. (2009). *Material Markets: How Economic Agents are Constructed*. New York: Oxford University Press.

Malmo, C. (2017, November 1). One Bitcoin Transaction Now Uses as Much Energy as Your House in a Week. Retrieved January 27, 2018, from https://motherboard.vice.com/en_us/article/ywbbpm/ bitcoin-mining-electricity-consumption-ethereum-energy-climate-change

Matta, M., Lunesu, I., & Marchesi, M. (2015). The Predictor Impact of Web Search Media on Bitcoin Trading Volumes. In *Knowledge*

Discovery, Knowledge Engineering and Knowledge Management (IC3K), *2015 7th International Joint Conference on* (Vol. 1, pp. 620–626). Lisbon, Portugal: IEEE. Retrieved from http://ieeexplore.ieee.org/abstract/document/7526987/

Mattila, J., Seppälä, T., & Holmström, J. (2016). Product-centric Information Management: A Case Study of a Shared Platform with Blockchain Technology. Presented at the Industry Studies Association Conference, Minneapolis, MN. Retrieved from http://escholarship.org/uc/item/65s5s4b2

Matzutt, R., Hiller, J., Henze, M., Ziegeldorf, J. H., Müllmann, D., Hohlfeld, O., & Wehrle, K. (2018). A Quantitative Analysis of the Impact of Arbitrary Blockchain Content on Bitcoin. In *Proceedings of the 22nd International Conference on Financial Cryptography and Data Security (FC)*. Christ Church, Barbados: Springer.

Maurer, B. (2006). The Anthropology of Money. *Annual Review of Anthropology, 35,* 15–36.

Maurer, B. (2007). Incalculable Payments: Money, Scale, and the South African Offshore Grey Money Amnesty. *African Studies Review, 50*(02), 125–138. https://doi.org/10.1353/arw.2007.0109

Maurer, B. (2015). *How Would You Like to Pay?: How Technology Is Changing the Future of Money.* Durham, NC: Duke University Press Books.

Maurer, B. (2016). Re-risking in Realtime. On Possible Futures for Finance after the Blockchain. *BEHEMOTH-A Journal on Civilisation, 9*(2), 82–96.

Maurer, B. (2017). Money as Token and Money as Record in Distributed Accounts. In N. J. Enfield & P. Kockelman (Eds.), *Distributed Agency* (pp. 109–116). New York: Oxford University Press.

Maurer, B., Nelms, T. C., & Swartz, L. (2013). "When Perhaps the Real Problem is Money Itself!": The Practical Materiality of Bitcoin. *Social Semiotics, 23*(2), 261–277. https://doi.org/10.1080/10350330.2013.777594

Mazer, R. (2014, December 12). Digital Currencies and Financial Inclusion: 5 Questions. Retrieved January 4, 2018, from http://www.cgap.org/blog/digital-currencies-and-financial-inclusion-5-questions

McDermott, B. (2017, July 14). IBM [Telephone].

McLuhan, M. (2003). *Understanding Media: The Extensions of Man.* (W. T. Gordon, Ed.) (Critical edition). Corte Madera, CA: Gingko Press Inc.

McLuhan, M. (2011). *The Gutenberg Galaxy.* Toronto: University of Toronto Press.

Mentzer, J. T., Min, S., & Zacharia, Z. G. (2000). The Nature of Interfirm Partnering in Supply Chain Management. *Journal of Retailing*, 76(4), 549–568. https://doi.org/10.1016/S0022-4359 (00)00040-3

Mettler, M. (2016). Blockchain Technology in Healthcare: The Revolution Starts Here. In *2016 IEEE 18th International Conference on e-Health Networking, Applications and Services (Healthcom)* (pp. 1–3). https://doi.org/10.1109/HealthCom.2016.7749510

Milkau, U., & Bott, J. (2015). Digitalisation in Payments: From Interoperability to Centralised Models? *Journal of Payments Strategy & Systems*, 9(3), 321–340.

Monax. (2017). Explainer | Dual Integration. Retrieved from https:// monax.io/explainers/dual_integration/

Moore, T., & Christin, N. (2013). Beware the Middleman: Empirical Analysis of Bitcoin-exchange Risk. In *International Conference on Financial Cryptography and Data Security* (pp. 25–33). Okinawa, Japan: Springer. https://doi.org/10.1007/978-3-642-39884-1_3

Mori, T. (2016). Financial Technology: Blockchain and Securities Settlement. *Journal of Securities Operations & Custody*, 8(3), 208–227.

Morozov, E. (2014). *To Save Everything, Click Here: The Folly of Technological Solutionism*. New York: PublicAffairs.

Mosco, V. (2004). *The Digital Sublime: Myth, Power, and Cyberspace*. Cambridge, MA: MIT Press.

Nakamoto, S. (2008, October 31). *Bitcoin: A Peer-to-Peer Electronic Cash System*. Retrieved June 3, 2013, from http://www.metzdowd.com/ pipermail/cryptography/2008-October/014810.html

O'Dwyer, K. J., & Malone, D. (2014). Bitcoin Mining and Its Energy Footprint. Presented at the ISSC 2014 / CIICT 2014, Limerick, Ireland. Retrieved from http://digital-library.theiet.org/content/ conferences/10.1049/cp.2014.0699

Office of Investor Education and Advocacy. (2017, July 25). Investor Bulletin: Initial Coin Offerings. Retrieved July 26, 2017, from https://www.investor.gov/additional-resources/news-alerts/alerts-bulletins/investor-bulletin-initial-coin-offerings

Ouyang, Y. (2007). The Effect of Information Sharing on Supply Chain Stability and the Bullwhip Effect. *European Journal of Operational Research*, 182(3), 1,107–1,121.

Pasquale, F. (2015). *The Black Box Society: The Secret Algorithms That Control Money and Information*. Cambridge, MA: Harvard University Press.

Peters, J. D. (2015). *The Marvelous Clouds: Toward a Philosophy of Elemental Media*. Chicago: University of Chicago Press.

Pirrong, C. (2016, January 31). CCPs & RTGS: Devil Take the Hindmost? Retrieved August 29, 2017, from http://streetwiseprofessor.com/?p=9810

Pitta, J. (1999, November 1). Requiem for a Bright Idea. *Forbes*. Retrieved from https://www.forbes.com/forbes/1999/1101/641139 0a.html#4a50a9cb715f

Plassaras, N. (2013). Regulating Digital Currencies: Bringing Bitcoin within the Reach of the IMF. *Chicago Journal of International Law*, 14(1). Retrieved from http://chicagounbound.uchicago.edu/cjil/vol14/iss1/12

Poovey, M. (1998). *A History of the Modern Fact: Problems of Knowledge in the Sciences of Wealth and Society*. Chicago: University of Chicago Press.

Popper, N. (2015). *Digital Gold: Bitcoin and the Inside Story of the Misfits and Millionaires Trying to Reinvent Money*. New York: Harper.

Popper, N. (2017a, November 21). Warning Signs About Another Giant Bitcoin Exchange. *The New York Times*. Retrieved from https://www.nytimes.com/2017/11/21/technology/bitcoin-bitfinex-tether.html

Popper, N. (2017b, December 19). How the Winklevoss Twins Found Vindication in a Bitcoin Fortune. *The New York Times*. Retrieved from https://www.nytimes.com/2017/12/19/technology/bitcoin-winklevoss-twins.html

Preda, A. (2007). Where do Analysts Come From? The Case of Financial Chartism. *The Sociological Review*, 55(2_suppl), 40–64. https://doi.org/10.1111/j.1467-954X.2007.00729.x

Reagle, J. M. Jr. (1996). Trust in Electronic Markets: The Convergence of Cryptographers and Economists. *First Monday*. Retrieved from http://firstmonday.org/ojs/index.php/fm/article/view/1509

Reijers, W. (2016). Digital Money Acts: A Postphenomenological Approach to Monetary Technologies.

Reijers, W., & Coeckelbergh, M. (2016). The Blockchain as a Narrative Technology: Investigating the Social Ontology and Normative Configurations of Cryptocurrencies. *Philosophy & Technology*, 1–28. https://doi.org/10.1007/s13347-016-0239-x

Roberts, J. J., & Rapp, N. (2017, November 25). Exclusive: Nearly 4 Million Bitcoins Lost Forever, New Study Says. *Fortune*. Retrieved from http://fortune.com/2017/11/25/lost-bitcoins/

Rogers, D. S., & Tibben-Lembke, R. (2001). An Examination of Reverse Logistics Practices. *Journal of Business Logistics*, 22(2), 129–148. https://doi.org/10.1002/j.2158-1592.2001.tb00007.x

RogomonZ. (2016, September 15). The Disaster that Is Bitcoin.

Retrieved August 24, 2017, from https://medium.com/@rogo monz/the-disaster-that-is-bitcoin-97f08f99a73e#.jv4fl97fc

Rosner, M. T., & Kang, A. (2015). Understanding and Regulating Twenty-first Century Payment Systems: The Ripple Case Study. *Mich. L. Rev.*, *114*, 649.

Rossiter, N. (2016). *Software, Infrastructure, Labor: A Media Theory of Logistical Nightmares*. New York: Routledge.

Russell, D. M., & Saldanha, J. P. (2003). Five Tenets of Security-Aware Logistics and Supply Chain Operation. *Transportation Journal*, *42*(4), 44–54.

Russell, J. (2017, August 21). Hackers Nab $500,000 as Enigma Is Compromised Weeks Before Its ICO. Retrieved August 24, 2017, from http://social.techcrunch.com/2017/08/21/hack-enigma-5000 00-ico/

Russo, C. (2017, July 18). Ethereum Co-Founder Says the Crypto Coin Market Is a Ticking Time-Bomb. *Bloomberg.Com*. Retrieved from https://www.bloomberg.com/news/articles/2017-07-18/ethereum-co-founder-says-crypto-coin-market-is-ticking-time-bomb

Santori, M. (2016, October 15). Appcoin Law: ICOs the Right Way. Retrieved from https://www.coindesk.com/appcoin-law-part-1-icos-the-right-way/

Saurwein, F., Just, N., & Latzer, M. (2015). Governance of Algorithms: Options and Limitations. *Info : The Journal of Policy, Regulation and Strategy for Telecommunications, Information and Media*, *17*(6), 35–49.

Schelling, T. C. (1960). *The Strategy of Conflict*. Cambridge, MA: Harvard University Press.

Schroeder, K. (2014, February). Deodands: DACs for Natural Systems. *Ethereum Forum*. Retrieved May 12, 2016, from https://forum. ethereum.org/discussion/392/deodands-dacs-for-natural-systems

Scott, B. (2014). Visions of a Techno-Leviathan: The Politics of the Bitcoin Blockchain. *E-International Relations*. Retrieved from http://www.e-ir.info/2014/06/01/visions-of-a-techno-leviathan-the-poli tics-of-the-bitcoin-blockchain/

Scott, B. (2016). *How Can Cryptocurrency and Blockchain Technology Play a Role in Building Social and Solidarity Finance?* Geneva: UNRISD Working Paper. Retrieved from https://www.econstor.eu/ handle/10419/148750

Seibel, P. (2009). *Coders at Work: Reflections on the Craft of Programming*. New York: Apress.

Shcherbak, S. (2014). How Should Bitcoin Be Regulated? *Eur. J. Legal Stud.*, *7*, 41.

Shin, L. (2016, April 21). Republic of Georgia to Pilot Land Titling on Blockchain with Economist Hernando de Soto, BitFury. *Forbes*. Retrieved from http://www.forbes.com/sites/laurashin/2016/04/21/republic-of-georgia-to-pilot-land-titling-on-blockchain-with-economist-hernando-de-soto-bitfury/

Shirriff, K. (2014). Bitcoins the Hard Way: Using the Raw Bitcoin Protocol. Retrieved April 3, 2018, from http://www.righto.com/2014/02/bitcoins-hard-way-using-raw-bitcoin.html

Simmel, G. (2004). *The Philosophy of Money*. (D. Frisby, Ed., T. Bottomore, Trans.) (Third enlarged edition). New York: Routledge.

Smith, M. A., Paton, D., & Williams, V. L. (2006). Market Efficiency in Person to Person Betting. *Economica*, *73*(292), 673–689. https://doi.org/10.1111/j.1468-0335.2006.00518.x

Stenger, A. J. (1986). Information Systems in Logistics Management: Past, Present, and Future. *Transportation Journal*, 65–82.

Stubbings, P. (2014, November 22). Limit Order Book Visualisation. Retrieved October 5, 2017, from http://parasec.net/transmission/order-book-visualisation/

Sulleyman, A. (2017, December 4). Man Wants to Dig Up Landfill Site after He "Threw Away" Bitcoin Haul Now Worth over $80m. *The Independent*. Retrieved from http://www.independent.co.uk/life-style/gadgets-and-tech/news/bitcoin-value-james-howells-newport-landfill-hard-drive-campbell-simpson-laszlo-hanyecz-a8091371.html

Sullivan, C., & Burger, E. (2017). E-residency and Blockchain. *Computer Law & Security Review*, *33*(4), 470–481. https://doi.org/10.1016/j.clsr.2017.03.016

Swanson, T. (2014). *The Anatomy of a Money-like Informational Commodity: A Study of Bitcoin*. Amazon Digital Services LLC.

Swartz, L. (2017). Blockchain Dreams. In M. Castells (Ed.), *Another Economy is Possible: Culture and Economy in a Time of Crisis* (p. 224). Cambridge, UK: Polity Press.

Szabo, N. (1996). Smart Contracts: Building Blocks for Digital Free Markets. *Extropy*, *16*. Retrieved from http://www.fon.hum.uva.nl/rob/Courses/InformationInSpeech/CDROM/Literature/LOTwinterschool2006/szabo.best.vwh.net/smart_contracts_2.html

Szabo, N. (1997). Formalizing and Securing Relationships on Public Networks. *First Monday*, *2*(9). https://doi.org/10.5210/fm.v2i9.548

Szabo, N. (1998). Secure Property Titles with Owner Authority. Retrieved April 27, 2017, from http://nakamotoinstitute.org/secure-property-titles/

Szabo, N. (2005). History and the Security of Property. Retrieved July

30, 2017, from https://web.archive.org/web/20060810175356/
http://szabo.best.vwh.net/history.html

The Trust Machine. (2015, October 31). *The Economist*. Retrieved from
http://www.economist.com/news/leaders/21677198-technology-
behind-bitcoin-could-transform-how-economy-works-trust-machine

Thrift, N. J. (2005). *Knowing Capitalism*. London: SAGE Publications.

Thrift, N. J. (2008). *Non-Representational Theory: Space, Politics, Affect*.
New York: Routledge.

Tsing, A. (2009). Supply Chains and the Human Condition.
Rethinking Marxism, 21(2), 148–176. https://doi.org/10.1080/089
35690902743088

U.S. Supreme Court. SEC v. Howey Co. 328 U.S. 293, 843 § (1946).
Retrieved from https://supreme.justia.com/cases/federal/us/328/
293/case.html

Velasco, P. R. (2016). Sketching Bitcoin: Empirical Research of Digital
Affordances. In *Innovative Methods in Media and Communication
Research* (pp. 99–122). Cham, Switzerland: Palgrave Macmillan.
https://doi.org/10.1007/978- 3-319-40700-5_6

*Vitalik Buterin: Cryptoeconomic Protocols In the Context of Wider
Society*. (2014). London. Retrieved from https://www.youtube.com/
watch?v=S47iWiKKvLA

Walch, A. (2017). Blockchain's Treacherous Vocabulary: One More
Challenge for Regulators. *Journal of Internet Law*, 21(2), 1–16.

Wang, K., & Safavi, A. (2016, October 29). Blockchain Is Empowering
the Future of Insurance. Retrieved from http://social.techcrunch.
com/2016/10/29/blockchain-is-empowering-the-future-of-insur
ance/

Weber, B. (2014). Can Bitcoin Compete with Money? *Journal of Peer
Production*, (4). Retrieved from http://peerproduction.net/issues/
issue-4-value-and-currency/invited-comments/can-bitcoin-com
pete-with-money/

Weber, B. (2016). Bitcoin and the Legitimacy Crisis of Money.
Cambridge Journal of Economics, 40(1), 17–41. https://doi.org/
10.1093/cje/beu067

Wilson, D. (2017, July 11). Maersk [Telephone].

Wilson, F. (2017, December 31). What Happened In 2017. Retrieved
January 3, 2018, from http://avc.com/2017/12/what-happened-
in-2017/

Winner, L. (1980). Do Artifacts Have Politics? *Daedalus*, 109(1), 121–
136.

Winner, L. (1997). Cyberlibertarian Myths and the Prospects for
Community. *ACM Sigcas Computers and Society*, 27(3), 14–19.

Wolfers, J., & Zitzewitz, E. (2004). Prediction Markets. *Journal of Economic Perspectives*, *18*(2), 107–126. https://doi.org/10.1257/0895330041371321

Wolfson, S. N. (2015). Bitcoin: The Early Market. *Journal of Business & Economics Research (Online)*, *13*(4), 201.

Wood, G. (2014). *Ethereum: A Secure Decentralised Generalised Transaction Ledger EIP-150 Revision*. Retrieved from http://gavwood.com/paper.pdf

Working Party 216. (2014). *Opinion 05/2014 on Anonymisation Techniques* (No. 0829/14/EN). Brussels, Belgium: European Commission, Directorate General Justice.

Yates, J. (1997). Early Interactions Between the Life Insurance and Computer Industries: The Prudential's Edmund C. Berkeley. *IEEE Annals of the History of Computing*, *19*(3), 60–73.

Yelowitz, A., & Wilson, M. (2015). Characteristics of Bitcoin Users: An Analysis of Google Search Data. *Applied Economics Letters*, *22*(13), 1030–1036. https://doi.org/10.1080/13504851.2014.995359

Yermack, D. (2013). *Is Bitcoin a Real Currency? An Economic Appraisal.* Retrieved from http://www.nber.org/papers/w19747

Yu, M.-C., & Goh, M. (2014). A Multi-objective Approach to Supply Chain Visibility and Risk. *European Journal of Operational Research*, *233*(1), 125–130.

Zamani, E. D., & Babatsikos, I. (2017). Diffusion and Adoption of Bitcoins in Light of the Financial Crisis: The case of Greece. In *Proceedings of the 11th Mediterranean Conference on Information Systems (MCIS 2017)*. Genoa. Retrieved from https://www.dora.dmu.ac.uk/xmlui/handle/2086/14418

Zeilinger, M. (2016). Digital Art as "Monetised Graphics": Enforcing Intellectual Property on the Blockchain. *Philosophy & Technology*, 1–27.

Zimmer, Z. (2017). Bitcoin and Potosí Silver: Historical Perspectives on Cryptocurrency. *Technology and Culture*, *58*(2), 307–334. https://doi.org/10.1353/tech.2017.0038

Zoey, Z. (2018, January 2). North Korea Accused of Stealing $25K in Cryptocurrency. *CBS*. Retrieved from https://www.cbsnews.com/news/north-korea-accused-of-stealing-25k-in-cryptocurrency/

Index